Conceptions of Institutions

and

the Theory of Knowledge

22 Sept 89

To Margo Nelson,
a source of continuing inspiration

Ed Koch

Conceptions of Institutions

and

the Theory of Knowledge

Second Edition

Stanley Taylor

*With a new introduction
and commentary by*

Elwin H. Powell

Includes three previously unpublished essays by

Stanley Taylor

Transaction Publishers

New Brunswick (U.S.A.) and London (U.K.)

New material this edition copyright © 1989 by Transaction Publishers, New Brunswick, New Jersey 08903
Originally published in 1956 by Bookman Associates

Library of Congress Catalog Number: 88-32627
ISBN: 0-88738-798-5
Printed in the United States of America

Library of Congress Cataloging-in-Publication Data

Taylor, Stanley, 1906–1965.
   Conceptions of institutions and the theory of knowledge / Stanley Taylor; with a new introduction and commentary by Elwin H. Powell; includes three previously unpublished essays by Stanley Taylor.
      p.   cm.
   Reprint. Originally published: New York: Bookman Associates, 1956.
   Bibliography: p.
   Includes index.
   ISBN: 0-88738-798-5
   1. Sociology—Methodology. 2. Knowledge, Sociology of. 3. Social institutions. I. Powell, Elwin H. (Elwin Humphreys), 1925–
II. Title.
HM24.T3 1989
301'.01—dc19   88-32627
                                                      CIP

Contents

Acknowledgments

For protracted correspondence on the Taylor Project I want to thank B. Wardlaw, Steve Sikora, Lisa Kruger, and Glenn Goodwin: their response to my letters enabled me to understand my own words.

For analyzing and debating sheaves of class handouts on Taylor's concept of the concept I am indebted to my students at the University of Buffalo.

For years of discourse on the Sociology of Knowledge I want to acknowledge Mark Kennedy, my alter-ego; each encounter with him left my mind enlarged.

For his continuing service in the preservation of the heritage of sociology I want to thank Irving Louis Horowitz, President of Transaction Publishers.

For arranging my initial encounter with Stan Taylor I would thank the "fates"—if I could name them.

Elwin H. Powell
Buffalo, New York

Introduction to the Transaction Edition

On Choosing Institutions: Ideas from Stanley Taylor

> The mind lives in perpetual conversation.
> —Charles Horton Cooley,
> *Human Nature and the Social Order*, 1903

In September 1950 I apprenticed myself to Stanley Taylor at the University of Texas. From him I took courses; for him I wrote my M.A. thesis. Through osmosis I learned the sociology which has since been the guiding project of my life. Twice a week I walked home with him, ambling through the green streets of Austin. Years later I fed on thought he left with me.

Quietly radiant, Stan Taylor had the charisma of purpose: his life was about the search for knowledge—and he knew it.

Everyone at Texas played with the golden words on the tower, the main building of the university: YE SHALL KNOW THE TRUTH AND THE TRUTH SHALL MAKE YOU FREE. Stan Taylor actually set out to decode the message: what does it mean to know? Is there an enduring truth beyond perishing opinion? Is freedom only anomie—another name for nothing left to lose?

Taylor lived ideas. For him the university was sacred ground, a place for discourse. A sociable introvert, he hated idle chatter—and idle writing even more. Steeped in the classics of philosophy, literature, and the social sciences, Stan Taylor's lectures were a kind of "oral publication."[1] After recording his words in class I retyped them at night and thus discovered questions that have lasted a lifetime.

Resonant in both voice and spirit, Taylor attended carefully to

1

the words of others; since he wanted to be heard, he listened. A cantless man. Droll. Warm. Exacting. Rightly he called my first M.A. thesis proposal "an awful jumble of non-sequiturs." Crushed, I worked for three weeks to rewrite four pages, and then he said, "That's better." "He is sparing in his praise," I recorded in my journal of February 17, 1951, "but he will talk as long as I care to converse and that is encouragement enough."

Although twenty years my senior, Taylor treated me as an equal, a co-participant in the process of inquiry. Dealing in questions rather than pronouncements, he was more a freelance philosopher than an academic man. Having neither position nor reputation to defend, he could follow his mind where it led him. Graduate students clustered around him, and people listened to Taylor because he seemed to be listening to himself. A man of intelligent laughter, he was both secure and searching.

Born in England in 1906, Taylor grew up in northern Ontario (the town of Barrie) and graduated from the University of Toronto in 1932 with a B.A. in English literature. Supporting himself as an occasional office worker and spending his free time in the public library, Stan studied with H.A. Innis in the 1930s and entered the Canadian army in 1939. An enlisted man, he spent the war in England with the coast artillery. Afterward he returned to the University of Toronto, took an M.A. in philosophy, and then moved on to graduate school at the University of Chicago, where he studied with Louis Wirth, Herbert Blumer, and Phil Hauser and connected with Ivan Belknap, who brought him to Texas in 1950.

Years of material hardship and military servitude nurtured in Stan Taylor a free spirit and calm self-sufficiency that contrasted sharply with the status anxiety of the Texas professoriate. Unstylish in dress, bespectacled, with a slight "scholar's stoop," tallish, he seemed to belong to another time and place and was therefore comfortable in the world. Thus I wrote in my journal: "Feb. 20, 1951...tomorrow I will walk home with Stan Taylor, live in the Platonic world of ideas. Knowing him gives me courage to scorn success and search for Truth...He lives in serene obscurity...in a rented apartment five miles from the campus...has neither telephone nor automobile. Never seems to hurry...laughs a lot. He has taken knowledge as its own reward. His lectures are works of art, made with reverence." Stan Taylor was not a rebel but an alternative.

In 1939 a graduate student named C. Wright Mills found the University of Texas "a thoroughly exhilarating place."[2] In 1950 the campus, still teeming with veterans from the "good war," had about it the silent excitement of impending doom. Everyone expected the bad war (Korea) to end civilization, if not humanity, once and for all. Casually people talked of dropping atomic bombs as a final solution to the communist problem. The spirit of adventure, even peace, of the earlier postwar years had by 1950 become a mood of sullen drift.

Outrage became enrage. Between 1937 and 1967, five deaths occurred by falls from the University of Texas tower—two accidental, three suicides.[3] The suicides happened between 1949 and 1951. (Cynics observed that the truth can make you flee.) For their inner grievance against a mysterious system that lured them into self-betrayal people sought redress in alcohol. Everyone felt like a potential Winston Smith: *1984* was a book we knew by heart. Stan Taylor's words had power for those walking on the rim of the abyss.

> Oh the mind, the mind has mountains, cliffs of fall,
> Frightful, sheer, no man fathomed,
> Hold them cheap
> You who have never hung there
> —Gerard Manley Hopkins

Although in the university by choice, we felt like conscripts; formally free, we were servile to those in authority. Segregated like officers and enlisted men, faculty and students held each other in mutual contempt. Professors celebrated the scientific method but were careful to see that critical intelligence was not exercised in their presence. A distinguished psychologist canceled his seminar because too many of us—twenty five—signed up for it; he wanted to study the rat mind, not the student mind.

In happy contrast, the sociology department actually liked people, invited disputation, and encouraged unorthodox research. Thus a venturesome circle of eccentrics, most of us bored out of psychology by the behaviorists, collected around Garrison Hall, the seat of sociology at Texas. Twice a week we listened to Stan Taylor lecture on the sociology of knowledge and then joined him for a two-hour lunch, indulging in "the leisure of the theory class," as E. Gartly Jaco put it.

Afterward Stan and I sauntered toward his apartment and the grey pall of *1984* lifted as we started rewriting our own history. With automobiles flowing around us we refought the street battles of realists and nominalists at the University of Paris in the thirteenth century... helped storm the Bastille on July 15, 1789. Standing by San Jacinto Creek, Taylor explained Kant's categorical imperative and what Hegel really meant by the dialectic. Mere names became people and dead script acquired a voice.

Cardinal Newman (1801–90) defined a university as a community of scholars where the conversation of each is a series of lectures to all. This I experienced in Garrison Hall at the University of Texas in 1950–51. Graduate students expounded on their research to anyone who would listen—Mark Kennedy was using Fichte (1762–1814) to understand the Texas oil-field roughneck (circa 1948), and Charlie Whately had found in Durkheim the answer to the riddle of existence. One aspiring scholar showed how Talcott Parsons's sociology could explain group sex; he sent his manuscript to Professor Parsons but never received a reply. Another denizen of Garrison Hall played the stock market and ended up a millionaire. Sweet are the uses of sociology!

Vigorously we debated the methodology of the social sciences—we saw ourselves as creating, not merely studying sociology, an attitude proudly fostered by Warner Gettys, Harry Moore, and Carl Rosenberg, the senior people in the department. Classrooms became a dialectical arena, energized by native Texas contention. "The positivists disgust me," I wrote in my journal on November 15, 1950, after a stormy meeting at Walter Firey's seminar on social planning. "They expect to find Truth by taking a vote."

At twenty-five I was looking for a grander truth than offered by main-line sociology, which was only "counting people doing things," as Mark Kennedy put it. In letters to Ivan Belknap and Charlie Whately in 1950 I said I wanted a sociology that would (a) define the Good Society and (b) recognize the principle that individuals have some control over their own destiny. To my profound surprise, I discovered Stan Taylor had wrestled with the selfsame problem for twenty-five years, probing in depths I could not even name.

Notes from Taylor's lectures in the sociology of knowledge reveal the cogency and coherence of his mind. Each meeting from February 6 to April 30, 1951, has a defined theme with the main ideas pared down to seed, the foliage stripped away. Outside the lecture hall, Taylor speculated and sloshed around through three thousand years of history; inside, he was always precise, centered. From this course emerges the narrative that reappears in *Conceptions of Institutions and the Theory of Knowledge* (1956) and comes to final fruition in his unpublished papers.

Behind all of Stan Taylor's thought is a single question: what is the connection between Concept and Conduct? My notes record a continuing dialogue that went on between Taylor and me and a community of people—some present as percept, others as only idea. To quote Robert Merton: "The significant aspect of oral publication is found in the distinctive social networks of students and teachers, masters and apprentices and collegial peers at every phase of academic life which feed back to affect the kinds of cognitive development resulting from the oral transmission of knowledge... the cognitive interaction between printed and oral publication is central to the transmission of knowledge between generations... and the further *advancement* of knowledge within them."[4]

Naturally my notes are what I heard—and wanted to hear—not what was objectively uttered in the classroom. Nor can I now say how much of "my" Taylor is fiction and how much is fact—I can only hope that both are true. At twenty-six I was urgently seeking a vocation—a calling—I could choose as my own, and I was discovering in sociology a rhythm congruent with my nature. This quest for location colored all of my perception. What I now think I heard Taylor saying was this: yes, obviously institutions determine our behavior, but only if we choose to obey them.

However, my friend Mark Kennedy, who was there at the time, remembers the story otherwise; in a recent letter (1/7/87) he writes: "...looking at your outline [On Choosing Institutions] I am convinced that you and I re-read Taylor in different ways. You chase down one set of implications while I chase down another set. This fact tells me that what Stan gave us both, not merely in his books and papers, but also in his lectures and private discussions with us, was a conceptual system, a most dynamic one, that would allow each different student of his to incorporate it into his own frame of reference.... Thus you saw 'choosing' as the outstanding [implication] while I saw cultural relativism as the essential dilemma."

What does it mean to choose an institution? What is an

institution? Entering the English language in the thirteenth century the verb "to institute" means to give form, to establish (*Oxford English Dictionary*). In 1987 Wlad Godzich defined an institution as "a guiding idea and a set of procedures," echoing (without citing) Sumner's words of 1906:[5] "An institution consists of a concept (idea, notion, doctrine, interest) and a structure. The structure is a framework, or apparatus or perhaps only a number of functionaries set to co-operate in prescribed ways.... The structure holds the concept and furnishes instrumentalities for bringing it into the world of fact to serve the interests (of people) in society." From the concept, the invisible essence of every institution is derived a body of rules defining the expected pattern of behavior called a social role. And the roles we play make us the person we are; as Gerth and Mills[6] suggest: "Institutions not only select persons and eject them; institutions also form them, imprint their stamps upon the individual, modifying his external conduct as well as his inner life. For one aspect of learning a role consists of acquiring motives which guarantee its performance."

But, psychologically the role is only as significant as the person chooses to make it. From 1944–46 I was a Seaman in the U.S. Navy: the role did not stamp me. My years at the University of Texas as a biology and chemistry student (1946–50) left scarcely a mark on my mind. Then in 1950 in choosing to write a M.A. thesis I restructured my consciousness—the role became my project, turned me into a sociologist. With the project came new rules, shared by others, thus creating for me a new society and institutional order. "We construct our world," writes Henrietta Spencer[7],

> and on that structure we drape our values. We choose our essence, and we are responsible for that choice. The person formulates a basic set of choices, and in the parlance of Humanistic Existentialism those choices are called one's 'cosmology,' 'myth' or 'project.' This does not necessarily mean that we choose to be poor, weak or inferior, conditions Sartre called our 'facticity.' Within these objective limitations, however, there still exists the subjective choice of how to view them.... Although existentialism puts its cornerstone on the choice a person makes, the Other is inescapable. 'I recognize that I am as the Other sees me,' says Sartre. 'Through the engaged encounter I discover who I am. The Choice of one's being does not exist in a vacuum, but with the Other.'

And the Other is always a personification of an institution; every Significant Other is a partial representative of a Generalized Other, (G.H. Mead).[8] Thus I first encountered Stan Taylor as an embodiment of the Generalized Other of the institution of scholarship. As my project took form I selected friends who could teach me sociology; virtually all my associates were aspiring scholars. Through this micro-society—we called ourselves the Austin circle—I found objective validation for my own subjectivity. We were a structure because we shared a concept. "Concepts are beliefs about the nature of things" says Stan Taylor, "and are translated into values. A belief is what people think to be real; a value is their opinion of what ought to be." *(Conceptions of Institutions . . . p. 76)*

But only those concepts I choose to believe have determining effect on my conduct. Why did we believe Stan Taylor? Because he made sense? Because he listened? Because he spoke the truth? Because, perhaps, he recognized the reality of the "ought" in a time of cynical relativity? He spoke as one having authority. That authority which comes of being the author of your own acts. He spoke out of wisdom. Out of knowing. And also out of silence. And it was really none of these. We listened to Stan Taylor because we knew he sought the truth.

That spirit permeated his lectures in the Sociology of Knowledge and the dialogue which developed around them. I took notes during the sessions and later reorganized and re-typed them, no doubt selecting what I myself needed to know. But in presenting that material here I have tried to avoid interpolation and to remain faithful to my own typescript from the Spring of 1951. Let me now pass on brief excerpts from my notes on Taylor's lectures.

Lecture I. Feb. 6, 1951. Definitions:

Sociology—the science of society (Comte).
Science—a way of knowing, of testing theory against fact, combines deductive and inductive method.
Society—an "interpenetration of minds"; through the concept, we share in the life of one another. We come to self through the other: consciousness means to "know together."
Socius—the Latin root for social, means friend, ally, companion. Sociology studies the process of association.
No accident that sociology arose in France . . . in a time of disillusion, like our own. The French Revolution was

the greatest attempt yet made to control the social environment, its failure not in intention but method.

Saint-Simon (1760–1825) and Comte (1798–1857) say the new society must be built on the authority of science. But at what cost? Scientific explanation requires that you show the unique to be an attribute of a more general law. Without uniqueness there is no poetry, art, religion....

Feb. 10. On Comte's Law of the Three Stages of Thought:

1. Theological (animistic) thought explains things in terms of gods, wills. Even the stars had their psychology. Will is in the object, thus the idea of Free Will, i.e., the assumption we are capable of exerting influence on the world around us...

2. Metaphysical thought formulates general laws. Aristotle--body has "essence," i.e., heaviness, therefore falls to earth. Motion of bodies explained in terms of its nature. E.g. today—sex, instincts [sought inside the organism rather than in relationships—EHP]. Objects form a class, exhibit certain features, therefore the feature is the consequence of the class. The class is then spoken of as the nature of the object. Galileo made a vast class of all objects we call matter, then studied relations of parts to one another. The object is not explained in terms of itself but in relation to other bodies... Newton's law of inverse squares is not a statement about the body itself but a relation to other bodies in a system of forces.

3. Positive science...the Third Stage, describes as real that which occurs in space and time, wants to deal with the "is" not the "ought"... would rule out will and choice to create a science of human affairs, a determinant system.... Comte dispenses with the category of causality as a metaphysical concept with no reality. But Kant locates cause in "consciousness as such." Whitehead says science is founded on faith in the law of causality (Hume has never been answered). Still it is the idea of cause which enabled us to gain control over nature and evolve.

Ultimately, science itself still rests on the law of parsimony, on "Ockham's Razor" which states of two equally plausible explanations of an event, choose the simpler one. Thus the ultimate criterion of truth is aesthetic (read Croce)...and does in fact rest on a kind of choice...

Feb. 16. On Predictability through Mathematics:

Comte thought all reliable knowledge would someday be written in mathematics. But thought can't be reduced to mathematics—those who think they have done so have merely shown that thought is logical.

We cannot predict human behavior with mathematics. In fact, people do not behave as if they are determinate. No one in the practice of his own life assumes determinancy. Durkheim showed that the suicide rate is determinate but the individual is scientifically inexplicable.... Last year a man jumped from the 35th floor of the tower, after writing on the wall: "I did not fall. I was not pushed. I jumped."... Was his act determined or free?...

Feb. 22, 1951: on Voluntarism v. Determinism:

...neither is satisfactory, the former implies Free Will, the latter mechanism. But once we become aware of the mechanism determining our behavior it is no longer a mechanism. Is our subjective life determined by objective conditions? No. What the object is depends on the way we are prepared to respond to it. Even physical phenomena appear differently in different cultures—e.g. W.J.R. Rivers, an authority on vision, found that South Sea islanders could not distinguish red from green. We see through concepts, not with our eyes only.

Feb. 24 ... On the Making of Objects, the Direction of Life:

So the objective world is a conceptual construction. How are concepts formed? We abstract common elements and neglect differences in perception. A concept is an agreement of at least two people on a segment of reality. To know about a situation does not mean it is necessary to know all. Concepts cannot exhaust the empirical system.... We never have the same experience twice.

Never have the same experience twice? How many hours of perambulation went into that proposition! Knowing changes the knower so that which is known is never reknown in the same way. Yet the craving to reexperience past joy is the source of all our frustration (and perhaps of meaning?). Do I not feel it even now—

June 14, 1988—as I in my mind walk with Taylor in Austin sunshine? Nature may repeat itself, but consciousness moves on

- perpetual revolution of configured stars,
- perpetual recurrance of determined seasons,
- world of spring and autumn, birth and dying.
                                —T. S. Eliot,
                                "Choruses from the Rock"

Feb. 27. Concepts Create Objects, Selves:

The concept is always social, not individual; the rational is the universal, the sensory is particular. But truth is independent of the individual subject. Francis Bacon said the world is a world of individual things. This is a fallacy. The world of real things is itself a social product. Every object is a telescoped act (G.H. Mead) and thus "determined" by our response to it. So objects are not things and subjects are not individual minds but social selves.

Mar. 8. On Knowing the Self...Mannheim:

Classical theory of knowledge explores the relation between experience and reflection; the sociology of knowledge asks how participation of the thinker in society effects the process of thought itself (Louis Wirth, Preface to *Ideology and Utopia*, p. xxix):
Man's nature, his rationality, emerges out of interaction with the external world. Out of this interaction comes the categories by which he knows himself... Understanding is impossible if we have to take ideas at face value.

March 10. Truth Is Determined by the Conceptual Scheme:

Husserl says "the genesis of a proposition is irrelevant to its validity." Truth spoken by a madman is still true. A concept is neither validated nor invalidated by the nature of its origin but by its fit in a conceptual scheme; e.g., Kepler's work in astronomy originated in neo-Pythagorean theories about the divine nature of numbers but he finally made his theory congruent with the facts as defined by the conceptual scheme.

March 12. Freedom through Meaning:

Meanings have historic origin but their validity is not affected thereby. The truth of a concept depends on its place in a complex of concepts.

Freedom is meaningful action in a situation... not indeterminancy. See Fromm on "freedom from" external restraints, and "freedom to" actualize potentiality (*Escape from Freedom*).

Determinate action [i.e., coerced behavior] is meaningless.

March 21. Concepts Are the Structural Beams of Civilization:

The western world has been imprisoned in Greek ontology, which paradoxically gives us our freedom.... In contrast to other peoples of the time, the Greeks thought reason could be used to direct political life—even deliberated and voted upon the decision to go to war, unlike the Persians who acted on the dictates of an Emperor who was a virtual god-king. Herodotus says that even Greek slaves defended Greece against the Persians.... From living under the force of the popular assembly came the idea that law could be changed. Hebraic law was more rigid, written in stone by Moses with the help of God (or vice versa). The Greeks did not worship their gods, but made them into companions, at home in the world.... The *Iliad* was always being rewritten, or at least added onto; certainly the work is not the creation of a single man named Homer since 250 years separate the *Iliad* and the *Odyssey*. An evolving open work, in contrast to the sacred writings of the Hebrews which strove for absolute and unchanging exactness.

March 23. Clashing Concepts [Greek and Hebrew] Drive Western Civilization:

An irony of history—little is preserved when much is written. In the last days of Rome there were many books but few are left. With the closing of the schools in Athens in 529 A.D., medieval time begins. The Middle Ages were an attempt to reconcile the Old (Hebraic) with the New (Hellenic) Testament. Both Greeks and Hebrews were ground down by superior empire (Rome)—religion develops in such an atmosphere, its idealistic character

springing from materialistic defeat. But Greek and
Hebrew points of view were irreconcilable, and the attempt to fuse them may account for the continuing
tragedy—and dynamism?—of western civilization. Conformity to nature constituted a virtue in the ancient world
but not in the Middle Ages when the individual is made
part of the divine scheme, a realm superior to the natural...

March 29. Books Preserve the Conceptual Scheme:

Christianity brought an emphasis on the text, a belief
in books—scripture. There was a great use of books in the
Middle Ages—even though it required 8 to 10 months to
make one copy of one book. In Irish monasteries even
Greek was copied and in the 9th century Irish monks
moved south as Bible missionaries to rekindle the flame of
learning on the continent. [Monasticism spread from
North to South?] The Benedictine monasteries, established 3 centuries earlier, kept learning alive but were only
interested in the preservation not the development of
ideas. The Irish Platonist Erigena (815?–877) had his eyes
gouged out by his students—was this resistance to the
light of learning?...
  In the early Middle Ages (500–1000) the ideas of
Plato and Plotinus had come to fruition in Augustine;
theorists were preoccupied with saving man for the next
world. Aristotle had ceased to have any influence by the
6th century but when he returns in the 10th century is an
empiricist, founder of the conceptual framework of modern science.
  Aristotle was translated by the Arabs and passed
through Spain, reaching Paris in the 12th century, regret-
tably diverting attention from the original work of Alber-
tus Magnus....
  The logic chopping of the theologians made for the
precision and clarity of the French language....

On the eternal return of Aristotle: because the idea of Form is
the kernel of information theory, Jeremy Campbell has proposed
that Aristotle be given a posthumous Nobel Prize.[9]

April 3. Institutional Determinants of Medieval Life,
Roots of Freedom:

Celibacy in a world of primogeniture meant that new
blood was constantly recruited for the church, which was

governed for the most part by intellectuals ... Until the 12th century the superior was selected by the subordinates; afterwards superior selects the subordinate. Church resists organization.

Emphasis on Latin represents unity of Church, rise of the vernacular its breakdown. Peaks at 1300. Church laid down universality. Rise of the Dominicans and Franciscans indicates the Church is having to develop new programs to hold its adherents. ... The growth of distant authority made the individual freer; earlier Barons had had practically absolute control over their serfs.

Development of a money economy means the emergence of a cohesive society ... energy tends to pass from religion to acquisition of wealth. [From the thirteenth century; see Tawney.]

1150–1250: Unparalleled prosperity. Period of cathedral building. Development of City-Republics provided an escape from feudal domination. A serf who could live in the city for a year and a day was declared free, could not be returned to the land. City air makes one free, says the German proverb. Der Stadt macht Frei.

April 1. Medieval Universities Canonize Public Opinion, Manifest/the Realist/Nominalist/Controversy:

Benedictine monasteries kept learning alive in the early Middle Ages but the resurgence of urban life [1000 A.D.] brought the cathedral school, out of which evolved the university. Because books were scarce, great emphasis was given to lecturing. While mysticism dominated the monasteries of the 13th century, the Realist/Nominalist dispute permeated the universities, was in fact the main controversy of the Middle Ages.

Realists believed in the reality of the universal: ultimate categories are part of the structure of the universe ... an idealist position which goes back to Plato. Nominalists, on the other hand, believe that universals are only names, labels ... flatus vocus, mere waves of air ... and only individual things really exist, an empiricist position that goes back to Aristotle and forward to positivism. Duns Scotus, William of Ockham and Roger Bacon. Provides the metaphysic of modern science.

Abelard was able to question dogma and develop a conceptualist philosophy which synthesized and perhaps transcended both realism (Platonic theorizing) and nominalism (Aristotelian empiricism). In Paris, realist and nominalist fought each other in the streets. Dissension brought migration to Oxford and Cambridge ... the medi-

eval university system was not a monolith ... Usually nominalism was a progressive force, though at Prague it had
become reactionary.

The dispute between realism and nominalism started
over the question of transubstantiation: did the bread and
wine of the mass become the "real" body and blood of
Christ or was it only nominal, in name only, a symbol? If
you are into theology and have plenty of time you can see
how scholars could get carried away with the issue. The
Middle Ages loved argument. Helen Waddell tells the
story of two medieval scholars in the 7th century who
"argued for fifteen days and nights without sleeping or
eating on the frequentative of the verb to be, till it almost
came to knives."[10]

The universities were in fact canonizing public opinion, giving expression to a weltanschauung. The University of Paris was the fountainhead of ecclesiastical thought.
The connection between staff and student was very close
in the beginning; this changes with the introduction of
marriage. University was a commune, a guild. As clergy,
university personnel were under canon law; universities
even had their own jails for unruly members. Students
were rebellious, disruptive ... shot dice on the altars of the
Cathedral of Notre Dame. The word "nation" originates
in the national groups which made up the university
community of the 13th century.

April 3. Universities in Decline:

Learning in the universities is almost extinguished by
the 15th century ... became places of reaction. Parallel
today with the emphasis on natural science and the
neglect of ethics. Indicates crisis. It became increasingly
difficult to treat theological issues in the vernacular. As if
physics today had to be translated into everyday speech.
Scholastics were not understood, thus scorned.

After John Wycliffe (1330–84), "the morning star of
the Reformation," translated the Bible into English, the
people could go directly to scripture for confirmation of
their religious conceptions. In Bohemia John Huss, later
to be burned at the stake, followed suit.

The great theologians were ceasing to be the vehicle
of ideas. When people carried scripture in their head it
became necessary to destroy the person to stamp out
deviance—hence the burning of people by the Inquisition. Later they burned books for the same reason.

April 7. Truth Compartmentalized,
the End of the Middle Ages:

Significant scholarship shifts outside the university.
Main writing is commentary which does not go beyond the
framework of theology, except perhaps for Thomas Aqui-
nas (1224–1277). William of Ockham, however, deserves
special attention: with him comes the idea of a truth of
Faith and a truth of Reason. Thus you cannot think your
way to truth. But man is a moral being precisely because
he is a thinking being. So now the Middle Ages has arrived
at two disparate truths. The whole of scholastic philosophy was an effort to mediate, to synthesize these two
frameworks [faith and reason]. But Ockham plunges the
whole structure into ruin, with a compartmentalization of
mind which denies that Truth is one.

April 9. Protestantism, a New Conceptual Scheme?

Writing does not necessarily make for social change.
In ways writing fixes ideas—that after all is its purpose, to
keep the record straight.
The new literature of the 15th century was used
against the clergy. But by the end of the 16th century the
Church had worked out an index of banning books. Even
the Bible was banned—like closing the barn door after the
cow is out.
The Renaissance was a reaffirmation of classical values, the Reformation of medieval values. The printing of
the Bible reaffirmed the medievalism which killed off the
Renaissance.
John Milton's *Paradise Lost* fixes the Puritan Tradition, a conceptual framework holding in tension Hebrew
Rebellion and Greek Reason, a picture of life as argument.
Max Weber located the source of modern individualism in the asceticism of the Middle Ages, an asceticism
which enabled the Protestant to win out in the economic
and military battles with their "cavalier" opponents. But in
the process, says Weber, "the Protestants turned the whole
world into a monastery, created a hitherto unheard of
inner isolation" (*The Protestant Ethic and the Spirit of Capitalism*—1905).

April 11. The Conceptual System Creates Choice:

Writing brings with it the possibility of vicarious
experience. In folk societies decisions are arrived at on the

basis of the conceptual scheme at the surface. But writing brings the past into the present thus making possible the envisagement of alternative futures.

Choice is at the core of Western myth of creation: Adam and Eve choose to eat the forbidden fruit, thus become conscious, become as gods knowing good and evil.

Has the sphere of choice enlarged over the past 2000 years? In its early years [say until 400 A.D.] Christianity was a chosen, i.e., voluntarily selected, rather than imposed, inherited institution—an existential fact crucial in shaping our conception of freedom, according to Fustel de Coulanges (*The Ancient City*, 1864).

After the Church became the State, Christianity became compulsory and in the Middle Ages you had to be a Catholic. But the rise of the medieval city made possible an alternative to feudalism, the beginnings of capitalism, creating new and real choices in everyday life. (See Mannheim on social mobility in the Middle Ages, on how the same world begins to look different to those who move around.)

After the Reformation you could choose your religion, Catholic or Protestant... which came in more and more varieties... And after the Democratic revolutions you could choose your politics. In the American and French revolution came the hitherto unheard-of idea of choosing to set up a new government. Thomas Paine sets out the choosing process clearly in *Common Sense* and *The Age of Reason*.

Rousseau said (1770s) we were now forced to be free.

So if "freedom" is our fate how best does sociology deal with the fact? Today people long for connection, not detachment, community, not individuation.

April 19:

Today we are in the midst of a deluge of ideas; there is no anchorage, no permanence. There is unity of thought in astronomy but division at the human level. And natural science has nothing of consequence to say on social issues.

Actually we are still in the Copernican Counter-Revolution, as Nietzsche called it: "displaced from the center of the universe, man is hurled to the periphery and is now exhilarated by the thrilling sensation of his own nothingness." [Does that happen with the suicide? Is this the state of anomie?]

Nietzsche thought that religion was dying out with

the man in the street by the 15th century. But the Reformation brought the Counter-Reformation which kept the institution alive for 4 more centuries.

But now we have new institutions, new religions. Positive science. The State. Technology. Money. And in Texas, oil. But be careful about your opposition—you may reinvigorate a collapsing structure.

Mannheim says "the sociology of knowledge is the systematization of doubt" [*Ideology and Utopia*, p. 45]. What can that mean? That we create a new conceptual framework for the reclassification of old knowledge, remembering that it cannot be done alone and it need not last forever. No concept ever exhausts reality, yet it is only through the concept that we apprehend reality at all. To reason is to reason together.

Strangely, Taylor's sociology evolves into gnosticism, not agnosticism. Knowing gives us freedom. When we understand the institutions (rules) that determine our conduct, we can then reformulate them to suit our own aspiration. Such were the approximate ideas of Stan Taylor's concluding lecture, where he read out loud these difficult words from Karl Mannheim: "Man attains objectivity and acquires a self with reference to his conception of his world not by giving up his will to action and holding his evaluation in abeyence, but in confronting and examining himself. The criterion of such self-illumination is that not only the object but we ourselves fall squarely within our field of vision. We become visible to ourselves, not just vaguely as a knowing subject as such but in a certain role hitherto hidden from us.... In such moments the inner connection between our role, our motivations, and our type and manner of experiencing the world suddenly dawns upon us. Hence the paradox underlying these experiences, namely the opportunity for relative emancipation from social determination, increases proportionately with insight into this determination" (Mannheim, *Ideology and Utopia*, p. 43).

The nadir of my sixty-two years on this planet came in January 1951. Broke, I eked out spending money as a tutor to the University of Texas football team; living in monklike solitude on a country estate where I received room and board for caretaking, I worked on my M.A. thesis, *The Limitations of Sociological Positivism*, and soaked in Gregorian chant and Gustav Mahler trying to heal the wounds of a broken love affair. Each morning's radio news announced the next step toward Armageddon. Taylor was the light of my life, but I distanced myself even from him. Although I had known him since September, I see that I wrote in my journal on January 25 "even though others call him by his first name, I have not yet taken that liberty."

But by April my life was turning around and I remember (through the help of my journal) a glorious day when Stan and I merged into a crowd in front of the co-op bookstore on our main street, the Drag. General MacArthur's speech to the Congress was coming to us by live radio broadcast, and people on the street were jubilant: Thank God that bastard's gone. That day the Drag had the feeling Ronnie Dugger described in the sixties, the feeling of life in love with itself.[11] We browsed in the bookstore, and Stan said I should buy the paperback of Huizinga's *Waning of the Middle Ages*, recalling he spent whole days reading the book in the Toronto library where it was treated as an uncirculating rare volume: how extraordinary to realize you could now own it for one dollar— enough to make you believe in progress.

We moved on talking of everything at once. Whitehead's idea that science is founded on faith, faith in the law of causality—really Hume has never been answered: all you can know is conjunctive occurrence, the sun may rise because the cock crows. . . . Still cause is the master category—the "illusion" that gave us control over nature. . . . And why were Hegel's lectures so much better attended than Schopenhauer's, Stan wondered, when the former is so dull and the latter so dramatic, at least in writing. . . . Of Kant's twelve categories Schopenhauer discarded eleven, keeping only cause. . . . Recalling Huizinga, Stan said the inquisition in Spain killed off the cats to get at the witches and this caused the rats to grow and spread the bubonic plague, which killed a third of the population of Europe and ended medieval society. What a shame they did not pay more attention to Aristotle's category of efficient cause, which caused me to recall a fellow Texan, a football player who in his education course learned that "Aristotle was the son of a bitch that caused the Dark Ages. . . . " Not an easy concept, cause.

Stopping for coffee at the Toddle House at Nineteenth and Guadalupe Street, we savored MacArthur's passing and talked of Roman commanders who came back from the field and took over the government. And Stan told of criminals hiding out from the Roman cops in religious communities and ending up as saints. Did that happen today? What could you make of Sutherland's theory of "differential association" as a cause of crime? Certainly it's true that criminals learn their roles by associating with each other—just as do scholars. Both live in networks of significant others, and both fail at their jobs if they don't believe in what they are doing, if they don't have the calling. Stan quoted that passage from Max Weber on how you have to believe that the fate of your soul hinges on making the right conjecture in a manuscript and if you don't have that feeling of vocation for scholarship you should do something else. "For nothing is worthy of man as such unless he can pursue it with passionate devotion."[12]

After an hour, we walked on, talking about MacIver's rebuttal of George Lundberg, who had argued that for methodological purposes you study a man fleeing from a pursuing crowd as if he were a piece of paper flying before the wind; in both cases the salient data is the movement of an object through space and time. MacIver said no, you have to look inside the man because for him "the image of what is yet to be informs the process of becoming."[13]

And then Stan recalled commentary by Huizinga on the unpredictability of life in the late Middle Ages, how crowds who had come out to see a hanging would unexpectedly be moved by pity and demand the release of the criminal—and the authorities would comply. Moral of the story: it's never over till it's over.

So now we were almost downtown, crossing the grounds of the state capitol, and Max Weber was eating on me and I blurted out "Look, Stan, I've got to know: do I have the calling for sociology?" And he said yes, without hesitation. What else could he say? Still his response meant for me the end of anomie, and I don't think I have known thirty-seven days of despondency in the subsequent thirty-seven years of my life.... We stopped for a last cup of coffee and drifted into talk of Hegel, who, said Stan, defined happiness as "a dream in youth realized in age."

For several years thereafter our paths parted. I went on to Tulane, wrote a doctor's dissertation on the medieval city, drawing on the 'heritage' Taylor and I had created in our Austin walks. In my journal in New Orleans I remembered Stan Taylor as the "only original thinker I have ever known" adding "but now it seems certain the rest of the world will never know of him."

Everyone recognized Taylor's creative genius but no one expected him to transcribe his thought into written form. Then at

forty-seven he returned to the University of Chicago, finished his
Ph.D. dissertation which is revised as *Conceptions of Institutions and
the Theory of Knowledge.* The postman brought me the book as a
complete surprise in 1957 when I was teaching at the University of
Tulsa; it has since been my constant companion.

Helen Waddell finds "the first articulate credo of the scholar's
religion" in these words by Hbranus Maurus[14] penned for a friend
in 911 A.D.:

To Eigilius, On a Book That He Wrote

No work of men's hands but the weary years
Beseige and take it; comes it evil day.

The written word alone flouts destiny,
Revives the past, and gives the lie to death.

Stan Taylor called my attention to the poem in 1951; the message
seems even more apposite now.

Notes

Introduction: CHOOSING INSTITUTIONS—A NARRATIVE
FOR THE SOCIOLOGY OF KNOWLEDGE

1. Robert Merton, "On the Oral Transmission of Knowledge"
in *Sociological Traditions from Generation to Generation: Glimpses of the
American Experience* (Norwood, N.J.: Ablex Publishing, 1982), pp.
1–35.

2. Irving L. Horowitz, *C. Wright Mills: An American Utopian,*
(New York: The Free Press of Macmillan, 1983), p. 35.

3. Data from *Time,* August 12, 1966, in the story on the sniper
Charles Whitman, who shot forty-four people from the tower.
(Fifteen of them died.) Four months earlier Whitman had told a
university psychiatrist that he was "thinking about going up on the
tower with a deer rifle and start shooting." The remark did not
particularly upset the psychiatrist because it was "a common
experence for students who came to the clinic to think of the tower
as the site for some desperate action."

4. Merton, *op. cit.,* p. 5.

5. William Graham Sumner, *Folkways: A Study of Sociological Usages, Manners, Customs, Mores and Morals* (New York: Mentor, 1960), pp. 61–62. cf. Wlad Godzich, "Afterword," Samuel Weber, *Institution and Interpretation.* (Minneapolis: University of Minnesota Press, 1987), p. 156.

6. Hans Gerth and C. Wright Mills, *Character and Social Structure: The Psychology of Social Institutions* (New York: Harcourt Brace, 1953).

7. Henrietta Spencer, "Through Projects, the Self is Actualized: Depression in Women as Seen by Humanistic Existentialism," *Catalyst,* 16 (1985), 28–34.

8. For elaboration see Taylor's "Conjure with the Self as Actor" in the Afterword.

9. "Afterword: Aristotle and the DNA," Jeremy Campbell, *Grammatical Man: Information, Entropy, Language and Life.* (New York: Simon and Schuster, 1982), pp. 266–73.

10. Helen Waddell, *The Wandering Scholars: The Life and Art of the Lyric Poets of the Latin Middle Ages* (New York: Doubleday Anchor, 1955), p. 30.

11. Ronnie Dugger, *Our Invaded Universities: Form, Reform, and New Starts. A Non-Fiction Play for Five Stages* (New York: W. W. Norton, 1974), p. xx.

12. Max Weber, "Science as Vocation" in Logan Wilson and W. L. Kolb, *Sociological Analysis* (New York: Harcourt Brace, 1949), Weber's lecture was given in 1919.

13. R. M. MacIver, *Social Causation* (Boston: Ginn and Company, 1942), pp. 8–9.

14. Waddell, *op. cit.,* p. 57.

CHAPTER ONE

Introduction

The Problem

The classical, or traditional, theory of knowledge is anchored to the Lockean sociology, or to put the matter in more familiar terms, to the individualism of Locke.[1] This institutional conception detached the knowing subject from the social context, and yet sought to validate knowledge by an analysis of the subject. In this there was a change of emphasis from the uncertainty of a dogmatically given ontological order to an attempt to attain surety by discovering in the subject the limiting conditions of knowledge. Empiricism aligned itself with rationalism and endowed the individual with reason, or a kind of absolute rationality. For the latter to operate it was necessary to strip away such factors as personal and emotional bias, class and institutional interests, and all that appeared to make for prejudice and passion. Further, in order to establish logical nexi between the objects of its apprehension this rationality required universal and necessary categories of thought. These were provided by the philosophy of Kant. In this way objectivity came to be regarded as residing in the inner necessity of thought.

It was the achievement of Marx, Durkheim, Mannheim, and Mead in the theory of ideology and the sociology of knowledge to restore the individual and his thinking to the social context. This made impossible the formulation of the epistemological problem in terms of the subject-object polarity as originally conceived for the subject *knows* only through institutional structure, or as the member of a class, age, party, society, or other social grouping. Once again it became necessary to consider the implications of the fact that thinking bears this continuous relationship to the forms of social existence. With the ever-increasing emphasis upon social structure the limitations of the older view of objectivity, and rationality, became apparent. A turning point was reached when social phenomena were viewed no longer as sources of error, illusion, and superstition, but as positive factors in the determination of thought.

These positions form the main outlines of a problem which appears in increasingly sharpened form with the further development of the sociology of knowledge. It is, however, of significance, not only to the historian of ideas, but to the sociologist whose method and subject matter constitute its core. Despite the seemingly contradictory character of the individualistic and sociological approaches to the problem of knowledge, it is *the thesis of the present study that the current disparity of viewpoint is not inevitable, and that the mediation of these perspectives is possible within the theoretical development of sociology.*

The Epistemological Status Of Social Elements In Knowledge

It has been implied in the opening statement that the classical theory of knowledge involves a concept of objectivity, or idea of truth, that structures the role of social factors in knowledge in purely negative fashion. Further, it was pointed out that, contrariwise, the sociology of knowledge insists that the realm of the theoretic is not autonomous, and that the effective penetration and disclosure of reality requires that the positive significance of social elements in the process of thought be explicitly recognised.[2] Because of this position in regard to the social conditioning of thought, the sociology of knowledge gives to the present period of social science its most characteristic feature. It is this notion of the positive role of social factors in the processes of human thinking that has permitted the sociology of knowledge to assume with almost dramatic suddenness a position of strategic importance.[3] Thus it may be helpful to indicate briefly some of the steps in the transition from the view of social elements as factors of bias through to the logical inversion of this conception in the sociology of knowledge.

The idea that social existence may be involved in the validation of thought can be found in one form or another in the methodological and metaphysical inquiries of various thinkers of modern times.[4] Among the earliest to express such a view in clear and intelligible form was Francis Bacon.[5]

English philosophy is especially distinguished for its continuous protest against Scholasticism. It is no exaggeration to say that the classical period of English thought is an unremitting effort to show on an epistemological basis the utter impossibility of a valid metaphysic. This critical movement which did not exhaust itself for almost four centuries begins with Bacon. Never weary of assailing the curiosities, subtleties, and "word-wisdom," of the schoolmen as fruitless and barren logomachy, Bacon, on the objective side directs attention to nature and actuality.[6] This setting up of experience as an independent object of thought to be studied by the inductive method, has won for him his place at the head of modern philosophy. Somewhat less acclaimed has been the subjective side of Bacon's contribution. Not only is it necessary to reduce science to nature and experience, but the intellect must be kept free from a certain "infusion" that perverts and falsifies its work.[7] There are, says Bacon, factors that lead the understanding to erroneous conclusions. These sources of error, bias, and prejudice, he calls, "Idols." The most troublesome of all are the "Idols of the Market Place,"[8] which are brought about by man in social intercourse, especially by language, in the tendency to substitute words for ideas. Thus Bacon is the first of that series of thinkers who seek to explain certain aspects of bias, error, illusion, and superstition by their social origin. In an essential sense Bacon conceives of mind as capable of objective knowledge. Given the proper methodological safeguards science is possible.

The problem, then, for Bacon is to unveil, strip away, and remove from the processes of rational thought the obstructions which arise out of man's social life. He is fully aware that. "every day experience is no sure basis for a true knowledge of nature," but his admission of the skeptical argument in nowise destroys his faith in an objective order which can be known, and which will assure man his power over things.[9]

Bacon in his derivation from Medieval nominalism has taken from his precursors the belief in things (particulars) and the Divine mind which provides for their necessary connection (order, laws).[10] This is Bacon's objectivity. He does not appear to be committed to a belief in an absolute reason. On the contrary his critique of the understanding would seem to show a strong belief in man's tendency to "rationalization" rather than rationality. For him the cloudy thinking capacity of man attains knowledge only where there is a constant alertness to the falsification of experience by the idols, and when the intimate, immediate commerce of the senses with external nature is rigorously subjected to the inductive method. Since some classes of idols are deemed to be merely adventitious, but others innate, Bacon can have but little confidence in reason as such. Like all nominalists he tends to subordinate reason to the primacy of will, as if knowledge followed from what is *done* rather than from what is thought.[11] Hence, the emphasis upon method.[12] Indeed, that distrust of reason which was to reach its culmination in the twentieth century is present already in Bacon. Of course, for the early investigators of the physical world the implications of this distrust in rational thought are tempered by a firm belief that nature constitutes an order, and also by the confidence inspired by the inductive method.

The full significance of the idols makes itself apparent only when attention is directed to the study of human relations. The idols mean that historical social structures are edifices of prejudice, bias, and error. The latter having their foundation in expediency, interests and passion, they become the instruments of exploitation, and at the same time, the living repository of the past stupidities of mankind. It is these implications of the nominalism of Bacon (and at a later date, of Locke) which on being transplanted to France become the revolutionary thought of the *philosophes* — Voltaire, Diderot, D'Alembert, Helvetius, Holbach, and La Mettrie. Finally, the view that society and its institutions are the chief source of human error is taken up by the *idéologues,* or ideologists, whose task becomes that of first identifying, and then separating the rational idea from its institutional husk.

The *idéologues* — Condillac, Cabanis, Maine de Biran, Destutt de Tracy, and Degérando, to mention only the more familiar

names, differ from their brilliant predecessors, the *philosophes*
in the specific program of their efforts, but scarcely at all in
the spirit of them.[13] The passionately cherished end of human
freedom; the hatred of hierarchical and state intolerance; a deep
contempt for the simply dictated — these characteristics animate
the French *illuminati* from first to last.

The logical consequences of the implicit thought of the
Idols of the Market Place are set forth by the *philosophes* in
extreme radical form, sometimes with the most unhesitating har-
dihood. Directing their polemics and sparkling satire against the
whole world of authority, tradition, and received opinion, they
endeavored to point out as the epitome of contradiction the
contrast between Church and state on the one hand and the
demands of reason on the other. Bacon, of course, had been
content to comply with a blind submission to the authority of
the state.[14] Apparently satisfied to point out how the distorting
effects of the Idols of the Market Place could be minimized
in the study of physical nature, he was able to suggest no "help"
by which a systematic elimination of error might be effected
in the social realm. Indeed, the latter as constituted by "the
intercourse and association of men with each other," is, for
Bacon, the very fountainhead of error. Now the *philosophes*
seized upon the view that the vitiation of reason by social life,
especially in its phases of greed, prejudice and superstition was
responsible for the institutional framework that presently existed.
They held that it was no longer possible for men to reason
with accuracy because the latter are impelled to prejudice by
their respective positions in the social structure. However, the
philosophes were not content to maintain a position of relativism, where as they envisioned it, one set of prejudices would
confront another. Instead, they hastened to establish a mode of
thought that would be detached from the distorting influence
of social factors.[15] It will be seen that while it was the *philosophes'* conception that bias and error are intrinsic to institutions, they, nevertheless, believed that it was possible to reach
the reasoning process as such, and having accomplished this end,
to find ways to eliminate, or control the virus of error, constituted, so to speak, by social existence. Foremost among the
idéologues to attempt this analysis of the human mind was
Destutt de Tracy who took up the term "ideology" as descriptive

of his task and goal.[16] Firstly, he hoped to show how institutional structures arose; and secondly, to lay bare the foundations of reason. He felt that only by building anew upon such a base could a rational collective existence become a possibility. To achieve his aim of separating out from the tangle of social structures the idea in its purity, Destutt de Tracy turned to the philosophy of Locke. The Lockean theory of knowledge (like that of Bacon) involved the nominalist premise that things alone are real, and that abstract ideas, or universals, are valid only insofar as they correctly express as symbols the particulars to which they refer. The *idéologues* discovered in this position a weapon for their attack upon the abstractions which supported the various institutional forms. If the universals had no reality in themselves then institutions such as the Church and state were but individuals and their relationships.[17] Thus, it seemed to the *idéologues* that it would be possible by means of an analysis to reduce the institutions into the relationships of individuals in whose minds alone the universals had any existence.[18] The *idéologues* felt that they were in possession of a method that would hasten the destruction of the existing social order made up of institutions, of superstition, prejudice, greed, and exploitation, and which at the same time would facilitate the construction of the rational society of the future.

It may be well to summarize quickly certain resemblances and differences in the positions of Bacon and the *idéologues* respectively.

As has been shown Bacon posits the object as a discrete entity; the subject is equally discrete. Except for the refracting process of the idols no emphasis is placed upon the interrelationship of subject and object. Bacon does not consider the object as a product of a conceptual apparatus. Since no attention is given to the conceptual framework as constituting, in form at least, the object, so there can be no recognition of the positive part played by social, or interest bound, factors in formulating what is the object through their determination of the conceptual apparatus. Bacon has identified nature with ontological reality, and objectivity, or objective thought, is no more than its unclouded image.[19] The great obstacle to truth is the deceptive and falsifying influence of the idols. There is no awareness in Bacon that the reliable and coherent aspect of experience is, to an extent as yet not clearly established, a function of the fixity and universality of categories. Bacon did observe that the social process refracted the object, but he regarded this as accidental in the achievement of objectivity; he did not see that this same process is responsible for both the fixation and dis-integration of the categorial framework necessary to any kind of objectivity. Further, he could not recognize the variability involved in human thinking — a feature logically implied in the consequences of social processes in widely different human groups giving rise to equally different categorial structures.[20]

Turning to the *idéologues* one finds the acceptance of nature as the real world (a view deriving from Bacon, Newton, and Locke), but there is a great deal more weight placed upon the role of the intellect in objective knowledge. This is shown, first, in the negative, or adulterative sense, in the socially derived tendencies to prejudice and error; secondly, in a positive man-ner in the possibility of thought existing in a pure form — as reason.[21]

These differences in emphasis are readily explained in terms of the history of nominalism in English thought and medieval realism in that of France. It need only be pointed out that the latter mode can be observed with marked clearness even though enclosed in the transplanted empiricism of Bacon and Locke. In addition to the point of agreement on the thesis of the distorting influence of social factors in knowledge there is a second, already implied in the first: the belief in a sphere of truth that is in itself absolute.[22] This realm is believed to be independent of the human coefficient and all social perspec-tives. Indeed both Bacon and the *idéologues* hoped to explain the illusions, superstitions, and prejudices of man by either their social origins, or their private passions. The sphere of truth is reached only as there is an unmasking, or unveiling, of the motivations that give rise to the propositions in question. Thus, for Bacon and the *idéologues* objectivity is possible only when those elements of an assertion having their origin in class, in-stitutional, or other sociological sources are disentangled and removed. It is characteristic of the conventional theory of knowl-edge to regard the residue alone as of objective importance. It is but a step from the position of Bacon and the *idéologues* to that of Kant where to obtain objectivity the residue must be referred to an absolute conceptual scheme, or more narrowly, to final criteria of validity. As is well known, the basic categorial apparatus is, for Kant, *a priori*.

The dominating feature, then, of the belief in a sphere of truth as such is that knowledge consists of ideas detached from, or transcendent to, the world of social experience. Although only two positions received any analysis, the most cursory examination of many other thinkers will exhibit the same belief in regard to social processes on the one hand and knowledge on the other. This seems to be the case even when the thinker in question has some grasp of the role of social factors in knowledge. For example, this is to be observed in Auguste Comte who in the famous, "Law of the Three Stages," presupposes a connection between the stages of the development of a society and kinds of knowledge. Thus, for him, theological, or religious knowledge, belongs to an old type of structure; metaphysical knowledge, to a kind of feudal structure; positive, or scientific, to an industrial social structure.[23] One notes a primitive sociology of knowledge in this correlation of types of social structure with types of knowledge. However, in following Comte further, it is important to mark his assertion that objective knowledge is attained only in the positive stage when knowledge becomes causally determinative of the form of society, and not, as when vice versa, in the theological and metaphysical stages, society is determinative of the form of knowledge. In other words, for Comte, objective knowledge is possible when the dependence of thought upon social structure ends or when the point of reciprocal dependence of thought and social structure disappears. Thus the positive, or scientific, stage is that of disengagement or liberation of thought from class, institutional, and other social forms. In this it is not difficult to see how closely related the thought of Comte is to that of the *idéologues*.

The notion of an absolute sphere of knowledge pervades the thinking of Karl Marx as is evident in his discussion of ideological superstructures.[24] The latter has reference to the way in which Marx in his empirical analyses found social and political ideas to be conditioned by the social milieu — to reflect the economic interests of those participating in the conflict of classes. In this connection Marx carefully separates the natural, and mathematical, sciences from those of human behavior as e.g. political science, sociology, etc. He finds that in the latter group objective knowledge is presently impossible since the influence of social structure is such that only ideologies, and not objective ideas arise. To be sure Marx believes that objective knowledge for the human studies is possible, but only when the distorting influence of existing social structure ceases — that is, when the class struggle is ended. Thus with Marx, as with Bacon, the *idéologues,* and Comte, the dominating thought is that objectivity can come about only as ideas are purified, or as they break out of the falsifying ambiance of the social. Marx like his predecessors views the social perspective in pejorative fashion, as derogation from the autonomy of reason.

Mannheim has followed Marx closely in this regard. He, too, views knowledge of the social realm as qualitatively different from that of physical nature and as requiring its own distinctive thought model.[25] He appears to have abandoned the view that objective knowledge would follow upon the close of the class struggle for he insists upon the premise that all thinking in sociohistorical terms is ideological. However, his effort to set up a class of "intellectuals" which is to be "loosely anchored in tradition" indicates clearly that he has not escaped from the notion of a sphere of pure objective knowledge.[26] Indeed, the kind of knowledge which Mannheim envisages as the goal of the intellectuals is quite the same as that which Marx had in mind, and which was to appear with the classless society. It has an affinity too with the completely positive knowledge of Comte which the latter declared would become a reality in the third and final stage when thinking had become independent of social structure. Further, it closely resembles, if it is not quite the same, as the reason, or pure ideas uncolored by social perspectives, to which the *idéologues* aspired in their analysis of human thought. Hence, despite the advances made by Marx and Mannheim in drawing attention to the social context of thought, there is at the same time no full relinquishment of the views that objective knowledge is one cleansed of the bias of its social origin. Indeed, in some respects there is in the Mannheimian conception of the intellectual almost a reversion to the traditional theory of knowledge.

There are, however, two sociologists who, unlike the men touched upon above, do not regard knowledge of social phenomena as in a distinct category from other knowledge and as requiring a special treatment to render it objective. Émile Durkheim[27] and George H. Mead[28] regard all knowledge as arising in the social process. Further, it is implicit in their writings, when not actually expressed, that objectivity consists in referring knowledge back to the social process, or the institutional structure. It is important to note that the setting up of institutions as a basis for objectivity completely reverses the conception of the traditional theory of knowledge which viewed social factors as contingent elements.

In regard to social factors and the objectivity of thought it will be seen that four possibilities now present themselves: (1) On the assumption that objectivity is attainable in the natural and the exact sciences to apply their methods rigorously to the study of social phenomena with the purpose of minimizing and ultimately eliminating the perspectival distortion. The achievement of this goal would be to incorporate the study of society in the same general system of knowledge as the natural sciences. On the whole this has been, and remains, the position of positivism. (2) On the same assumption of objectivity in the natural and exact sciences to divide the field of knowledge cleanly and finally between the natural and exact sciences on the one hand and the social sciences on the other.[29] The latter as concerned with "relational" knowledge would develop its own canons of objectivity through the study of "stylistic structures" and their mediation by a class of intellectuals. This is the position developed by Mannheim on the insights of Marx. (3) To view all knowledge as arising in the social process, and objectivity as subject to the dynamics of that process. This possibility has been seized upon by the social psychologist, G. H. Mead, and in a somewhat different way by Durkheim, but only in the final stages of the latter's theoretical development. (4) To follow Mead and Durkheim in viewing all knowledge as arising in the social process, but at the same time, to insist upon the distinction drawn by Marx, Weber, Dilthey, Mannheim, etc. between the natural sciences and the social sciences.

The first position adheres to the notion of objectivity in the usual positivistic sense of the classical theory of knowledge. It denies that other cognitive conceptions in regard to reality can have any final meaning. The second position sets up two orders of reality and of knowledge; it seems to imply the need for some modification of the concept of objectivity as developed in the classical theory. The third position raises in acute form the problem of historical and cultural relativism. The fourth position is confronted with the problem of assimilating at least two diverse kinds of knowledge to one another; in addition, it must bridge the gaps between socio-historical periods, etc. of a single culture and find the common denominator in various cultures.

To summarize: It is clear that in the earlier period of modern science the presence of the social factor in scientific method was either overlooked, or neglected. Insofar as social elements were thought of in connection with knowledge they were conceived to be obstructions to objectivity; indeed, as accidental, foreign, strange, contingent, and contaminating. The problem was to find a way to the systematic elimination of these sources of interference with reason. The question remained at this level even with the *idéologues* but had advanced to a somewhat sharpened form. Like the *idéologues,* Comte and Marx were intensely aware of the important part that social elements had played, and continued to play, in human thinking. Nevertheless, they regarded the liberation of thought from such elements, not only as a desirable goal, but one historically now close at hand. With Mannheim, Mead, and Durkheim came the realization that thought is always bound up with social processes and structures — that the autonomy of a theoretic sphere conceived of as in separation from the social process is delusory. With Mannheim alone there remained attenuated and vestigial traces of the old ideal of "freeing" thought from its anchorage in classes and institutions. With Durkheim, however, there is no longer an acceptance of objectivity detached entirely from the on-going social process. This may be said likewise of Mead. With these men what was once a concern with features of contingency in knowledge e.g. idols and ideologies develops rapidly into a sociology of knowledge, or more clearly, a theory of knowledge.

The traditional theory of knowledge had found its criteria of validity in categories of an innate and transcendent character. It had carried to their logical conclusions the presuppositions contained in the theory of the vitiation of the understanding by the Idols of the Market Place, which as the *idéologues* had demonstrated, meant the refraction of reason by institutions and by

position in the institutional structure. As already shown it pos-
ited a hypothetical sphere of truth or pure reason. To attain
thinking of this undistorted kind it became necessary to effect a
separation of the individual from the institution — that is, from
the context of historical social structures. In this is expressed
the dominating thought of individualism. However, in the extreme radical form of detaching the individual entirely from institutional bases, individualism has never been permitted to realize
itself in history.

It has been noted that Durkheim took up an inverse position
to the traditional theory of knowledge insofar as he endeavored
to derive the categories — criteria of validity — from the institutional
structure, and thus make the latter the basis for objective thought.

From the foregoing it becomes evident that institutions must
occupy a significant place in any effective discussion of the theory of knowledge and the latter's central issue, the problem of
objectivity. However, it will be observed that it is not only, or
necessarily, the way in which institutions are constituted as observable phenomena that is of importance. Equally significant
are the conceptions (also a feature of social existence) which
men form of their institutions.[30] Thus before proceeding to an
analytical treatment of the theory of knowledge as formulated
by thinkers of representative schools it seems relevant to consider
more directly, if briefly, the relation of the concept of institution
to the problem of objectivity.

Institutional And Methodological Issues

It has often been said that the focus of sociology must be
the institutional problem;[31] it has almost as frequently been
said that research into the general question of institutions has
achieved only the vaguest and for the most part unsatisfactory
results. However, it must be admitted that studies in institutional analysis occupy a prominent place in modern thought.
Indeed, so much is this the case that the concept of institution
has emerged as the basic predicate of recent sociological investigation. That institutions are not only the constitutive tissue of
human social existence as exhibited in the patterns of moral
conformity, but are also bound up in a fundamental way with
the structure of thought is a fact that has been apparent to a
series of sociologists including Marx, Durkheim, Mead, Lukacs,

Scheler, Sorokin, Mannheim, Halbwachs, and Granet. The reflections of these brilliant thinkers upon the interrelated questions of social organization and human knowledge indicates that the direction, and in a sense the validity, of sociological research turns upon the correctness and clarity with which these relationships are described.

A singular feature of almost all studies of institutions is the neglect of any systematic analysis of the general conceptions that have obtained in regard to them. This is all the more strange since the general conception is the initial stage in the process of the isolation of the material as an object of study. It may be objected that general conceptions in fact have been studied but as an essential part of the institution itself and its historical transformations. In other words no explicit separation between the value and its empirical expression on the one hand and the general conception on the other has been felt necessary. In any event no matter what position is taken up on the question, it is of moment to recognize that the general conception is an important element in the basic meaning which an institution has for its participants. At least some attributes of the institution appear to be in conformity with the general conception. It follows from this that since the general conception undergoes mutations no statement regarding such attributes would be valid for all periods. The question arises: Is there any principle in terms of which the general conceptions can be ordered, and which will exhibit, or reflect, in the conceptions what in a primary sense the institutions actually are for the members of a given society or historical epoch? Now it will have been seen that any answer to the thesis hinges upon what is connoted by the concept of objectivity. Indeed, the connotations placed upon this concept are the datum and logical terminus of the thinking processes of a society. Hence, if a relationship does obtain between social structures and thought, it may be expected that this basic notion will manifest itself in the way the institutions are related to the general conception of them.

Turning to concrete societies and making use of the notion of objectivity as an instrument of classification in respect to conceptions of institutions, three situational types are distinguishable:

1. That in which the institution is the basis of the individual's thinking, feeling, and acting. In this situation the insti-

tution is sacred, and the thought forms embodied in it have an eternal validity guaranteed by an ontology deriving its authority from some transcendental stadium, e.g., God, etc. Strictly speaking the objectivity of this situation is best described as a conception, or norm, of "truth."

2. That in which the institution is viewed in separation from the individual and in a pejorative connotation becomes the object of critical reflection and analysis. Objectivity is no longer grounded in the institution but in the cognitive act of a rational subject.

3. That in which there is a sociological reconstruction of the significance of the institution but upon a platform of validity measured by secular criteria, e.g. science, etc.

Methodologically, these three conceptions of institutions together with their corresponding notions of objectivity are constructions similar to the kind theoretically formulated by Max Weber as ideal-types.[32] They are in no respect metaphysical entities but devices intended to stylize actual structures of mentality. However, they do not carry the implication that any concrete society, or individual mind, in its thinking corresponds to a type in an exact or complete sense. Rather, the types are statements of the norms which govern thinking in various societies and epochs, but with the reservation that a given socio-historical situation, or its representative thinker, is likely to reflect only an imperfect compliance with one of these normative orientations, or perhaps exhibit traces of more than one norm. It would seem justifiable to speak of a mentality of one or other of the three types provided that the norm described by the construction infuses, permeates, and dominates the mental content of a given society, school of thought, or individual thinker. The ideal-type, then, may be used in the analysis of concrete structures of thought, and indeed, constitutes the frame of reference for the subsumability of particular instances.

It is evident that each of the three situational types serves as a very general conceptual scheme and determines for given subjects the form, or mode of statement, of the facts of experience, their classification and validation. The experiences of every day life are reclassified according to the concept of objectivity obtaining, and each conception, or situational type stands, as the case may be, in a positive, negative, or mixed relationship to the actual institutional structure. Indeed, the conception of the institutional field is an integral part of the latter and determines the nature of the subject's reception of reality. So much is this the case that empirical data considered to be existing in direct significant relationships when subsumed under one situational type may well be differentiated by the entire dimension of being when the subsumption is in terms of another type.[33]

It is well to perceive at once that the "thingness" or objective aspect of the world is given to us not by its ontological status as such, but by a peculiar relationship between this ontological reality and some general frame of reference. Empirical experience does not in itself permit its own validation; it cannot distinguish clearly between truth and error, objectivity and illusion. Experience has always to be corrected, or validated, ultimately by one or other of the three situational types mentioned although a number of conceptual schemes may be found in the continuum between the experience and the validating situational type.[34]

The three conceptions of institutions and the theories of knowledge they involve are, perhaps, the most general schemes of validation that have been used. As previously suggested each conception functions as a norm of thought, and designates in and for the subject a fairly definite mentality.[35] The close connection of the first conception (Type 1) with sacred and religious truth is obvious. Similarly, the second conception (Type 2) is clearly related to secular thought and describes the attitude developed and expressed in the classical theory of knowledge. The third conception (Type 3) is characteristic of various schools of the sociology of knowledge. Since this type makes the institutional structure the source and warrant for the logical categories operating in the subject's thought, it is the inverse of individualism as conceptualized and formulated in the classical theory of knowledge.

The ideal-type procedure is frequently employed to determine how much the sociological type diverges from reality and vice versa. However, the three types discussed here have been constructed with the purpose of precipitating the varying assumptions regarding the nature of objectivity to the surface of thought; to throw into sharp relief the forms by which experience is validated; to clarify generally the issues involved in the investigation. Above all they are intended to demonstrate the difficulty that resides in the current concept of objectivity as a result of the contradictory views that obtain with respect to the epistemological status of institutional and other social elements in knowledge. The resolution of this difficulty would effectively mediate the classical and sociological positions. An important step in achieving this end appears to lie in determining with greater precision the nature of the relationship between institutions and knowledge. The character of this problem discloses that the investigation falls definitely within that sphere of research which has come to be designated the sociology of knowledge.[36]

The major assumption upon which the present inquiry proceeds is that of the logical interrelatedness of all experience. This is no more than the principle of sufficient reason, and there would seem to be no escape from this premise unless one is prepared to accept the various discontinuities in experience as final. The latter alternative is the abandonment of explanation in favor of the pluralistic position that the discontinuities are non-rational limits to disparate implicative systems.

Together with the primary assumption that all experience is bound together in the unity of thought is the second assumption that no intelligible answer to an experiential question is possible that fails to recognize clearly the distinction between thought and things. To state this proposition otherwise, it is meant that in the very asking of a question, or setting of a problem in regard to experience, a separation of the metaphysical unity into the order of thought and the order of things has already occurred.

With this complex of theoretical goals and assumptions in mind the attempt is made to reach a position that would be favorable to a direct attack on the question — the character of the relationship between the institutional structure and the forms of thought. In order to achieve this limited objective it seems relevant to examine representative statements of certain positions — individualistic and sociological — in respect of this relationship. By such a procedure it would seem possible to bring to light the basic presuppositions involved. However, the main object of the analysis and comparison of viewpoints is to seek out the causes of their inadequacy in order to move forward with some assurance toward a more satisfactory formulation of the problem.

The systems selected for examination are individualism, sociological positivism (Comte, Durkheim), and historical relativism (Mannheim), respectively.

While there is nothing that is not material for scientific research, certain methodological limitations are imposed by the nature of the facts to be comprehended. Since the empirical basis of the present study consists of the objective traces of thought in the form of written records, an important difficulty presents itself. It is necessary to note that the content of the data are subjective and in a double sense. They are the product of the mental processes of various authors but are subject also to the transforming effect of the emotional and categorial apparatus of the investigator's mind. The leading assumptions making up this mental set, insofar as they can be made explicit at all, have been scrutinized above. However, the presence of assumptions means that the deductive processes based upon them will be present also in all the inductive inference of the research.

The particular inductive procedure to be employed is that based on the theory which claims to trace and build the systematic connections of the facts themselves. In this instance the facts are subjective and are governed by a certain kind of norm — that of objectivity. More correctly one might speak of norms, each of the latter answering to a definite conception of objectivity as set out in the three situational types. The facts, then, are to be considered as fragments of systems; the goal is to show that given certain conceptions as to the nature of institutions these systems follow from the actual relationship between institutions and the forms of thought. It must be remembered that the chief data of the study — the schools of individualism, sociological positivism, and historical relativism are attempts at systematization. The application of the method suggested where the facts are ideas must consist in showing that the attempts mentioned are in terms of their objectives either incomplete or self-contradictory, or both. Thus the investigator's interpretation should complete the integration of the facts and remove the contradiction if the analysis indicates the necessity of the two operations.

In regard to the interpretation placed upon any one of the three schools referred to above, internal proof would consist in pointing out the ways in which it functioned to order the detailed data of the system. External proof would consist in deducing from a general postulate the set of postulates of the system in question, or again, the capability of this general postulate to subsume the data of all three systems.[37]

The first system of ideas to be examined is that of individualism.

CHAPTER TWO

Individualism

Historical And General Features

Historically, the rise of pronounced individualism whether ancient or modern is paralleled with the decay of religion and the growth of secular knowledge.[1] As the structure of religious myth collapses, philosophy and science attempt to discover solutions to those questions of human life and of the universe to which religion at an earlier period supplied a ready answer. But whereas the sacred framework is social in the broader sense of the term, philosophy and science present an appearance of individuality since it is at scattered points in the social milieu that the disintegration appears. These points — the foci, in fact, of new social forces — are individual minds. The passing of religious belief is not confined to a disdain for miracles, omens, and auguries; the negative, critical attitude extends into the social and political sphere in the undermining of class stratification and the overthrow of institutions. The usual constraint and obligation that flows from the institutional structure becomes mere irksome restriction; the thought forms embodied in that structure lose their universal and eternal validity, and they are reduced to targets for popular wit, and sometimes the most vicious satire. The individual justifies to himself the breaking up of the sacred system into a multiplicity of concepts as a protection against political and hierarchical absolutism, and as rendering explicit the concept of change. The latter from the individual's standpoint is envisaged as progress.[2] The individual regards institutions as having functioned as instruments of social control largely successful through the fear and terror they inspired but as now devoid of

41

meaningful content. To him ritual and ceremony seem even less rational than other institutional practices, but all alike are suspect, and he anticipates their disappearance with the growing rationality of man.

In individualism the stadium of rationality and objectivity is transferred from the social framework to the cognitive act of the subject. Each man becomes a rational agent and all men may enter into contracts. Indeed, much of the attitude of the individual toward fundamental institutions can be traced to the ascendancy of contract.[3] Now the possibility of contract can arise only with the correlated rise of the concept of free-will. Generally, that point in history when institutional norms can be written down is the one when law emerges. Early law appears to be rigid but this would seem to be a consequence of the anchorage of written concepts. In any event this inflexibility passes away with the rise of contract. However, the very carrying out of contract interferes with the privileges, duties and obligations of status. Hence, with the rise of individualism basic institutions such as marriage, family, and social class, which define status systems, exhibit a marked decline.[4] Sociologically, this means that an individualistic society endeavors to transform these institutions into contracts.[5] Indeed, civil law, or contract, shrinks the area of status rights and duties so characteristic of the sacred viewpoint; instead, it emphasizes the contractual bond as the most significant one obtaining between men. Contract, however, is possible only when the individual believes he is free to act and direct.

It will be seen that two predicates — perhaps incompatible ones — are essential to individualism. These are (a) the belief in the rational nature of the individual, and (b) the belief that this rational individual is free to choose between alternatives (volitional indeterminacy). Together with these positive assertions as to the nature of man is the negative formulation of institutional structure as the product of irrational social forces — a structure for the most part non-rational, coercive, and restrictive.[6] The difficulties involved in these assumptions will be examined later.

Looking more particularly to the rise of individualism in modern Europe, certain unique features present themselves. Despite the dissolution of the Medieval world-view into a multiplicity of competing ontologies, modern individualism has retained the basic conception of Christianity in respect to the infinite worth of the soul, but in the mundanely transmuted sense of the human individual. During the long centuries of the Middle Ages faith in the individual soul had become positively formulated. With the transition to another age the universe itself came to be reconstructed in terms of self-conscious reason. Hence, the early modern period is almost wholly individualistic. Ages of preoccupation with the inner worth of the individual developed a fundamental conviction that even the universe must conform to the individual, and with the passing of the emphasis upon the soul as such, this meant conformity to the thinking subject. The ascetic isolation of the subject from the world, together with the ever-increasing inflation of his ontological significance which this separation from the stream of reality involved, finally effected a remarkable circuit of theory. It shifted the location of the real itself from the externality of the visible universe to the internality of thought. Thus, the assurance and sense of dominion which modern individualism displays has in this important respect almost no counterpart in other societies, or in ancient times. It is important to note that this new power of the individual is conceived of as proceeding from himself as autonomous and self-sufficient. It is in sharp contrast to the view of the individual as powerful in terms of an institutional base. Indeed, to this individualism, the very notion of institution is of doubtful value. Unlike other periods, in the individualistic epoch the institution is seldom conceived of as necessary to a rational social life. In most ages the individual grounded his speculations upon some philosophy, or religion, and found objectivity and authoritative statement in some such source. The rational interference with the non-rational forces of nature, or of social processes, had been in terms of some divinely revealed truth, or institution so-established. However, in the high-tide of individualism toward the close of the eighteenth century the rights of the individual ceased to be regarded as an ordering fiction merely but were now a reality founded upon experience and discovered inductively.[7] The dispersion of coercive authority among various powers — political, industrial, and ecclesiastical — is believed to be essential to the individual. The welfare of the individual came to be the sole criterion of the worth of any institution whatever. Indeed, the

fundamental institution of the modern world has been the individual. As an institution he became sacred and central; what
had been sacred and central (the state, Church, etc.) became
peripheral and only with difficulty justified their existence. In
a way this is the same view more succinctly expressed by Descartes:

> I was convinced of the necessity of undertaking once in
> my life to rid myself of all the opinions I had adopted,
> and of commencing anew the work of building from
> the foundation, if I desired to establish a firm and abid-
> ing superstructure in the sciences.[8]

The Cartesian method of doubting the validity or sufficiency of
what is already known is fundamentally a doubt of the "opinions" developed in social life. It indicates a deep distrust of
those historical and institutional formulations which hitherto had
constituted the conditions of intelligible meaning and valid inference. Descartes, like Bacon, takes social elements — institutions,
class position, etc. — into account, but only as sources of confusion and obscurity. Descartes' assertion is the expression of a
conviction that the individual has both the capability and the
need to detach himself from the socio-historical process and its
more stable aspect — the institutional framework. Through this
separation, individualism declares, it becomes possible for the individual to attain that purely abstract rationality essential to the
validation of his experience. Hence, from this standpoint knowledge must rest upon an inner, but universal predicate, common
to all men, independent and inderivative from any conceivable
historical social structure, or position in it.

While other ages have been strong in faith, the Cartesian
method of explicit and systematic doubt expresses what is characteristic of all modern life. The notions of "false consciousness,"
self-deception, disguise, and simulacra, together with the doubt
that they inspire, anticipate the universal debunking atmosphere
of the twentieth century. In the individualistic society the individual above all else fears to be duped and misguided.[9] Psychologically, he looks for the "rationalization" in thought, feeling,
and action; similarly, from the sociological viewpoint he seeks to
separate out the interest-bound, ideological element in socio-historical judgments by an examination of the latter's class and
institutional roots. This widespread, pervasive doubt is but the

reverse side of the coin which on its face bears the image of an absolute "reason." Thus again it must be reiterated that the Marxist and Mannheimian conception of ideology, insofar as it connotes falsity, remains attached in this respect to the standpoint of individualism with its emphasis upon a rationality free from the refractions and sublimations contingent upon position in class and institutional structure. Of course, one should not overlook the fact that the legitimacy of any form of doubt requires some ideal of perfect knowledge. Certainly, in principle this ideal does not require a fixed, or *a priori* form, and quite conceivably, might be constituted by a process, e.g., the social process. It is the express goal of the sociology of knowledge to pass beyond the implication of falsity contained in the ideological concept to the insight that the social process is the basis of all knowledge.

The vast, complex dimensions of individualism make difficult any single definition of it that would be empirically and logically adequate. No important thinker of individualism formulates its meaning in a manner that would be acceptable to all other thinkers of the same movement. However, for all the diverse ways in which individualism is socially expressed and theoretically presented, this much may be said: Firstly, it can be identified by its ahistorical, critical attitude toward class and institutional forms; secondly, as philosophic affirmation it always asserts the ethical and rational finality of the individual, as opposed to society, in the ontological conception of the world. This view of the profound nature of the individual remains characteristic of individualism whether the metaphysic that purports to express the reality of things is materialistic (La Mettrie, Holbach) or idealistic (Kant). For the most part individualism is a social theory and an ethic; its premises signify "that there is no such thing as an abstract good of society apart from the good of persons composing it."[10] Yet, since the meaning of individualism is inserted in the metaphysical finality of the individual in a rational, as well as in an ethical sense, there can be no dependence upon tradition, custom, and institutions for universally valid standards in thought any more than in ethical norms. In the thinking of individualism, institutions lose their unity and universality, and are resolved into relationships between individuals — become mere organizations of the latter. The continued existence of such struc-

tures is to be justified only in their service and critical subjection
to the purposes of individuals.[11]

These remarks seem to suggest that the problem of the validation of knowledge is an aspect of the larger problem of the
relation of the individual to the institutional structure, or more
accurately, of the way in which the individual conceives of this
relationship, and of how he defines that structure. It is typical
of individualism to deny that institutions, or more broadly, social
existence, can have a positive bearing on the validation of knowledge, and it seeks its criteria of validity in transcendental, or
metaphysical sources.[12] Negatively, however, individualism regards
social existence as affecting the validation of thought — viewing
it as a source of error.

The peculiar import of these remarks arises from the depth
of the antithesis of individual and institution — an antithesis that
appears only with individualism, and which, as has been shown,
carries consequences not only for the meaning of ethical norms,
but for the theory of knowledge. With the abstraction of the
individual from a social structure and its theoretical under-
pinning, the individual can no longer validate his experience,
either in regard to empirical factual relationships or ethical ends,
by reference to a divine source, but only on some *a priori* ground,
some metaphysical principle.[13] There is the alternative of proceeding to the concrete individual, and on the basis of what
appears to be his nature, establish standards of thought and action.
A third possibility is to refuse to pass beyond the immediacy of
experience, to accept an absolute relativism of the subject (individual), and thus abandon the search for ultimate standards of
validation. In modern individualism these three possibilities exhibit themselves as actual developments and may be expressed as
follows: (a) In the pursuit of rational certainty by substituting
a metaphysical reconstruction of ultimate principles in place of
the earlier divinely supported unity of institutional and ontological orders now splintered and atomized by individualistic,
critical attitudes (Kant). This metaphysical reconstruction is to
be seen in various philosophical systems. However, it is the pecu-
liarity of the system of Kant that it arises within individualism
instead of in opposition to it as, for example, the system of Hegel.
Different as are the two systems mentioned, both strive to overcome the caprice and arbitrariness of the concrete individual, and

in this one respect may be said to be animated by the same intent.[14]
(b) In the ethics of sensibility, or hedonism. This is particularly
so in that form of the latter known as utilitarianism, in which
the effort is made to erect as a norm what is believed to be the
actual nature of man.   (c) In subjectivism.

Before attempting to comprehend the character of the relationship between the above-mentioned forms of individualism and
the process of validation, some additional remarks may be offered
with reference to the grounds upon which these particular kinds
of individualism have been selected for examination.

For the purposes of this study the significant element in
individualism is its negative, critical attitude toward institutional
and class structures. The accentuated formulation of this element
in the inquiry should not obscure the widely varying range of
individualistic positions in which it is to be found. The most
cursory survey of these positions reveals a continuum at one end
of which is an extreme singularistic and nominalistic subjectivism.
Opposing itself to institutional standards, rules, and definitions,
and finding its criterion of validity for thought and conduct within the subject — usually, in the act of perception — it stresses the
individual in his discreteness, autonomy, and independence. The
opposite end of the continuum is marked by an individualism of
universalistic and idealistic emphasis. Here the criteria of validity
are sought for in universal predicates of thought and action —
categories, categorical imperative, etc., — while institutions, and
all finite communities of men, are regarded as limiting, contingent factors.

In order to cover the wide range of individualistic thought
with some effectiveness, it would seem desirable to consider these
extremes of the continuum together with one type, at least, that
stands midway between them. The polar opposites are well represented by the subjectivism of Protagoras and the universalism
of Kant respectively: the middle variety, by utilitarianism.

These three forms of individualism now will be examined
separately.

Subjectivism

That there is nothing absolute, that all is a matter of individual perception, opinion, and arbitrary will — these are propositions characteristic of the intense subjectivism that emerges upon

the break-up of institutional frameworks, particularly, when the change in question is one of decay. The dissolution of ancient institutions gives rise to the conviction that there is no such thing as objectivity, that no universal order exists; that, on the contrary, there is only a conventional order resting upon the interests and opinions of men. Depending upon the various contingencies of one's life situation, the individual may develop a sense of unlimited superiority and defiance of any kind of authority (intellectual and moral); or in his effort to escape from the difficulties of life, his thought may turn inward to a morbid preoccupation with itself. Exceptional individuals may attempt a metaphysical reconstruction of their former world, but more frequently the attempt to solve primary philosophic problems for their own sake is given up. Social and ethical problems tend to replace the metaphysical endeavors of earlier men, and the practical becomes the issue of the moment. Thought turns away from the wider universe to man himself. Such a trend in making the individual the pivot of all existence necessarily becomes both pragmatic and relativistic.

Subjectivism is representative of thinkers as widely different in the detail of their works as the Sophists, Stirner, Nietzsche, and Bakunin. All exhibit the principle of Protagoras that "man is the measure of all things." While this phrase may be variously interpreted, its context reveals that it means man as individual and his renunciation of all universally valid standards.[15]

The Protagorean theory of knowledge reduces to a theory of perception, and insists that there is no other knowledge than perception.[16] A very brief examination of this claim indicates the contradictions in which it becomes entangled: Firstly, the view that knowledge is perception leads to the statement that what appears to be true for an individual is true for that individual. However, this frequently shows itself as false since future events from time to time refute what has appeared to be true for the individual. Secondly, perception does not yield consistent impressions. Any object appears larger, smaller, darker, lighter according to distance and atmosphere. In one light it is green, in another blue, in yet another it is grey. Geometric figures assume a variety of shapes according to the position of the observer. But if individual perception is the only objectivity one perception cannot be preferred over another. All constitute knowledge although inconsistent. Thirdly, that individual perception is objectivity for the individual makes all discussion, proof, or disproof, impossible. The perceptions of any one are as good as those of another whether scientist or child. This means that nothing can be taught since all perceptions have equal epistemological validity. Yet, since persons do discuss problems, it is clear that they are not prepared to allow equal validity to all perceptions. They know that contradictory perceptions cannot have the same objectivity. If all the perceptions are objective, there is nothing to discuss or dispute, and the theory is futile. Fourthly, the distinction between objectivity and subjectivity is destroyed. On the basis of the theory it makes no difference whether it is said that a perception is objective, or not, which is only to say that it does not mean anything. Fifthly, in all perceptions there are elements not contributed by the senses of the perceiver. For example, comparison in terms of difference and resemblance is a part of the perception, and yet difference and resemblance are not sensory phenomena. These non-sensory elements (concepts and categories) remain totally unexplained in the individualism of the subjectivist type. It is possible to take these elements into account by the introduction of a metaphysic (Kant), or by an empirical mode of explanation to demonstrate their emergence in the socio-cultural process (Durkheim).

It is readily seen that perception as such cannot be regarded as knowledge.[17] To possess knowledge one must not merely perceive but relate the disparities of perception by concepts. Thus a conceptual (or categorial) scheme is a necessary condition to objective or valid, knowledge. When objectivity becomes identified with subjective impressions it has disappeared. The impossibility of objective knowledge is always implicit in any form of individualism which bases itself upon the individual in his separateness and discreteness.[18] This is readily apparent since the universal element in objectivity requires that the disparity in the perceptions of diverse individuals with respect to the same ontological reality be overcome. Having no way of establishing a ground or relationship between perceptions, that is without concepts or categories, the Protagorean theory becomes an identical proposition, — namely, what an individual perceives, that individual perceives — a most empty and trivial tautology.

It is well to remember that this hopeless result of radical

individualism follows logically enough from the premises of Sophistic thought. The separation of the individual subject from the authority of Grecian institutional structure meant the abandonment of the thought forms embodied in that structure, and which for an earlier period had provided a validational ground. Sophism in its attempt to dispel every illusion, to state the content of existence in terms of reality instead of myth, transferred the basis of validation to the perceiving subject. The fruitless consequences of this operation as worked out in the Protagorean theory of knowledge has led many thinkers to feel, that in the nature of the case, objective thought must be conceptual thought. Objective knowledge must be knowledge through concepts. It was seen to be absurd to regard knowledge as being confined to the separate perceptions that are apprehended by an individual at any particular time. Without the recognition of fundamental orders furnished by the master concepts, or categories, there is no passing beyond the immediate perception to a coherent system of connections. The first question in the problem of knowledge becomes that of introducing such various modes of connection (categories) by which a "manifold of sense" (perception) can be reduced to systematic order. However, beyond the question of what categories adequately perform this ordering function is that of discovering the source, ground, or basis of the categories, and accomplishing their derivation, or deduction.

Now it is possible to view the categories as constitutive of the world in an ontological sense. Thus a category has reference to the most general kind of existence or reality which any object can have. When the categories are predicated of reality in this way, the institutions which embody them carry also an ontological meaning. This conception of the categories, and as a corollary, of institutions, has played a role of the greatest importance in the history of European thought. In this connection Plato, the Medieval Realists, and Hegel, come to mind at once.

Again, the categories may be viewed as the immanent laws of the intellect,[19] necessary principles that are essential to every experience, yet inderivative from experience. They are the indispensable, logical prerequisites of thought. Thus, the basis of validation passes from an objective ontological order as expressed through social institutions to the logical requirements involved in the experiential act, or more simply, in the understanding of any experience. Such is the position of individualism as developed in the philosophy of Kant.

Kant

Nominalism in its long struggle against Medieval Realism and institutional authority at first endeavored to achieve objectivity in knowledge by direct reference to things (Nature). Especially was this true in British empiricism with which individualism has been closely associated. It was felt that a method of observation was vital, but it was also important to eliminate as far as possible the distortions that entered into observation as a consequence of emotions and social existence. Experience, it continued to repeat, was the only source of knowledge. However, as with the individualism of Protagoras, it became increasingly apparent that empirical observation could not accomplish its own validation. In terms of then existing theory, there could be no real knowledge of anything but a series of individual perceptions — whether the lively ones that are called impressions and beliefs, or the fainter ones that are called ideas and fancies. Hume stated the problem very clearly thus:

> There are two principles which I cannot render consistent; nor is it in my power to renounce either of them — viz. *that all our distinct perceptions are distinct existences,* and *that the mind never perceives any real connection between distinct existences.* Did our perceptions either inhere in something simple and individual, or did the mind perceive some real connection among them, there would be no difficulty in the case. For my part, I must plead the privilege of a skeptic, and I confess that this difficulty is too hard for my understanding.[20]

This skeptical result of centuries of philosophical individualism is the problem taken up by Kant.

Now while Hume on the one hand reduced the categories to subjective illusions,[21] Kant insisted on the other that scientific knowledge, which is equally valid for all, requires regulation and grounding by categories. Thus, for science, the relation that a judgment establishes between subject and predicate must be a necessary one, not merely accidental. Hume took it for granted

that we have no other source of knowledge except experience.
Kant declares that experience furnishes only a limited number
of cases. Therefore, it cannot yield universality and necessity.
Hence, a judgment based solidly on experience, i.e., a *posteriori*
cannot constitute scientific knowledge. In order to be necessary,
or scientific, a judgment must rest upon a rational basis, i.e.,
upon *a priori* grounds as well as upon observation. This rational
element in scientific judgments is constituted by general concepts
(the categories). *Scientific knowledge requires that the categories
have no element of contingency* and hence the categories must
be innate to the understanding, that is *a priori*. Thus, if it is
true with empiricism that experience is the only field of knowledge, that to experience one owes all the matter of knowledge,
it is equally true with idealism that there exists in our knowledge
a factor not derived from experience, that is, the categories.
Were there no external world there would be no perception, and
were there no innate categories, these perceptions would constitute
an indefinite, formless plurality.

Kant tends on the whole to make "relation" the chief category, or perhaps, one should say "cause," but cause conceived of
as the necessary relation between phenomena. Unlike Aristotle,
he pretends to derive his table of twelve categories from the
logical judgment. Just as there are four types of judgment, each
with its three sub types, so also there are an equal number of
general concepts or categories.[22] Kant regards these as *a priori*
but not as constituting the structure of reality.[23] They have
validity only in application to sensory perception. They are *a
priori* functions of the understanding, means of knowledge, and
not objects of knowledge.[24] Of the twelve, as already indicated,
the category of relation is seen as most general since every judgment whatever expresses a relation.

One of the pervasive difficulties in the work of Kant is the
indefinite character of the concept of "subject."[25] As a consequence of both his individualism and his idealism, Kant has
always a subjectivist bias. This is clearly seen in his view that
his philosophy constituted a Copernican revolution — a movement
from a cosmocentric to an egocentric position. Yet it is also evident that by subject, Kant means not the individual ego but
mankind as a whole, or a universal ego. For Kant the problem
is: In what sense is objective knowledge a possibility for this

universal ego? Nevertheless, the Kantian philosophy is a shift of reality from object to subject. He was never able to bring a positive contribution to thought of the same convincing kind as his negative criticism. It has become difficult since Kant to view man in the old way as part of the world which includes him as part of its framework. The subject has become the starting point, and is, indeed, himself an organized structure upon which the phenomenal world depends. But it is impossible to admit that this subject has its own sphere without making it much more than the individual of immediate experience. Just what it is that differentiates this subject, or universal ego, from the concrete individual, what gives to its activities a universal validity, Kant is never able to demonstrate.[26]

In the classical theory of knowledge a wide range of meaning is involved in the term "subject," connoting as it does a somewhat psychological entity in Locke and a metaphysical one in Kant. However, the conceptual model that underlies the whole development of the epistemological recourse to the subject is that of insight into the cognitive act as furnishing a basis for objective knowledge in the place of the discredited and competing institutional representations of objectivity as resident in the various ontological orders. The institutions came to be regarded as intellectually bankrupt, and the ontological orders, whose reality the institutions purported to express, were felt to be the chimera of ancient ignorance and superstition. Various groupings, each with its institutional organization and ontology, laid claim to absolute knowledge. In this situation the tendency was to search for objectivity, either in the things observed in ordinary experience, or in the cognizing subject. For nominalism, until its climax in Hume, these two sources remained the basis of objective knowledge. Thus the role of the subject in the cognition of things became the focus of attention and remained the central problem of philosophic individualism. The role of institutional, class, and social factors generally, except as mere negation, was to be rediscovered belatedly only in the second half of the nineteenth century. From the standpoint of sociology the most serious criticism that can be leveled against Kant is that he evidences no appreciation of the social nexus in which all individual experience takes place. The context of institutional and class structures which provide the concepts and values for individual experience is given no place in his analysis. The framework of problems, and the conceptual tools for their solution, are both, without residue, rooted in specific historical social textures. No epistemology which disregards the empirical evidence of sociology, and social psychology, as to the social character of knowing is likely to meet with anything approaching complete success. The failure of the Kantian Critique to recognize in any way the group matrix of thought is in part a consequence of various limiting conditions of the era of the Enlightenment.

It has been pointed out that the Critical Philosophy began as an attempt to overcome the impasse reached by Hume.[27] The two irreconcilable principles which Hume enunciated were denied in fact by Kant, and the solution to the problem was effected through a consideration of the categories as constituting fundamental determinations, or permanent conditions of all experience. However, there was at this point a shift of levels — from a rigorous empiricism in Hume to a pure metaphysic in Kant. To some minds the Kantian answer to the problem posed by Hume is unacceptable simply because it is a metaphysic — it does exceed experience.

With the development of the sociology of knowledge the whole question of the categories may be viewed in a new perspective. It has become possible to resume the path marked out by British empiricism and to attempt an empirical account of the categories. The description of their emergence in the context of social life would continue to recognize the great importance which Kant attributed to them as criteria of validity.

Kant makes use of the antiquated psychological principle of faculties of the soul (or mind) in order to separate clearly the latter's functions. These faculties, or functions, are cognition, will, and emotion, but it is the first which contains the regulating laws of all three. So far as cognition contains the principles of its own act it is theoretical reason; of will, practical reason; and of feeling, judgment. Now with respect to categories, Kant limits himself to theoretical reason and takes as the basis for them, Aristotle's analysis of the logical judgment, but as developed in the Formal Logic of Kant's own time. Thus, he is lead to taking up Quantity, Quality, Relation, and Modality as his chief classes and under each of these finds three categories giving the complete list of twelve as enumerated above.[28] It is interesting to note, however, that Quantity and Quality are schematized as extensive and intensive magnitude respectively, so that both sets of categories are, in effect, Quantitative categories. In the proper sense of the word there is in Kant no category of Quality at all. Further, since Kant restricts his list to the theoretic reason, such categories as Value, End, Perfection, Beauty, etc. do not appear.[29] The gravity of these omissions seems great.

Philosophers have shown marked disagreement upon what conceptions constitute categories, and even upon the definition of the term category. Perhaps, no one today would be prepared to accept the list given by Kant. The exact claim of the respective members of the list to be regarded as categories is for the most part an academic question. But what cannot be so easily passed over is the general character of the Kantian categorial scheme. What significance is to be attributed to the fact that the Kantian Critique refuses to include Value, Perfection, etc., among the field ideas making up the background of thought? Now it is precisely this order of category — Value — that is embodied pre-dominantly in institutions. Societies in which the conception of institutions is sacred find the validation of thought in institutional structure and hence, largely in Value (Situational Type 1). Now the categories of Kant have only logical and not ontological significance. But the category of Value as found in the sacred society, like the categories of Plato and Aristotle, is presumed to run through all reality as well as through all thought about reality. Indeed, its meaning is primarily ontological. This, too, has a certain importance for the kind of objectivity that is found in the sacred society.

The basic determination of thought and condition of experience in the sacred society is in terms of the valuations placed upon objects, activities, and relationships by institutions — usually religious ones. The sacred and profane, holy and unholy, good and evil, sinful and taboo, etc. are values and refer to the general kind of existence or reality which objects, individuals, and relationships are deemed to possess. But the sacred value, or more simply, the sacredness may flow from one object, or person to another; likewise the profane contamination passes with contact from object to object, and object to person. He who violates a taboo becomes himself taboo, etc.

In such societies there is no clear separation of the object as a part of nature from the value that is presumed to inhere within the object. It is evident that under these circumstances, while objects may be brought into a unified totality by virtue of the values being classified or pyramided in some fashion, yet the establishment of relations of objects to one another in terms of their natural properties will be obscured. Empirical knowledge will rise above a mere minimum only with the greatest difficulty, since objects classified in terms of the values of religious institutions would be classified very differently if their physical properties as such were known.

No society has been able to demonstrate with certainty that values have any objective existence, or reality, other than as ideas in the mind. It follows that the objectivity which obtains in a sacred society rests entirely upon agreement concerning the values and their possible hierarchical arrangement. Objective thought will be based upon values that have been universalized, that is, wholly agreed upon within the limits of a given society. Such agreement will constitute the predicate, or fundamental condition, for the cognitive experience of all its members. There is, of course, some doubt whether the term objectivity is genuinely applicable to experience for which the validational basis is the category of Value.

Returning to the Kantian Critique it becomes evident that Kant in setting up his criteria of validity with the omissions mentioned was setting aside the validational procedure common to sacred societies and present in varying degrees in all societies. What Kant has substituted for the values embodied in institutional structure, and which are the basis of the individual's thinking in a sacred society, is a set of forms according to which one judges, but judges upon the relations between objects. The scheme may be said to be limited to objects and their interrelations. This only means that an observer judging upon the interrelations of objects according to Kant's categories will arrive at conclusions regarding these interrelations which will differ from those reached when the judgment is on the basis of Value.

For Kant, objectivity is attained when the judgment expressing a relationship between objects is in accordance with his categorial framework. From this framework the disparate values of historical institutional and class structures have been excluded.

Kant does not regard his categories as resting upon an agreement, as having been built up in a social process, but as the conditions universally necessary for rational thought. If Kant has not taken from the past the conception of an absolute ontology, or truth, resting upon a stadium such as God, he has none the less made the forms according to which one judges just as absolute. As pointed out earlier, Kant goes so far as to say that in order to eliminate all elements of contingency from knowledge — to render it truly scientific — the validating criteria must be *a priori*.

To this the sociology of knowledge must take objection. It would hold that the validating framework is built up in the social process, and hence, the view of an absolute rationality is untenable. If, as the sociology of knowledge would hold, the categories have a history, this would mean that the objectivity given by the Kantian categorial scheme, like that given by the sacred society, has its basis in agreement. To say this is to indicate that knowledge validated on the basis of the Kantian criteria is perspectival knowledge, is knowledge from one point of view, and that all knowledge is perspectival in this primary sense.

Although the sociology of knowledge would assert that any validational scheme is thus limited by the circumstances of its particular socio-cultural history, it does not mean that the validational schemes of the sacred society and of Kantian individualism give the same kind of objectivity. The Kantian scheme has the closest possible relation to scientific method and enables judgments to be made about the interrelations of objects in a manner markedly different from the scheme of the sacred society.

The work of Kant may be viewed as an end product in the long development of individualism. The latter transferred objectivity from the institutional structure, and from an ontology of Divine origin, to the cognitive act of the subject. Institutions were viewed as sources of error, bias, and contingency. In effecting the separation of the thinking subject from the institution, individualism separated him from the values the institution embodied. Thus individualism discovered a way of thinking about objects in detachment from the values the institutions had imposed upon them. This exclusion of values from the objects scrutinized, and from the relation of the object to the observer, meant a more effective knowledge of what constituted the relations between objects. Individualism itself may be viewed as an institution. Like other institutions it has a value, or perhaps, many values. In its form as contract it reduced the burden of institutional status obligation and ritual practice, and thus developed a new kind of social relationship (the contractual). In its theory of knowledge it excluded values, but in such a way as to develop a new order of objective knowledge. Viewed from the standpoint of knowledge, the chief value of individualism, considered as an institution, resides in the fact that it is the institution which has enabled a contemplation of the object in detachment from other institutional values. As shown, this feature has been incorporated in the clearest form in the Kantian theory of knowledge.

Utilitarianism

The utilitarian view of institutions is set forth with the utmost clarity by the psychologist Allport. "In the natural science sense institution is not a substantive concept at all."[30] Expressly recognizing his derivation from nominalism Allport insists that science can deal only with actualities (particulars). To exist means to be an individual. Since an institution has no particularity in this sense, Allport openly antagonizes a science of institutions as an absurd system. Like most of the utilitarians who long precede him, Allport regards the problem of institutions to be spurious — a consequence of the fallacious belief in the reality of universals.[31] What is explicitly stated by Allport is expressed in varying ways in many Continental, and the majority of English thinkers of the nineteenth century. Although the high-tide of modern individualism had been reached with the publication of Kant's *Critique of Pure Reason* (1781), the individualistic mode of thought continued to spread, and in one form or another was the dominant social and political concept of the Western World.

On the Continent the prevailing type was the revolutionary individualism of Rousseau,[32] whether as exemplified by the Girondists and Jacobins, or as tamed and humanized by Kant[33] and by Fichte in his earlier philosophy. A milder form was displayed by the great Wilhelm von Humboldt who regarded government as a necessary evil, urged that its functions be restricted to the mere protection of life and property, and contended that the unfettered freedom of the individual in both speech and action was the indispensable condition of human progress.

Another type of individualism was the romantic. The tendencies of hero worship like those of Thomas Carlyle, which Windelband regarded as isolated in the nineteenth century, had their parallel on the Continent in the work of Friedrich Nietzsche. This peculiar variety of individualism is related to the irrationalism of Schelling and Schopenhauer rather than to the quasi-rationalism of British empiricism.

In England anarchic individualism had some vogue. The works of Thomas Paine were frequently reprinted, widely read and were regarded as the gospel of advanced British Radicalism.[34] However, the prevailing type of individualism was the reforming utilitarianism of Bentham.[35] It was an individualism understandable as a reaction from the excessive and disastrous government "interference" which had characterized the eighteenth century; unintelligent interference; corrupt interference in the interests of privileged classes and favored persons; persecuting interference in religion; mercantile interference in commerce; anti-labor interference in industry. The cry of *laissez-faire, laissez-aller,* raised in France by the physiocrats, was caught up in Britain by non-conformists like Godwin,[36] by economists like Adam Smith, by champions of labor like Francis Place, and by political reformers like Bentham and his disciples. It was the dominant cry until the early days of Queen Victoria, and it aroused the Radicals to secure the abolition of countless iniquities.

The prolixities and intolerable jargon of Bentham was rendered intelligible to the public by his disciple, James Mill. Like his master and with Hobbes, he held that man is an entirely selfish animal whose main characteristics are love of liberty and lust for power. He urged, therefore, that if this self-regarding individual assisted in founding institutions, e.g., the State and setting up a government he did so for purely personal and utilitarian ends, these ends being the defense of his own life, liberty, and property.

He further maintained that all persons entrusted with governmental authority, by reason of their human nature, would inevitably lust for more power, and would endeavor to encroach on the liberties of their subjects. He consequently, urged upon his fellow citizens the need of eternal vigilance, and advised them to curb the might of the executive by a single chamber of representative system marked by a wide suffrage, frequent elections and vote by ballot.

With John Stuart Mill the hard logic of his father's utilitarianism began to disintegrate.[37] He became a utilitarian who admitted qualitative distinctions in pleasures; an empiricist who claimed the force of institutions; a realist inspired by lofty idealism; an atheist with a strong sense of religion; an individualist with a strong leaning toward socialism. Nevertheless, he was predominantly an individualist. He pleads for freedom of thought and discussion, and for freedom of action in so far as such freedom does not interfere with the equal freedom of others; he emphasizes the inestimable worth of personality. He exalts self realization, rather than happiness, as the final aim of existence; finally, he sets rigid limits to the authority of the State over the individual.[38]

From this brief survey it is apparent that much of the thinking of the nineteenth century was characterized by the basic assumption of the rational nature of the individual, and by the ideal of freedom. Implicit in the predicate of rationality, and in the ideal of liberty is the further assumption of volitional indeterminacy — that the rational man is free to choose between alternatives, that modes of action are not bound in a set of necessary relationships.[39] But other aspects of nineteenth century thought are logically inconsistent with these postulates and ideals. For example, the same century emphasizes natural law and linear evolution. Indeed, leading thinkers demand *laissez-faire* declaring that only through non-interference can this natural law work itself out. Thus with the predicate of freedom there was interwoven a curious thread of fatalism. The question is: How is this autonomous, rational individual consistent with that other predicate of the nineteenth century — the determinism of natural science? The tendency was for the observer to see every individual activity as entering into two distinct orders of relationship. In the first place the occurrence was deemed to have an immediate significance for the individual whose activity it was — a significance due to the supposed fact that it was an attempt on the part of a free agent to realize an end.[40] On the other hand the occurrence was placed in a scheme whose relationships were understood in a completely non-teleological, in fact, mechanical way. This dual manner of viewing things has continued to the present time. The same contradiction is implicit in the view that the more knowledge one has about nature, or about society, the better one is able to make use of this knowledge to serve human interests. On the one hand human activity is seen as voluntaristic, that is, autonomously determined. On the other hand nature is separated from the essentially human and regarded as a system of law bound, mechanical relationships.

The concept of *laissez-faire* translates this contradiction of natural law and the free, rational individual into economic terms. On the one hand it is felt best to allow natural law to determine economic relations; on the other the rational individual should be left free to pursue his own self-interests. The utilitarians oppose the institution both to natural law and to the free individual. Mill, Spencer, and Marshall regard institutions as but external obstructions to the working of individual rationality.[41] Interference with the rationality of one by an external, coercive institution is also an interference with the rationality of many, since society is conceived of as simply a sum of rational individuals.[42] Culture was regarded as an outer, or formal aspect, of life. Tylor's definition of culture seems to indicate that nineteenth century man felt that some small part of man's thinking was socially derived. However, the general view was that thought was a universal process, the same in all times and places. Culture on the other hand was but local and temporary.

At the core of nineteenth century thought is the idea, that with the increase of scientific knowledge and with the increasing rationality of man, the need for an institutional structure will be outgrown; that the state will "wither"; that ceremony and ritual will pass; that religion will relax its grip; that marriage will become completely contractual, and that a community of "free" men will shape itself as an actuality. Mill, Spencer, Tylor, and Westermarck imply throughout their writings that man is now partly rational and growing more rational. On the other hand the institutional structure with its interpenetrating attributes of rational and magical authority appeared to these men as creations of primitive ages and often constituting rationally unjustifiable, non-logical "survivals."[43] Religion and the state especially were looked upon in this light. Indeed, to be consistent the utilitarians should have evaluated every institution in terms of its efficiency to achieve hedonistic ends. Almost no writer of the utilitarian group states this explicitly but such a position is implicit in the writings of all.

The individualism of the Enlightenment and that of Victorian utilitarianism mark the points in the history of nominalism when the individual and the institutional structure came to be viewed almost as if they were antitheses. Thus Spencer labors to prove that the moral and the institutional are not the same. He declares that "this sense of coerciveness becomes indirectly connected with the feelings distinguished as moral . . . since political, religious, and social restraining motives are mainly formed of represented future results." But, "Emerging as it does from amidst the political, religious and social motives, it long participates in that consciousness of subordination to some external agency which is joined with them," and "the sense of duty or moral obligation is transitory and will diminish as fast as moralization increases."[44] Although the English utilitarians are never able to draw in full the implications of their position this is done unhesitatingly by Max Stirner who declares that the sense of institutional conformity or moral obligation is the last form of superstition.[45] For him, the ego can come into his own only where the sentimental supposition of duty, together with belief and submission, have vanished in the rational knowledge of the real relations between man and the external world. Thus institutional authority shorn of its falsifying nimbus of the traditional and sacred is to vanish like the phantom that it is.

Summary: It has been shown that historically the rise of individualism whether ancient or modern coincides with the collapse of religious myth and the decline of institutional and class authority. In its initial stages individualism accords the individual, as over against society and its institutions, an ontological finality. It ceases to view the institutional order as the ground of universal standards either in thought, or in conduct. Indeed, on the one hand it skeptically questions all stable and objective "truth," and on the other, insofar as there is any acceptance of the concept of validity, declares that the individual as the highest existence is the "measure of all things." Typical of this intense subjectivism and singularism is Protagoras who insists, that in order to dispel the illusions embodied in institutional predicates, it is necessary to transfer the basis of validation from the traditional authority of institutions to the act of perception. However, it is soon seen that objective knowledge is possible only as concepts and categories are introduced to bring the immediate perceptions into a coherent system of connections. The Protagorean individualism renounces the conceptual framework provided by the institutional system, and yet fails to suggest any other concepts, or categories, that might permit an objective order to arise out of the disparities of individual perception.

Similarly, on the dissolution of the religious structure of the Middle Ages into a variety of competing ontologies, modern individualism attempts to find a basis for objectivity in the cognitive act. Here, too, it recognizes in due course that knowledge which is valid for all requires to be grounded by categories. Taking up this problem as his own, Kant endeavors to set out specifically the character and number of the fundamental categories. Thus individualism shifts its emphasis from the immediate perception, and from the individual in his separateness and discreteness, to the universal predicates of all thought — to a search for criteria of validity common to all men and inderivative from experience. Since the conceptual frameworks of institutional and class structures, because of their historical particularity, cannot provide the universality desired, individualism continues to view such structures in negative, critical fashion, as factors of distortion and bias.

Midway between the singularistic and universalistic forms of individualism lies utilitarianism. Holding closely to the nominalistic tendencies of the earlier phases of individualism it denies and derides the ontological significance of institutions, and attempts to establish standards for human conduct by a consideration of what it believes to be man's nature. Although the latter is hedonistically conceived, utilitarianism stresses that fully adequate empirical knowledge of the means to be employed in the attainment of goals can be discovered only by the employment of "reason." This reason, or rationality, is formulated in universalistic terms, and hence, viewed as at variance with historical social structures.

Despite the significant differences between the three types of individualism discussed, they are at one in their repudiation of institutional and class structures as a basis for objectivity —

in their rejection of historical social forms as providing a validational criterion for either thought or conduct. Each type
separates the individual from the traditionally established institution. The effect of this separation is to separate in turn the individual from the values which the institution embodies. Thus
the objectivity of individualism is characterized by a description
of the object, and its relationships to other objects, in detachment from the valuations imposed upon the object and its relationships by institutional forms.

CHAPTER THREE

Positivism

Comte

Turning from individualism the next position to be examined is positivism. More particularly the question is that of the meaning of institutions in the positivistic framework. While the latter has much in common with individualism — empirical positivism, at least, being little more than a variant of the nominalism of Locke and Hume — yet in the hands of Durkheim it transforms the significance of institutions such that their understanding in positivistic terms becomes impossible.[1] Whereas in individualism, and in empirical positivism, institutions are viewed in opposition to the autonomous, rational individual, in the final work of Durkheim they become the ground of mind itself, the sole basis of meaningful activity. Moral freedom in the individualistic sense becomes absurd since an institutional framework determines conduct. Likewise rationality becomes a function of institutional structure, and ceases to be a faculty of discrete, isolated, human atoms.

Durkheim's conclusions are slowly and painfully attained. The dialectic of his thought struggles forward almost tortuously as if in fetters. It may be objected, and with truth, that Durkheim never does set forth explicitly the theory outlined in the above paragraph. Nevertheless, the basic structure of such a position is evident in his work. In order to formulate for the present inquiry the implications of this inversion by positivism of its own premises a more detailed study and understanding of how this remarkable result was reached must be undertaken. Before proceeding to the institutional theory of Émile Durkheim, it becomes

65

necessary to consider the conceptual scheme (empirical positivism) which dominates his research, and which, perhaps, limited his success. This can be done best by examining empirical positivism in the work of its founder, Auguste Comte.[2]

Until the advent of Comte the study of social phenomena was by all investigators completely subsumed by philosophy. Comte had concluded that the social, unlike the psychological, could be made the subject matter of a science.[3] He was convinced that the study of social phenomena would show the presence of invariable relationships, or laws. Society as a part of nature possessed its own sequences and coexistents, and a science of society was to be the accurate and formal description of these relationships.[4] However, Comte emphatically denied and reversed what may be regarded as a chief postulate of Western thought. On the whole the West has concurred in the search for an ultimate principle that would make intelligible the fluctuating, ever-changing, phenomenal object. Always the question has been, What is the nature of the object? To explain a thing was to deprive it of its singularity by finding its membership in a class of objects, or by reduction to a common ground of some class. Complete explanation was to show how it was imbedded in some final ground which was the constitutive tissue of the universe.[5] But for Comte a final principle has no reality; there is nothing but phenomena. Empirical processes alone constitute reality and the essence of knowledge. The description of facts and their order is science; philosophy, when legitimate, is but methodology. Comte goes on to say that the methodologist, like the scientist, must eliminate as metaphysical such concepts as substance, causality, and force. This insistence upon not passing from the phenomenon to its logical presupposition is the keynote of positivism.

Comte, like Bacon, is in a sense not a philosopher but an exponent of method. Hence his emphasis upon a classification of the sciences according to the properties with which they deal. It is to be noted that his attitude toward psychology, logic, and metaphysics is wholly negative — in fact constitutes a denial of their very existence. Wholly dogmatic he exhibits no appreciation of the problems of such sciences, and thus contemptuously disposes of a large part of the vast edifice of human knowledge.

For Comte the limits of knowledge are set by time and space. Phenomena constitute the real, and, "every proposition which is not

reducible in the last resort to the simple statement of a fact . . .
must be without real and intelligible sense."[6] A law for Comte
is a statement of invariable relations between phenomena. He
includes only external facts; our intellectual and emotional processes are ruled out by Comte since they cannot be observed in
the framework of space and time. The ruling out of this order
of facts enabled Comte to erect a classification of the sciences
upon a single base. A discussion of the famous hierarchy of the
sciences need not be entered upon here. The important matter
is that sociology as the crown of the structure is limited to the
study of observable phenomena (as understood above), i.e., to sensible perception.[7]

Durkheim has followed Comte closely in this regard and
declared that social phenomena can be explained only by their
own laws. When the former defines a social fact as that which is
characterized by obligation, or constraint, it is seen that such a
definition is derived directly from human phenomena. It is not
an aspect of a social law derived in part from the inductions
of a lower level of a natural science, e.g., biology, physics, etc.,
to which something has been added as a sequel. On the contrary, the lower levels enter the sociological situation only as
conditions which in turn, due to their heterogeneity, modify the
application of general laws in any particular social instance. The
Comtean methodological inversion in respect to sociology, as suggested above, proved to be the basis for the Durkheimian attempt
to derive explanations of social facts only from social facts.

Durkheim was influenced greatly by the Comtean statement
regarding the metaphysical stage of human thought. Comte had
said that just as the theological view of causality was derived
from the analogy of human volition so also the habitual and
mechanical aspects of human life are projected into the universe
as metaphysical causes. The metaphysical cause takes charge of
a class of homogeneous phenomena. Such a cause is, indeed,
nothing but the abstract idea of the generic character of such
phenomena. For example, certain phenomena similar in character are grouped together in a class. Then the same class concept
is set up as the origin, or goal, of the phenomena, as the case
may be. Thus there arises the metaphysical double of the phenomena under observation. As nature falls more and more into
unvaried order before the observer these abstractions spread. They

are regarded as forming a framework for the universe as gravitation, force, vitality, essence, cause, etc. However, when the metaphysical causes vanish there are left simply the laws of coexistence and succession among phenomena. The laws as aforesaid are but statements of invariable relationships.[8]

The sketch just presented of Comte has not aimed at any complete compend of positivism but merely to bring together a small number of its numerous assumptions. In regard to these some comments may be hazarded. As has been said, Comte limits knowledge to the finite contents of space and time. But all cognition is the product of two factors, the cognizing subject and the cognized object. The external object contributes the material, the empirical aspect of knowledge, but the subject also contributes something, namely, the form — those logical categories by virtue of which any connected knowledge, any synthesis of individual perceptions into a whole of experience, is possible. Cognition fills up the frames of the categories with the matter of experience. Among the categories is that of "cause." Now Comte, like J. S. Mill, talks of invariable antecedents and invariable consequents. But this does not solve the problem for the latter is contained in this very invariability. In speaking of the relations of phenomena Comte is in effect only substituting one category for another, namely, the category of relation for that of cause. That this is any advance seems doubtful, particularly when one reflects that both are subjective elements in cognition. It must be owned, however, that Comte's insistence upon the category of relation is consistent with the ever-increasing use in science of the concept of function. In the same way the category of cause, like that of force, tends to disappear.

As has already been pointed out, Comte's philosophy is entirely a methodology — and its framework is more or less that of the physical sciences as this method was used by Bacon, Galileo, Newton, and others. Comte was among the first to see the underlying differences in the concepts used by the ancients and those used by the moderns. These differences are set forth with great clarity in his discussion of the metaphysical stage of human development.[9] What was for the early investigators of modern science little more than a rule of thumb became with Comte a highly refined technique. He saw that the presence of certain philosophical tenets was highly prejudicial to the fullest use of this technique. What Comte

did not see was that only certain aspects of the object, or phenomenon, were amenable to the new scientific approach, and that other
aspects—the qualitative—were neglected. Here the limitations of
the approach become apparent—for those aspects of the object dis-
regarded, or even denied, at the level of physics and biology ob-
trude themselves upon the investigator of the social. Comte had
declared that these aspects of the social object such as "value"
or "will" could be denied just as the metaphysical qualities of
objects at the level of physics could be denied. Thus he presented
to the world his sociology, or what was for him a social physics.

Now social facts are not given *per se* as Comte supposed but
are part of a framework of value.[10] Just as physical science is
imbedded in a metaphysic so the social sciences exhibit a tangled
skein of value conceptions. Indeed, the social actuality is largely
subjective — the reflection of an inner value structure. This subjective aspect is an essential attribute of social actuality. The
pure observation of Comte is a myth.

It should be noted that this component of social actuality
has a dual aspect. On the one hand it is an estimate of our past
social experience, and is now related to some goal, practical end,
or interest. In this aspect it is part of our social philosophy. On
the other hand it obtains in a specific situation and can be regarded as the property of that situation. As such it would be capable of objective description and is the concern of science. However, there are certain objections to this position and these will
be considered in another place.

Now the problem which Comte raises — that of method — is
fundamental. Without a basic approach it is doubtful if sociology
can lay claim to the name of a science. The physical sciences
found their method long since and the past three centuries have
witnessed its continuous refinement. The chief assumption of
the physical scientist in the past has been the postulate of the
reign of law. As has been noted, Comte defined law not as necessary relationship between phenomena but only as a statement of
the relations that do obtain between sequences and co-existents.
Thus Comte found it possible to accept Hume and remain scientific. The invariability in a mathematical equation states a necessary relation only between its own terms. The area of the universe
to which the equation applies may exhibit contingency. Although
this conclusion is implicit in positivism few proceed thus far, and

unlike Comte, postulate universal causation. The opposite doctrine—that of will, choice, decision, and plan usually have been considered to be the greatest hindrance to the progress of the social sciences. Most social scientists have been anxious to prove a law of universal causation to overcome the objection that social facts have no law. Thus, in order to subject social facts to law, many sociologists have resorted to analogies from the physical sciences—usually from biology. All such people have hoped to provide a foundation for social studies by showing that their method, or reasoning, was that of the physical sciences. However, logic cannot establish this doctrine, nor has it been borne out in empirical research. This has led many to think that the method of sociology must be determined from its own problems and crude analogies from the physical sciences discarded. Mere analogy carries little weight in itself.

From what has been said it is obvious that the positivism of Comte is not broad enough to meet the demands of the social thinker. The very things which Comte's method would disregard are those which provide the meaning of human existence. Comte's denial of the possibility of metaphysical knowledge means also the denial of moral values upon which all practical conduct must ultimately be based.[11] It would seem that the method of Comte needs to be supplemented. Although Comte's avowed aim was the reconstruction of human society, to find objective principles which he might oppose to the subjective freedom of the Enlightenment, he rejects philosophy. Yet science only provides a body of well-attested knowledge which may be used in the service of some end. If thought embraced only scientific knowledge, one would not know what end to pursue, what alternatives are possible, and which the more significant. It is this lack of a goal-setting counterpart together with the failure of his method to reach the meaning content of social actuality that constitutes the Achilles' heel of the Comtean position.[12]

Durkheim

Under the influence of Comte and empirical positivism generally there arose in France the vigorous sociological movement of which Émile Durkheim[13] may be regarded as the most profound representative. Although highly original Durkheim's work is tied to Comtean Positivism, and as may become apparent in due course, the paradox to which it moves is largely a consequence of this anchorage.

For Durkheim society is itself a reality *sui generis*. As such it is not assimilable to the linear evolution of the later utilitarians — that is, society is not reducible to the more fundamental laws of nature such as are found in physics or biology.[14] Society is itself the source of knowledge and the latter is authoritative insofar as it is an expression of collective, as distinguished from merely individual, thought. The Kantian forms of space and time are for Durkheim the products of social experience and arise as a condition for ceremonial activity.[15] What is true of the forms of space and time is also true of the so-called *a priori* categories. Indeed, all the fundamental concepts of modern science simply reflect the needs of man in Western culture. In the same way the mentality of primitive man exhibits another mode—the mystical, or pre-logical.[16] The general term employed by Durkheim for these thought-forms is "collective representation."

Durkheim also insists that while societies may be compared, it is impossible to understand a society by reference to the individuals who compose it. The social entity is not resolvable into biological entities. If the social constitutes an order of its own kind it must have properties unique to such an order. Such properties, declares Durkheim, are constraint and obligation. But these are essentially moral ideas—and society must be conceived of as a moral entity.[17] Thus Durkheim rejects all views which attempt to understand society primarily in biological, or economic, concepts. Further, this morality consists of established rules. The latter determines the actions of individuals by a coercive force which is felt both as immanent and transcendent — as obligation in the former case, as constraint in the latter.

The set of rules may be regarded as a value-system and this in turn constitutes for Durkheim the institutional structure.[18] Such a structure is moral reality. It is conceived of as defining specific ends for individuals and as an instrument integrating in some measure the wide diversity of individual ends into a social totality.[19] The efficacy of the ultimate value system resides in its moral authority. Sanctions in the form of punishment and other coercive pressures are entirely secondary. While Durkheim is content to equate the moral order and the institutional structure a

question arises as to the precise nature of these. In what does
the moral force consist? Evidently, morality is not a calculation
of individual interests in the utilitarian sense. Morality would
appear to be a social fact and hence capable of scientific description, and the latter is such when it is in terms of empirical positivism.[20] Social facts, then, are to be treated as things. Here one
would like a more adequate definition of a social fact. Usually,
a fact is thought to be empirical, that is, a sense datum whose
meaning is made explicit by conceptual subsumption. However,
many abstractions are spoken of as facts and yet no abstraction as
such is a sensory phenomenon. Now if social facts are rules, or
values, it seems clear that these are not sensory phenonena. Therefore, they are not amenable to scientific analysis in the empirical
positivistic sense — that is, they are not observable, concrete particulars. Nevertheless, Durkheim insists that social facts are *choses*.
The latter, like the "hard, stubborn facts" of British empiricism
are not regarded as subjective creations, but as objective actualities.
The social fact constrains, is exterior to the individual, and hence,
Durkheim feels, cannot be identified with the individual, nor with
a subjective mode of thought.

Although Durkheim never abandons his tendency to reification he declares that he does not mean that society or social facts
are material in nature, but only that society, or social facts, are as
real as material things. Nothing indicates Durkheim's descent from
the Medieval realists more than this emphasis upon the reality of
the social fact. Indeed, Durkheim never ceases to be imprisoned
by an ontology of Medieval realism despite his manifest effort to
follow a positivistic method. His various empirical studies increasingly exhibit the idealistic metaphysic.[21] This becomes strikingly obvious when Durkheim makes the *conscience collective*
the *representation collective*. In other words, the collective conscience has become a system of universals (concepts). If the an-
thropomorphic element is removed from this statement—that is,
if the *conscience collective* had been dropped and the system of
universals substituted, Durkheim would have arrived at the conclusion toward which his empirical researches were driving him.
At an earlier period *conscience collective* had seemed to mean
collective consciousness. Thus the tendency had been for the earlier Durkheim to confine the system of universals to moral concepts.
In the later Durkheim the emphasis is upon the conceptual sys-

tem as a rational structure. Hence he was close to a conclusion that he did not quite reach—that obligation and constraint, the unique properties of social facts are determinations by the system of universals. In other words the logical implications of the conceptual system (the universals) exhibit themselves as obligation and constraint in respect to human relationships. The institutional structure with its moral determinations is the translation of the content of the abstract metaphysic (the universals) into an observable pattern of conduct. This would mean that obligation and constraint which earlier had appeared to Durkheim as fundamental to the concept of the social, in fact as the constitutive principle of society, had now become secondary to the primary role of rationality.[22]

By the close of his career Durkheim may be considered an idealist, and his view of what is meant by institutional structure becomes strikingly similar to that of the Hegelian school. He states categorically that society "consists exclusively of ideas and sentiments,"[23] and that ". . . there is a realm where the formula of idealism applies almost literally; that is the social realm."[24] While Durkheim defined sociology as the "science of institutions,"[25] it should be noted that he came to regard institutions less as factors external to the individual and more and more as if they existed "only in the minds of individuals."[26] As Parsons has pointed out with marked acumen this is a position utterly untenable for a positivist. The institutions can not be "observed"—at least, they do not belong to the world of sense perception. Certainly, Durkheim continues to speak as if society—and by society he appears to mean culture—were a sensory phenomenon, but the logic of his work has driven him into a completely idealistic position where culture generally, and institutions specifically, are ideal, non-sensory entities.[27]

The fact that Durkheim refused to accept his own idealism is explained partly by his positivistic inheritance. But chiefly it is to be understood by the theory of knowledge which he had erected on the narrow base of empirical studies premised on Comtean positivism.[28]

Having recognized his mistake in attempting to explain social phenomena in terms of the material factor of population density, Durkheim attempted to take his fundamental principle more seriously. This latter was that religious, juridical and economic data must be explained in terms of their own nature—the social. He insisted that observed facts of this order must be placed within their own context if determinative causes are to be discovered. This only restates the Durkheimian dictum that the cause of a social fact is always another social fact. However, it would seem that Durkheim attributes to social facts a causal efficacy in an area beyond the merely social. He declares that the categories of thought themselves are social products. Space, time, number, causation, etc., are formed by and out of the institutional structure. Indeed, they grow out of the institutional structure. However, it should be kept in mind that the social for Durkheim is a *chose*, a thing; that it has exteriority as evidenced by its properties of constraint and obligation.[29] Such a definition enabled Durkheim to declare social facts to be observable entities. As such, social facts and certain other orders of facts, e.g., the biological, physiological, and the physical, can be subsumed under a common predicate. This procedure confronts Durkheim with the age-old and hopeless problem of showing how thought-forms can be derived from a non-ideal substrate. It is the same problem that has confronted materialistic theories (and in a somewhat different way, positivistic) for centuries. Put in this way it may be said that Durkheim hardly grapples with the problem at all. He seems to accept thought as such as given and then proceeds to show how the institutional structure—that is, the complex of social facts—determines the specific categorial forms that thought has taken in actual societies. Durkheim's positivism in this regard is set forth in *Les formes élémentaires,* but its development is more clearly seen in successive numbers of the periodical, *L'Année Sociologique.*

Early in the series Durkheim raises the question whether the forms of thought (categories) are caused by social forms or vice versa. His conclusion is that institutional forms are determinative of mental categories.[30]

At this point Durkheim still has to say explicitly that institutional forms produce mental categories. Thus far he has declared only that the categories do not operate to produce institutions.[31] Yet he does insist that the concept of society is cardinal and that (in the case of the primitive Australian, at least) all other knowledge must be shown to be in relation to it.[32] However, somewhat later in the series the assertion is made with an unmistakable definiteness that a direct and not accidental connection exists between the social and the logical.[33]

Following this Durkheim and Mauss proceed to exhibit the relationship between the institutional and logical systems of the Zuni, the Chinese, and the Greeks. The precise character of these comparative studies need not be taken up here. It is sufficient to state that the authors above mentioned find that the framework of logical classification by which the universe is understood by these societies respectively is in turn the institutional system of these societies. They do suggest that there is not a difference in kind between primitive classificatory systems and advanced societies but only one of degree.[34]

According to Durkheim and Mauss, man does not begin his thinking by representing things in connection with himself. The structure of the earliest theories concerning nature are not intellectual objectifications of the individual but of his society. Further, Durkheim and Mauss feel that what they have attempted to do in connection with the concept of classification itself might be done for other fundamental concepts. The categories of cause, substance, etc., should be illuminated by such an approach.[35]

Finally, they conclude that the first classes of things to be viewed as such were classes of men. Other things were then integrated with these classes. Since men found themselves in classes (groupings) they proceeded to classify (group) other things. These latter were thought of as composing part of society, and it was their place in the social order that determined their place in the natural order. Thus the first logical categories were social.[36] Further, the relation between things and between classes of things are determined by social relations. The class forms and their connections are of social origin. Because human classes are to be found enclosed within one another like so many boxes—that is, the sub clan within the clan, the clan in the phratry, the phratry, in the tribe—so classes of things are enclosed one within the other in the same box-like way. Thus the hierarchy and structure of knowledge is the same as that found in the social group and applied to the world in general.[37] The way any specific thing is classified depends upon its relation or impact upon the group. The sacred or profane character of a thing depends upon the relation to, or impact upon, the group.[38]

Admitting that the above summary of the Durkheimian theory of knowledge may be compressed to the point of caricature, nevertheless, it may serve to focus attention on two very different aspects of Durkheim's institutional and epistemological theory. The terms positivistic and idealistic may serve the purpose of designating these aspects. It will be observed that in the resumé just given Durkheim attempts to derive his forms of knowledge (the categories, etc.) from observable elements—the grouping of the tribe, the relation of the tribe to the phratry, the order of ritual, the periodicity of ceremonial, etc. There is an absurdity in this derivation that hardly requires comment. The introduction of certain physical factors into the understanding of social phenomena was exactly what the earlier Durkheim had repudiated. The theory can be used to show why time and space are subdivided as they are in a particular society. It may help to explain why the concept of death has such and such a specific content. It does not, of course, explain the presence of these concepts, and it was this that the theory purported to do.[39]

While noting the difficulties of this approach to the theory of knowledge it should be kept in mind that Durkheim in his institutional theory was *de facto,* if not admittedly, an idealist. If society consists "exclusively of ideas and sentiments" it is difficult to understand Durkheim's emphasis upon the aforesaid observable elements. However, Durkheim continually oscillates and presents a hopelessly contradictory position. A society (as defined by Durkheim) and a physical aggregate of individuals belong to different levels. Indeed, Durkheim has seized upon physical facts and treated them as social facts.

To understand Durkheim's failure to recognize the idealistic position into which the logic of his empirical research was driving him, it is necessary to remember Durkheim's derivation from Comte. The positivistic inheritance bequeathed by the latter to the former precluded an outright acceptance of the conclusions of his own work—that the key factor in the social is ideal. Above all else, the suicide study should have convinced Durkheim of the paradoxical character of his theoretical position. He had shown that a relationship existed between a value structure and the individual act of self-destruction. But a value is not a sensory phenomenon; it is ideal. The view that people hold as to what constitutes reality, that is, their beliefs as to the nature of things, are translated into values. The belief is what people think they know about the real; the value is their opinion of what ought to be. What appears to be actual, what appears as what ought to be, may for some people coincide, but they are logically separable. The values form a hierarchy, usually an illogical one, since irreconcilable concepts enter into the structure. The conflicts result from inconsistent or false views of the nature of reality. Human society, like science, is possible only where there are definitions. Words and language cut experience into a number of definable ideas and if they are illegitimate and contain a hypothetical treatment of experience so do every proof and disproof they exhibit. A value, of course, has a reality of its own, but such a value must be dis-. tinguished logically from that which is valued even though in the life of the individual the object and its meaning are one. To speak of values as social milieu, or social environment, only serves to confuse. Milieu, or environment, in ordinary usage as also in the biological sciences, refers to a sensory actuality, and as in all cases of the latter, open to sensory perception, that is, directly or indirectly to observation. The values are abstract in their entirety. It is the most signal error to regard this abstraction (the value) as of the same order with sensory elements of the social environment.[40] Now Durkheim persists throughout in treating these abstractions as if they were sensory phenomena. It is this that makes Durkheim's conception of the social a tissue of contradictions.[41] If it is asked in what does this ambiguity consist—the answer is—in the essential and insurmountable difference between the ideal and actual. What Durkheim meant to do was to give an empirical theory of abstraction. However, when Durkheim states that the categories grow out of the institutions of a society it is difficult to determine precisely what he means. If the institutions are ideal (abstractions) this could be interpreted that the categories are deductions from those abstractions. There are times when Durkheim expressly recognizes this ideal character of institutions. However, bound by the premises of empirical positivism he refuses to acknowledge the separate nature of these two aspects of the social—a difference that is one of genus and fatal to his famous dictum "that the cause of a social fact is always another social fact." His fundamental distrust of idealism forced him back to the side of positivism. Aiming from youth to provide a positivistic account of human action he was bound, perhaps, to minimize the abstract (ideal) aspect of his subject matter.

However, it is not true that the ideal has no place in sociology. To commit this error is to overlook both the nature of the social and of the cultural. Durkheim has shown conclusively that institutions do not have the properties of sensory phenomena. The system of "rules and sentiments" is entirely ideal; it does not exist in space, even if existence in time is admitted.[42] In Comtean positivism knowledge is limited to the contents of space and time. That knowledge is of this kind is also the view of the *Critique of Pure Reason* of which positivism is but another expression. The restriction to Comtean positivism is but the finicality of formalism itself; it converts the universe and the concrete life of human beings into mere externality—outsides. The recognition of this turned Durkheim in the direction of idealism. However, he remained anchored to Comtean concepts and refused to adopt a predicate, that might have led to a wholly different envisagement of his subject. It may be said that Durkheim never did solve the problem of the relation of institutional structure to the theory of knowledge. The problem occupied all the later years of his career for his work in the field of religion is an aspect of his epistemological inquiry. At best Durkheim has indicated something more than a mere relationship between the theory of knowledge and institutions. He shows that a basic connection exists between the theory of knowledge and religion. The former begins to pass over into the latter and vice versa. Certainly, he does not provide an acceptable account of the nature of the inter-relationships of society, institutions, religion, and the theory of knowledge, but the fact of such inter-relationships becomes indubitable. It has been indicated that his work contains an essential inconsistency due to his stubborn retention of an empirical positivistic approach while having at the same time reduced his subject matter to ideal elements. It would seem that the partial failure of his sociology of knowledge is a consequence of the implications of the positivistic premises of his institutional theory. The remarkable contribution which Durkheim makes is his discovery that institutions and the theory of knowledge exhibit a relation of dependency. The nature of this dependency he had hoped to clarify by his sociology of knowledge.

In order to facilitate a clearer view of the complicated structure which comprises the sociology of Durkheim, the following recapitulation of its fundamental ideas and a concise exposition of its chief propositions may be helpful.

Durkheim formulated his problem and established his methodology on the basic Comtean (and Kantian) proposition that phenomena are things or events, in space, and the space intended is the space of classical mechanics. This phenomenal world was accessible to understanding in terms of the natural sciences, and was to be treated logically and empirically as a closed system. A dilemma, or dualism, grew out of this proposition because man is not only a physical body, but is also a "knowing subject." For simplicity the horns of this dilemma have been labelled by some as idealism and positivism. In his earlier work Durkheim followed in Comte's path and adapted his research to the positivist, or radical empiricist, horn. Declaring that his social facts must be treated *comme des choses,* his difficulty in the adaptation of positivism in this manner arose because it could not logically embrace the "causal individualism" in the current positivistic theories — when treating social facts as "things," in the radical empiricist tradition, they could not be related to, or caused by, individual sensations, or men's ideas. Durkheim found that it was logically possible to escape individualism on a positivistic basis only by adopting a sociologistic positivism which was strongly rationalistic. His solution was to relate the existence and implications of social facts, treated *comme des choses,* to a social reality which was in his frequently repeated formula, a reality *sui generis.*

In his earlier theory Durkheim stated that the "concrete entity society" was an existent reality *exterior* to the minds of individuals. For social facts to be "things" they have to be related to a concrete reality exterior to the individual. It was necessary for Durkheim to alter this view in the light of his empirical research findings.

After explaining social phenomena in terms of the above theory in *De la division du travail social* wherein the "concrete exteriority" was population pressure, he found the theory no longer able to accommodate the facts in *Le suicide.* The concepts of egoism and altruism as causes of suicide did not fit into the "beyond individual" scheme. This trend of Durkheim's thought ends in the conclusion that "society exists only in the minds of individuals."

Beginning on the radical empiricist horn of the Kantian and Comtean dilemma, Durkheim was forced to the other horn (idealistic). The movement through this circle had been compelled by the necessity of taking account of individual factors in the social process.

The final phase of Durkheim's work is an exploration of the origins and development of knowledge itself, and constitutes a last attempt to find a basis on which to build a "science of sociology."

Durkheim emphasizes that beyond individual experiences there lies the realm of concepts and categories — the media by which individuals communicate. The concepts are held in common by men who have agreed on a classification of objects and experience on the basis of their common characteristics. Thus men are able to communicate and interact with each other on the expectation of being understood. The concepts are "impersonal" and "relatively immutable." They stubbornly resist change, but are altered when they no longer provide suitable universal meanings in slowly changing human activities and needs. The most general concepts are the categories and include representations of Time, Space, Number, Cause, Force, Substance, Personality, and Totality. These are the relatively permanent molds of thought from which it is possible to free one's self only with the greatest difficulty.

For Durkheim both concepts and categories fall into the class of collective representations. The concept capable of enveloping all other concepts and classes of concepts is that of Totality, which for this reason may be regarded as the principal category.

The conceptual system with its core of categories is for Durkheim the constitutive tissue of social life. The distinctively moral concepts, or rules, are a part of this system, and the system as a whole is the fundamental factor in subjective cognition. The system is expressed in institutional structure, and is the warrant and validational base for the entire thinking processes of a given group. In the institutional structure these ultimate principles (concepts, categories) and individual perceptions have their point of coincidence. Thus institutions are the means by which individual life is built into the net, or framework, of abstractions. Durkheim's phrase that the "categories grow out of institutions" indicates that he does not feel that categories and institutions are entirely different orders of reality, that standing in separation, somehow must be brought into relationship. The institutions, viewed as ideal entities, are nothing less than specific parts of the conceptual system (concepts, categories); viewed as social organization, the institutions are the means by which the conceptual system is translated into the thought, feeling, and action of individuals. The implication of Durkheim's analysis is that institutions are a process by which a conceptual system is brought into the life experience of the individuals of a group so as to meet the continuing needs of its existence. In this testing of the conceptual system by empirical reality and the group's changing needs, new concepts are developed and categories modified. However, the emphasis in Durkheim is in this matter pragmatic. He tends to see the needs of the group as giving rise to alterations in institutional structure and thus to changes in the ultimate categorial scheme. For him it is social existence which is prior, and the form of the conceptual system follows, and is dependent upon, that social existence. Yet the opposite view is implicit in Durkheim's idealism. Moreover, one is at a loss to see how there can be any social existence in the human sense unless the conceptual system is expressed through institutional structure in the concrete life of individuals.

At this point it may be well to compare certain of the findings of Durkheim with the position of individualism as expressed in the work of Kant.

For Kant the conditions of thought, or categories, are *a priori*. Thus they are inderivative from social process, or structure; independent of history and without empirical genesis. As prerequisites of the purely cognitive, they do not include Volition or Value.

For Durkheim the categories are a part of a total conceptual system. They differ from the other concepts of the system, sometimes in their greater generality, but if not in generality, always in their higher degree of impersonality. In these concepts and categories the cognitive and evaluative elements interpenetrate, and it is the entire conceptual system as embodied in institutional structure that forms the validational base for all experience. The categories have their origin, development, and modification in the social process as this takes place with reference to the changing needs and experiences of a given society. Thus the categories are not fixed, either as to their number or respective character.

It is clear that Durkheim would regard the Kantian categorial scheme as a special case only — one that reflects the peculiar needs of man in Western culture. The Kantian scheme becomes a specific instance of a generic process — the social process.

As pointed out heretofore, individualism in looking upon institutions as elements of contingency in knowledge was bound to exclude Value from its criteria of validity. This gave rise to a type of objectivity which is characteristic of the scientific outlook. It is an objectivity that is related to the objectivity of the total conceptual system as part to the whole. The objectivity that is involved in the Kantian criteria of validity has special reference to the objects of the natural world from which the values they possess for the observer have been removed — at least, during the observer's act of contemplation and observation.

It was the achievement of Durkheim to direct attention to the role of social existence in knowledge, no matter of what order that knowledge might be. However, the question arises whether the thought-model expressed in the objectivity involved in the Kantian Critique, and which has been of such inestimable service in the natural sciences, is capable of the same successful application in the study of social phenomena where volitions, values, and interest-bound elements are intrinsic to the subject matter. To this question Karl Mannheim has endeavored to give an answer.

CHAPTER FOUR

Historical Relativism

Mannheim

The sources of the sociology of knowledge are many. There is the line of descent that beginning in the positivism of Comte comes down through Espinas, De Roberty, and Durkheim. Again there is the tradition of Wundt and "folklore." In the United States the seminal writings of George Herbert Mead have focussed attention upon the social roots of knowledge. However, there is another principal stream which is developed in the tradition of history. The classical expression of such a theory of knowledge is found in the work of the sociologist Mannheim. This stream has its fountain head in the *Logic* of Hegel. The dialectic of the latter "inverted" by Marx is translated into a class theory of ideological superstructures. Later the concept of ideology is thought through by Mannheim with a vigor and determination that makes it the foundation for a new discipline and the starting point for a rigorous analysis and profound understanding of social life.

For Mannheim two inter-related basic issues in the problem of knowledge present themselves. First, there is the question as to whether theoretic formulations are a product of individual performances solely, or, on the other hand, of groups, classes, and societies, whose expression, of course, is necessarily through individuals. Nothing in the nature of a "group mind" is even remotely suggested by Mannheim. Secondly, there is the question as to whether thought is autonomous. Stated otherwise, does change in the realm of ideas proceed by an inner dialectic or, on the contrary, is the theoretic subject to, and modified by, existential conditioning of various sorts? An examination of the work of Mann-

heim indicates that he does not distinguish with any precision
between these questions but reduces both to the latter since for
him the existential conditions include the socio-historical (the
cultural-institutional) in addition to other elements. The consequences of lumping together disparate elements under the term
existential and thus constituting a conceptual congery will be discussed later.

In its attempt to answer these questions the Mannheimian
gnosiology turns to a consideration of the implications of the ideological concept. To view a thought content as ideological is to
take into account the socio-historical milieu from which it emerged.
It is this largely cultural-institutional base together with the co-
presence of other so-called non-theoretic facts that Mannheim calls
the existential conditions of intellectual activity. The same thought
content viewed in detachment from its social origins becomes only
an "idea." Mannheim declares that in the past thinkers have
failed to comprehend thought in its concrete setting of a cultural-
institutional situation. Indeed, philosophical schools of logic and
epistemology reflected only upon ideas, not upon ideologies.[1] According to Mannheim, "It is impossible to conceive of absolute
truth existing independently of the values and position of the subject and unrelated to the social context."[2] This does not mean
that Mannheim expects to find absolute truth by relating thought
structures to cultural institutional structures of history, but he
contends that such a procedure makes possible dynamic thinking,
enables the solution of concrete problems of existence, rather than
binding one to static modes of intellectual activity.

Now the term ideological as used by the Marxists implied that
the ideas of the bourgeoisie were distortions of the real nature of
the situation. If in any assertion the concealment of certain relevant
features of the facts is more or less conscious, the statements may be
regarded as a lie or a rationalization. The range of possibilities is
wide, but remains at the psychological level. The ideological in
this sense may be referred to as "particular."

However, when it is recognized, or implied that the whole
mind — the conceptual apparatus and its content — is ideological,
the merely psychological has been transcended. The ideological
so regarded may be referred to as "total."

In both cases it is recognized that the ideas of the individual
are a function of the cultural-institutional complex in which he

participates. The emphasis may be upon a specific historical epoch, a certain social class, a caste, etc. In any event the individual's intellectual formulations are related to an existentially determined perspective. Now when it is seen that all positions are ideological since noetic conditions underlie all judgments it becomes possible to designate the Marxists as ideologists as well as their opponents. However, in this last situation the connotation of pseudo-logicality, of falseness, disappears and the problem becomes one of seeing how the opposing judgments arose from the contradictory strata of the cultural-institutional world of the individuals, or groups, concerned. It is no longer possible to discredit an opponent by pointing out the ideological character of his ideas since in the total conception of ideology all ideas whatever are ideological.

At first sight this theory would appear to be a vicious relativism. It would seem to differ from the relativism of Protagoras,[3] of Lewes,[4] and Buckle,[5] in that these men assume the necessary subjectivity of all objects. Each says there is no truth but the truth for each. Truth has become as multiform as particular minds. Each truth, as equally authentic, is equally legitimate. There is no criterion of truth but what each particular man thinks — and thinks at that time. Now this kind of relativism is based on an untenable individualistic theory of knowledge.[6] It is sufficient to say that Mannheim is fully conscious of the inadequacy of any theory of knowledge based upon the predicate of individual thinking in its separateness and discreteness. Even so, it may be objected that Mannheim has succeeded in nothing more than a shifting of relativism from the individual to the group. It would be said that the perspectives of these social strata, whether whole societies, castes, classes, and factions, remain relative to one another as did the perspective of individuals in the outmoded relativism of the Sophists and of their modern exponents.

Now Mannheim meets this charge by declaring that his is a theory of "relationism" not of relativism. Now, "relationism means . . . that it belongs to the nature of certain statements not to be formulable absolutely but only in relation to the stylistic structure determined by the situation."[7] A modern theory of knowledge which takes account of the relational as distinct from the merely relative character of all historical knowledge must start with the assumption that there are spheres of thought in which it is impossible to conceive of absolute truth existing independently of the values and position of the subject and unrelated to the social context. Mannheim goes on to say, "even a god could not formulate a proposition on socio-historical subjects like 2+2=4, for what is intelligible in the socio-historical can be formulated only with reference to problems and conceptual constructions which themselves arise in the flux of experience . . . all historical knowledge is relational knowledge."[8] Thus Mannheim is insisting that relativism is bound up with a particular theory of knowledge. The latter is seen by him as having arisen on the one hand in consequence of the dominance of the natural and exact sciences, and on the other as part of an ancient, but continuing, philosophical ideal of knowledge. He believes this ideal of knowledge to derive from the high valuation placed upon the contemplative life. So high was this valuation that knowledge tended to become identified with contemplation. Indeed, knowledge was felt to require a passivity on the part of the observer. Knowledge acquired in this passive, contemplative manner was regarded as "pure" knowledge and designated "theoretical" as distinguished from less pure forms of knowledge associated with action. Mannheim calls this theory of the nature of knowledge an "aged," or "idealistic" one. He views it as positing a sphere of truth as such in terms of which the limited, incomplete cognitions of finite and historical creatures are measured. The notion of a sphere of truth, thinks Mannheim, is the counterpart of that sphere of perfection where the spiritual deficiencies of men are mirrored, and where the *relativity* of their perfection (and thus their imperfection) stands out in marked contrast to the complete and eternally perfect. As epistemology this so-called idealistic theory of knowledge has set up rules, standards, and norms for the validation of thought, but has lost sight of the fact that it is itself an emergent from a value and ontological conception which in turn stems from the religious life of Western society. Insisting upon the timeless character of "true" assertions, such a theory in the nature of the case cannot do other than pronounce upon the invalidity of socio-historical, or "perspectival" knowledge. Socially conditioned knowledge thus becomes "relative" — incomplete, imperfect, impure, and distorted.

Now Mannheim declares that the aged, or idealistic theory of knowledge has promoted the development of the natural and exact sciences, but he emphasizes that it rests upon a kind of thinking that may be described as static since its propositions are of a mathematical type (as quoted above). However, Mannheim believes this thought-model to be incapable of comprehending qualitative peculiarities, and at its best succeeds in stating accurately relations between formalized elements of a given situation. When it endeavors to handle socio-historical knowledge, which depends upon subjective interpretation of the data, it lapses into mere relativism. It is the belief of Mannheim that socio-historical material can be interpreted in a manner that permits not merely subjective relativism, but objective knowledge. Thus when differing ideologies are related to their respective cultural-institutional bases, it becomes possible to remove the distortions from the statements. More frequently it permits the rejection or acceptance, of one or other alternatives in lieu of the degree of adequacy displayed in the comprehension of the object.

Serious criticism may be levelled at Mannheim on two grounds; firstly, that the theory of relationism is a violation of Edmund Husserl's logical canon that a genetic account of a judgment is irrelevant to the question of its validity. Indeed, Scheler has attempted to demonstrate that both "psychologism" and "sociologism" exhibit the "genetic fallacy."[9] Secondly, in order to render a judgment on the validity of one or more ideologies it is necessary that the observer's position be not ideological in the sense that no concealed categories of thought be present. This would hardly seem possible. To have insight into one's own perspective it must be related to its existential conditions. But what can mediate a knowledge of the cultural-institutional framework itself? There is implicit in Mannheim's theory a regress which can be transcended only by immediate insight into contemporary categories of thought. Such insight is, on the basis of the theory, impossible. For the mind rises to an awareness of its categories when its products are viewed from the perspective of another set of contemporary social conditions, or in light of future conditions when the contemporary of one's discussion has receded into history.

In contrast to the static character of the positivistic framework of Durkheim, Mannheim has chosen to approach the problem of how objective knowledge is possible by concerning himself with the historical process, the flux of social actuality itself. He insists that institutions and other non-theoretical factors determine thought. It has been observed that he seeks to escape from relati-

vistic implications of his premises but despite his efforts there is
no way out of the inexorable closure of the circle in the doctrine
of perspectives. In this respect Mannheim and Durkheim are on
common ground for the positivistic framework did at the last
dissolve into a series of changing socio-historically determined categories. Thus, despite numerous differences in detail, Durkheim
and Mannheim arrive at very similar conclusions. This is indicated also by the way in which both sociologists find the self-
sufficient individual to be a myth and regard his thinking, feeling,
and acting to be a function of class stratification and institutional
structure.

Following this preliminary examination of the fundamental
conceptions of Mannheim and the theoretical difficulties they
raise, it becomes necessary to enter upon a more concise exposition
of his chief propositions and chief results. It is as exercising a
careful scrutiny of the ideological concept that the importance of
Mannheim resides; it is in consequence of calling attention to the
positive, as well as to the negative, elements in the relationship
between the social situation and the resultant thought that Mannheim's remarkable contribution to sociological theory is made.

Since the central task of Mannheim's sociology of knowledge
is to establish the relationship between modes of thought and existential conditions, it becomes important to enquire closely into the
meaning of the terms between which this relationship holds.

Investigation discloses that the "mode of thought" is a framework of categories which forms the validational base of the ideological judgment.[10] These categories through, and by which, a
subject, class, or age attempts to grasp reality, Mannheim calls "the
stylistic structure" or "perspective" (Denkstil, Aspekstructur).[11]
This constitutes the fundamental determination, or condition, in
the subject's apprehension of his socio-historical world. Unlike the
categorial scheme of the Critique of Pure Reason, but in common
with that of Durkheim, Mannheim's stylistic structure contains the
values, interests, purposes, etc. of the class, or epoch to which the
individual belongs.

In respect to the term "existential," Mannheim's account does
not exhibit clarity or distinctness.[12] A conceptual congery, referred
to as "factors of existence," its principal element is the social
situation. However, this too, although it is to be regarded
as a unity, is of great inner diversity. The social situation refers

not only to class in the Marxist sense, but to generations, status groups, sects, occupational groupings, schools, degrees of social mobility, etc.[13]

However, in addition to the stylistic structure and existential conditions Mannheim speaks of a third element in the ideological judgment. This consists of the *volitions* of the valuing subject. It was, of course, just this volitional element that Comte had excluded from the positivistic methodology and which he regarded as the distinctive category of the theological and metaphysical stages of human thought.

Now Mannheim regards the stylistic structure as emerging from the interaction of the subject with the existential reality. The volitions vary with the nature of the social situation, but the categories making up the perspective are a consequence of the volitional responses to the social situation.

It is evident that the existential conditions are not non-rational, or non-theoretical in any complete way for they include the social situation, as a principal element, and the social situation in turn involves a perspective. In other words the penetration of the theoretic by the social process is not, as one would gather from a cursory reading of Mannheim, a determination of thought by purely non-theoretic factors. The penetration is achieved only through the agency of a subject who in effecting the penetration does so on the basis of values, etc. derived from a past, or existing social situation. The rise of a new stylistic structure is in fact a consequence of the appraisal of his experience by a subject on the basis of an already existing stylistic structure. However, Mannheim's dichotomy of the existential and the theoretic definitely obscures, if it does not completely conceal, this feature. The presence of a theoretic within the existential is recognized by Mannheim himself in his distinction between "factual genesis" and "meaningful genesis." He asserts,

> "Social existence" is thus an area of being, or a sphere of existence, of which orthodox ontology which recognizes only the absolute dualism between being devoid of meaning on the one hand and meaning on the other hand takes no account. A genesis of this sort could be characterized by calling it a "meaningful genesis" as contrasted with a "factual genesis." If a model of this sort had been kept in mind in stating the

relationship between meaning and being, the duality of meaning and validity would not have been assumed as absolute in
epistemology and noology. Instead, there would have been a
series of gradations between these two poles, in which such
intermediate cases as "being invested with meaning" and
"being oriented to meaning" would have found a place and
been incorporated into the fundamental conception.[14]

It will be observed that the conception of the social situation,
as an order of meaningful being in contrast to mere physical being
is substantially the same as Durkheim's conception of society as an
order *sui generis*. However, both Mannheim and Durkheim frequently confuse this order with physical facts as such. Indeed,
Mannheim sees only gradations between the physical and social.
The sum of these various levels of being constitute the "existential."
To have been consistent Mannheim should have included the
theoretic as the upper level or limit of his gradations of being.
Instead he set up a dualism of various levels of being as making
up the existential on the one hand and the final level of being
forming the theoretic on the other. The views of Durkheim and
Mannheim in respect to social existence have an obviously metaphysical character. However, it is possible to translate much of
this esotericism into a formulation that is consistent with the
orthodox separation of thought and things. This is achieved
simply by saying that social existence (institutions, classes, etc.) is
the process in which concepts (collective representations, categories, stylistic structures, perspectives) are expressed as the life
activities of men and out of which activities new thought-structures
are formed.

   Mannheim has repeatedly said that to understand an assertion
it is necessary to refer the statement back to the existential conditions under which it was formulated and expressed. To do this is
to "particularize" the judgment in question — its partial, limited,
or perspectival character is made apparent. The referral is to the
stylistic structure involved in the social situation and the latter
makes up the principal element in the existential conditions. The
understanding of the judgment, and its partial character, follow
from having isolated the specific categories of the stylistic structure of a given social situation. Thus the element of validity, and
not merely of understanding, that is involved in the revelation of

the limited nature of the judgment is based upon the recognition of the inadequacy of the categorial scheme connected with that social situation, as over against the categorial scheme of a more inclusive social situation. It is important to observe that the validational base of such a judgment is ideal. The use of the terms existential and social situation tend to mislead one into thinking that the validation has been in terms of some sensory, or non-theoretic element.

While a judgment proceeding from the stylistic structure of some very limited social situation may be validated, or invalidated, by the categories of the stylistic structures of highly inclusive social situations, such a validation, for Mannheim, is not final. The ultimate criterion of validity is a pragmatic one. For example, a given class in the vicissitudes of its social existence may develop a stylistic structure, perspective, or set of categories, that runs counter to the whole conceptual scheme of society. The referral of judgments based on the perspective of this class to the wider perspective of the more inclusive social situation would invalidate the judgments. Nevertheless, the judgments may flow from concepts more in conformity with reality than those concepts of the more inclusive social situation. In other words the perspective includes new knowledge. However, the only proof of the objectivity of this knowledge will be the pragmatic test. In this regard Mannheim shows his close relationship to Hegel and Marx. The objective will be that which can actualize itself.[15] What does become actual or real has proved its truth. Thus, in this metaphysic of history, an objective which bases itself upon conformity with reality becomes one with an objectivity which utilizes the criterion of efficiency. The reality to which the criteria of objectivity conform is a changing, historical reality arising in the will, or efficiency, of a society, or class, which alone can bring the reality adumbrated in its "utopia" into actual existence. Such historical reality includes what can be realized in addition to what presently exists. It is to this more inclusive reality of history that Mannheim's criteria of objectivity and of efficency have application.

It has been shown that the validity of a judgment based on a given stylistic structure might be found in the more inclusive conceptual system of the society as a whole. However, since knowledge arises in the socio-historical process, it is not a question of validating the judgments based on the newly emergent concepts by a relatively fixed system of categories that are the perspective, or stylistic structure, of a whole society, or dominant group. Rather it is a question of integrating the new perspective, or elements of it, with the dominant perspective, or even with a number of perspectives. Instead of a fixed system of categories as in the individualism of Kant, which are the criteria of validity for all judgments, there is a dynamic change of standpoints. The method, then, is one of synthesis and Mannheim finds that history itself is a record of such syntheses.[16] However, he does not feel that the flux of standpoints can be organized into a system of affirmations and negations after the fashion of the Hegelian dialectic although the notion of such a dialectic is clearly visible in the background of his thought.

In a sense each ideology is an image of reality, but one which due to the social position of the thinker conceals aspects of that reality. Now Mannheim finds that these complexes of ideas (perspectives, stylistic structures) are of two main types: (a) Those that fix upon aspects of reality favorable to the maintenance of the existing order, and (b) those that direct attention to aspects of reality unfavorable to such maintenance. At this point in his theoretical development Mannheim drops the term "ideology" as a general term, for the various images that arise in the sociohistorical process, and substitutes the term "perspective." Henceforth, the term ideology is used to describe only the first of these types of image — that which directs attention to aspects of reality favorable to the existing social order. The second type of image — the virus of destruction in the established order — he now calls a "utopia," and henceforward, Mannheim's analyses are in terms of the ideology-utopia duality. A utopia, of course, can become an ideology as the continuing transvaluation of values is effected in the movement which arises in the tension between thought and existence.

Since Mannheim is concerned chiefly with the qualitative, or inner dimension of reality, he regards sociology as a discipline of interior comprehension, and like Dilthey and Max Weber, emphasizes the concept of understanding (*verstehen*). Thus the sociology of Mannheim is to be found dealing with the range of problems set by that line of thinkers who distinguish on the one hand between the natural sciences whose goal is explanation (*erklarung*) and on the other the disciplines of history, sociology, sociology of knowledge, etc. which are concerned with understanding or comprehension (*verstehen*). These thinkers — Dilthey, Croce, Simmel, Rickert, Scheler, Troeltsch, and Max Weber — extend their research and reflections beyond the limits of any single discipline. However, it is usually the question of the relationship between philosophy and the theory of history which consumes the energy of their thought. With each the problem is: How can one establish a scientific method, or failing that, a metaphysic that will permit of an escape from cultural or historical relativism and allow for valid historical and social knowledge? It has been pointed out above that, although Mannheim is unwilling to call himself a relativist, cultural relativism is his greatest problem. Each of these thinkers recognizes that the actual structure of social reality cannot be represented objectively in any single perspective. Each sees that the attempt to arrive at knowledge is relative to a given stylistic structure, or place in the socio-historical complex. Now it is evident that the relativism of all historical and socio-cultural accounts is due to the presence of conditioning valuational factors involved in the perspective. It is also these valuational factors that give rise to the "mentalities" which Marx, Mannheim, Weber and others have attempted to stylize in various ways. In these types of mentality one observes the relativism of the norms of thought — how these vary in historically differentiated periods, and even in class groupings in the present.

Summary: It has been shown that individualism in its effort to ground objectivity in the cognitive act of the subject repudiated institutional values in knowledge as sources of bias and distortion. Arriving at categories which it believed to be the universal and necessary conditions for rational thought, it could regard social existence in its particular historical phases only as a factor of limitation and contingency. Objectivity meant the transcending of all socio-cultural viewpoints and validation by universal reason.

Marx accepted this view of objectivity as applied to the natural and exact sciences. However, he declared that in the socio-cultural realm an inevitable distortion is introduced by the presence of unequal economic classes and their continuing struggle. For him, objectivity is possible at the level of social thought when the class struggle is ended. This is the well-known doctrine of ideological superstructures. The theory of ideology, however, is derived from individualism.[17] It is premised upon the conception of reason as an absolute, and upon the corollary of this conception that reasoning in the particularistic terms of class and institutional interests is of necessity a derogation from the autonomy of reason.

Mannheim like Marx tends to retain the notion of objectivity, although in a much modified form, but scrutinizes more closely than does his predecessor the connotation of falsity which individualism had attached to institutional and class thought. For Mannheim there is, in addition to the limitation and partiality imposed upon thought by class and institutional perspectives, a positive element. Facets of reality hitherto unobserved are brought into the focus of consciousness in the process of conceptualization incident upon the building of a stylistic structure. Thus the ideology contains new elements of knowledge but these elements are entangled in the prejudices, interests, wishes, etc. However, it was just these interest bound aspects of the situation that directed attention to otherwise neglected segments of that situation. Thus the referral of a judgment back to the social conditions under which it was formulated and expressed, is done with the purpose of synthesizing these new elements of knowledge, with other perspectives, and not merely with the negative purpose of unveiling the character of the distortion. This is of Mannheim's work the immeasurable worth — the discovery of the value of perspectival knowledge. That knowledge can arise only through a perspective, and, therefore, that all knowledge is perspectival — this point of view is set forth by Mannheim with such clarity and conviction that it may well be decisive for all the future.

Mannheim has equated perspectival knowledge with qualitative knowledge. Yet it is clear that the concepts that go to make up a given perspective need not be valuational concepts. Hence, the entire range of knowledge, and not only social knowledge, in principle can be subsumed under the category of Perspective. However, the knowledge which Mannheim discusses is political knowledge. This is the most partisan kind of all knowledge. The cognitive element in this knowledge is interpenetrated with hopes, desires, ambitions, and value judgments. Linked to propaganda platforms, parties, etc. it exists as an instrument of struggle in the seizure of power, and the creation of the social reality to which its cognitive elements will conform. The role of value judgments is so great that opponents are rarely permeable to the arguments of each other.

It will be seen that political knowledge involves more than one kind of knowledge, and that values are bound up with this knowledge in an almost inseparable manner. The objectivity which Mannheim envisages is a synthesis that gives agreement at the level of values quite as much as at the level of existential facts. Scientific research, however, is not concerned with the erection of a norm validating values; it has as its object the construction of a standard for the validation of descriptive statements regarding such values and their inter-relationships. The validation of values is both a practical and philosophical question; in regard to political knowledge, a matter of policy. Such validation is not the objectivity which science seeks.

It will be seen that Mannheim's objectivity of synthesis is very similar, if not the same, to the kind of objectivity which is to be found in the sacred society. In the latter, too, the categories include Value, and the existential knowledge of a thing is infused with the valuation placed upon it as sacred and profane, pure and impure, etc. The institutional structure binds knowledge and moral conformity together in the most inextricable way.

The synthesis of Mannheim likewise ties in a single unity the values and cognitive features of a social situation. If the term objectivity is allowed as descriptive of this kind of social agreement, it is evident that the content of this objectivity is markedly different from that of the natural sciences.

CHAPTER FIVE

Summary and Interpretation

A point has now been reached when it seems possible to summarize and interpret. Amid the confusions and uncertainties of sociological writing it is apparent that the problem of institutions and objective knowledge contained the three distinct tendencies discussed above. It is also clear that each tendency had its roots deep in the intellectual history of Europe. The first — individualism — is distinguished by its antithetical separation of the free, rational individual from the external, restrictive institution. It is true that the effort is made but rarely to carry out the principle of individualism in a complete way. Only a few attempt the reduction to anarchism.[1] Most thinkers in practice uphold individualism but partially, even if in theory they strive to make the part pass for the whole. In certain instances there is morbid sentimentality;[2] rhodomontades on eagles and lambs;[3] obscurantism;[4] and affected mysticism.[5] But generally speaking the discussion of the self-sufficient individual is based upon the intellectual conviction that egoism is a universal fact of human life. The native rationality of man is assumed, and the liberal thinker seeks to vindicate for him the consciousness of his freedom. More often than not the literary expression of the time is infused with a high regard for mankind who, it is felt, requires only the independence, the intrepidity and the courage to oppose its rationality to slavish obedience, tyranny and hypocrisy in order to liberate itself from institutional bondage.[6]

Paradoxically, the effort to escape from institutions but serves to institutionalize the individual. For modern individualism the

97

taking of what is most individual in the individual as the point of
departure for an assured dominion over the world had its roots
in Christianity, in the premise of the infinite value of the human
soul. The subject who began by ideally isolating himself from the
world, now starts from his own center to critically reconstruct the
world. Both Augustine and Descartes set up the thinking, percipient subject as a metaphysical entity discrete and independent
of others, and of the system of things. In Augustine the principle
of metaphysical certainty implied in thought is dependent upon
God. By the time of Descartes this theological support has vanished. In the nineteenth century the rational, free, autonomous,
self-sufficient individual is taken for granted. It has become a
structural beam in the edifice of thought.

While the rationality of the individual could be uncritically
accepted, what could not be so easily justified was the institutional framework (the state, Church, etc.) whose officers are hard
pressed in its defense. The sharper the distinction between the
rational individual and the restrictive institution, the more the
latter appears a mere "survival."[7] As such it is regarded as defunct
and soon to be replaced by science. It is felt that man will eventually grow out of his institutions as a child emerges from external,
paternal authority to rational self-responsibility. Indeed, contract
presupposed a self-responsible, free, rational agent. On the whole
there is a marked impatience with ritual and ceremony which is
presumed to be a mere vestige of non-rational institutional forms.

In attempting an interpretation of the individualist approach
to the institutional problem two things must be kept in mind.
The first is, as mentioned earlier, that it constitutes a metaphysic
on the nature of man; secondly, that it is a theory concerning the
origin of our ideas, a set of presuppositions and explanation of
the phenomenon of mind — a theory of knowledge. While these
involve one another it is the second that particularly concerns this
study. The theory of knowledge that underpins, or that is individualism (for no sharp distinction is possible) derives from the
breakdown of Medieval Christendom which had regarded its
"truth" as grounded in God, or more concretely in the sacred
institution of the Church. The latter was the depositary of divine
revelation and for long no other source of "truth" was recognized
or permitted. As this world view collapsed it became increasingly
necessary for thought to find an anchorage that would guarantee

the same truth to all. Out of the fragmentation of Scholasticism
and the Church there arose a variety of ontologies. The appearance
of a multiplicity of truths each struggling for dominance could
only produce more uncertainty and atomize yet further the already
disintegrating society. One way of regaining the certitude that
previously had been found in the Christian ontology was to anchor
truth in the cognitive act itself — in the individual. The psychological preparation for the transference of objectivity from an
ontology of divine source to the cognizing subject had been effected
by the whole history of the Christian metaphysic. The individual
had been made ready to believe that truth and reality resided in
himself. The man who separated the concept of the rational from
its scholastic shell — himself a product of the schoolman — was
Descartes. With him the specifically modern appears.[8] Henceforth, the attempts will be: one, to produce the world from the
rational individual, or two, to make the rationality of the individual the criterion of the truth of the world. Thus epistemology
and psychology become the preoccupation of the age.[9]

It is, perhaps, not altogether strange that the concept of
rationality upon its emergence at the beginning of the modern era
should have been identified with individualism. Tradition, history, custom, institutions were associated with society and these
were regarded as the antithesis of rationality. The new revelation
of Descartes presumed to reduce all problems to unquestionable
principles. Against the intellectual perfection of the mathematical
image in the Cartesian "reason," history and its institutions assume
a marked negligibility. As this conception of reason came into its
own, ancient usages, traditions, and institutions receded into an
ever-deepening shadow. The lord of this reason, this rationality,
was the individual; the bearer of tradition was society and its
institutions.

Thus it is that individualism is both a metaphysic and an
epistemology. As a theory of knowledge it assumes that the individual has an absolute, rational capacity independent of a socio-
cultural context. There are indications among proponents of
individualism that they understand the autonomous, rational, self-
sufficient individual to be an abstraction, a fiction, and that
concrete, historical human beings are in fact shaped and made what
they are by human society. Nevertheless, the belief in this fiction
has very real consequences. It means that the cultural institu-

tional context of thought was for a long while almost wholly neglected. When obvious differences in the individual's processes of thinking in various societies, and even historical epochs of the same society, were discovered, no explanation of the differences was possible except by the *ad hoc* theory of social evolution which declares that these societies and epochs represent stages of development. Although this has been called social Darwinism because of its tendency to regard the human mind as developing through stages from non-rationality to rationality with pre-literate societies at the base and Western Europe at the apex, it might better be regarded as a curious distortion of Hegelianism — that is, self-realization of absolute rationality through the stages of human society.

It was shown also that in the Kantian metaphysic individualism abandoned the nominalistic emphasis found in the earlier stages of the development of the classical theory of knowledge and sought for a validational base in *a priori* categories.

Now it is with this question — that of the character of human thinking — that Durkheim comes to grips at last. His early studies and his later research on suicide and religion had forced it upon him. Just as individual action had appeared to him as determined by the system of institutional relationships, Durkheim now suspects that individual thinking is a function of institutional structure. If this could be shown then the concept of institution would have become the predicate of sociology — the fundamental principle to which any aspect of the social would be reducible. Indeed, the final stage of Durkheim's work is an intensive struggle to verify this thesis.

Thus it was that the problem to which Durkheim was led by the inner dialectic of his development was that of the nature of the relationship between institutions and the structural beams of thought — the categories. That some kind of relation did exist between institutions and categories was readily demonstrable. Comte had suggested such a relationship in his Law of the Three Stages; the Hegelian philosophy had taken the variety of institutional structures as exhibited historically by the nations of the world to be but stages in the self-development of the Idea. Almost contemporaneously with Durkheim, Marxism in its inversion of the Hegelian position had stated that thought systems are "ideologies" and that the form of the latter is determined by the socio-historical milieu, not vice versa.

This type of problem (the categories) indicates the seemingly wide remove of Durkheim's task in the sociology of knowledge from the empirical positivistic questions with which Durkheim began. However, there is no hiatus in Durkheim's intellectual progress, and except for a certain stubborn hesitation in effecting the transformation — one never wholly completed — of his methodological framework from empirical positivism to idealism, the movement is remarkably even, being compelled, of course, by the logical interpretation of his empirical research. Reaching the point where it becomes evident that valid knowledge cannot be obtained on purely empirical grounds, Durkheim is driven to a consideration of the *a priori* element in knowledge — hence to the categories.[10] Thus, the sociology of Durkheim is, like the philosophy of Locke, Hume, Kant, etc., essentially criticism. The spirit of the theoretical endeavors of Hume, Kant, and Durkheim, are identical. Their aim is not to renounce thought but to establish it upon a firm and certain foundation. Like his predecessors Durkheim's work is an inquiry into the pre-conditions of knowledge. Further, it attempts to ascertain the origin of religious and metaphysical ideas. It sets forth the limits of human knowledge and yet indicates a new horizon for human thought of almost boundless dimensions. Like all the thinkers of the critical school, Durkheim insists that the grasp of empirical reality is dependent upon the categories. However, he declares (and this revolutionizes the critical standpoint) that the categories are socio-historically determined — their *a priori* character in the absolutist sense of Kantianism must be abandoned. The boundaries of thought are constituted by institutional structure and this structure determines the history of thought for it is itself a history having a past, a present, and a future. The categories, then, are fixed in only a relative sense as making up the field ideas under which individual experience must be subsumed. But the categories are permanent, no more and no less, than the institutional structure. The categorial framework of all logic and science, of all knowledge whatever, may be altered to the extent that changes, reformatory or revolutionary, are effected in the institutional base. Thus time, space, cause, etc., lose their status as absolute concepts and become relative to the various stages of institutional history. Thus for Durkheim the narrow limits imposed upon thought by the absolute Kantian *a priori* are transcended.

At this point it can be reiterated that Durkheim has passed from the fixed framework of positivism to a form of historical relativism. This is not so much inconsistent with positivism as it is with the idealism that also permeates his thought. Durkheim nowhere declares himself to be a metaphysical monist yet his idealism had seemed to leave him no other alternative. However, by holding on to his empirical positivism he has transformed the fixed categories of idealism, the "eternal objects," into the temporal products of human institutions. Durkheim has become relativistic in the same way as Mannheim. Thought ceases to have validity within itself; its reality is grounded in institutional structure, and no idea can be considered as "true" or "false" except as it can be understood in terms of the socio-historical process.

It should be noted that the sociological approach to the problems of epistemology and logic as exemplified by the school of Durkheim, and later that of Mannheim, was paralleled by an equally vigorous one in psychology. Both of the approaches were dominated by empirical positivism and were an effort to reduce logic to empirical law. The influence of Wilhelm Wundt and Franz Brentano was to underpin a theory of knowledge that made logical and epistemological problems special cases of psychological ones. That the essential theoretical basis resided in psychology was also the view of J. S. Bain, Lipps, and Meinong. According to these men even the acceptance of logic as an ethics of the mind — that it is a normative and practical discipline — did not make it any the less psychology. Indeed, some felt that ethics should be expressed as physics. Such a position was taken up by Herbert Spencer, who, it should be remembered, worked in psychology, sociology, and ethics. Spencer exhibits conduct as being in relation to action, and finally, to mere movement. Thus the inroads made by psychology into logic were a segment of a large attack by the empirical sciences generally upon the ideal and normative sciences. It was this attempt to find a validational base in psychology, and other disciplines that Husserl spoke of as the "genetic fallacy," and with special reference to sociology, "sociologism."

It is his contention that an account of origins, either individually or socially, can never tell us why ideas, or concepts or judgments are true. There is always the question of their logical validity, which, in the last analysis must be the final criterion. It was his attempt to establish the criteria for logical validation. He seeks for that which is deepest, for that which is final, self-sufficient — for an absolute which is the opposite of relative. In his quest he reduces the bulk of Kant's philosphy to a "psychologism," and Hegelianism to a "relativism." Philosophizing, he thought, was difficult and prolific of error because the methods of philosophy were confused and philosophers seldom tried to agree among themselves. These facts are mentioned here to indicate the scope of his interests and investigations, and to suggest to what extent his logical attacks penetrated the prevailing ideologies and nostrums, even to the great philosophical systems of his age. In the formulation of his own philosophical system of phenomenology, and although he could devise no satisfactory test for error in it, he, nevertheless, defined the limits of truth by a method of his own designing.

Husserl had come early to the conclusion that empiricism and naturalism could not be the basis for logic and mathematics, which to him were the roads to a validating absolute. So when empiricism and naturalism are applied to the field of sociology, only sociologisms are the result. Facts of experience and man's so-called natural rights, or natural heritage, are not valid criteria of the truth of the idea or of the right. Neither is an idea true simply because it has practical consequences for society; nor can it be made true by the process of institutional propagation. From anthropology he had seen that knowledge always works one way or another, but the fact that it does work is no certainty of its validity for truth. A sociology that considers only the experiential data, the natural phenomena, and the practical consequences in its field is committing the same error as philosophy and morality — it is incapsulating itself within a sociologism by an irrational process. In the last analysis origins in sociology are without significance from the standpoint of "truth."

Husserl also directed his attention to the realm of psychology and found the same conditions prevailing there as he had found elsewhere. Since the days of Hume the philosophers of empiricism had regarded psychology as the science of human nature. But Husserl was opposed to any form of over-individualism, and regarded with suspicion any tendency to look upon the human organism as an ultimate basis for truth. Any view which tried to make categories relative to a stage of development or to the psycho-physical constitution of the organism or the species he called a psychologism. By this term he meant any procedure which makes reason dependent on something non-rational in character, and all relativism, skepticism, idealism and subjectivism, have this common trait. It is what Plato called sophistry, and spent much time in its refutation. Much of contemporary psychological thought was of the nature of these ancient sophistries. The non-rational procedures, Husserl thought, had grown out of a confusion of logic and psychology, out of a confusion of formal structure and a psychological act. For him the results of an empirical investigation come to be expressed as truths, and the latter as propositions containing a subject and predicate constitute the standard by which the claim to be scientific is judged. Husserl took this to mean that such truth cannot be derived from the empirical disciplines but from logic itself.

Now the problem of the determination of the ultimate validity of a belief is not one that concerns this study. However, the question of the genetic fallacy enters into the inquiry directly since it is the position of Durkheim and Mannheim that the recognition of existential factors in knowledge compels revision of the thesis that the genesis of an idea is at all times irrelevant to its truth. It has already been pointed out that Mannheim holds the existential conditioning of thought to be a fact. That every theoretical work is limited by sociological, psychological, geographical, historical, and other conditions would seem to be indisputable. However, what Husserl has said is that the validity of a judgment does not depend upon referring its content to these conditions. On the other hand Mannheim and historical relativism generally, contends that knowledge must be referred to the processes under which it arose and can be understood only with reference to those processes, the ideal and material aspects respectively of those conditions.

Assuming that all thinking is situationally bound (and this seems undeniable) it is important to separate the components of the socio-historical situation. On the one hand the situation includes an ideal component — concepts and values (the stylistic structure); and, on the other, a set of non-ideal components — spatial and temporal position, geography, varying vehicles of communication such as stone, papyrus, parchment, paper, newsprint, and many other things.

It is not the purpose of this study to examine the role of these non-ideal components of the situation. However, it should be obvious that the non-ideal components do have a different significance for thought than do the ideal components — the several parts of the stylistic structure. The latter may be regarded as the conceptual scheme of a class or society at a given stage of its development. This ideal component in the situation is bound by the non-ideal components, but the latter can be regarded as only negative factors — a set of limits to the construction and expression of the conceptual scheme (the ideal component).

The distinction that is being insisted upon here owes its origin to the sharp scission created by Descartes between mind as *res cogitans* and the world as *res extensa*. In the work of Descartes thought and matter are conceived of as two distinct substances which have nothing in common, which are separated as to their nature by the whole diameter of reality. The Cartesian dualism cleft a deep chasm between thought and things and it is difficult to escape the implications of the Cartesian position.

The separation between thought and things has had as a consequence the neglect of qualities and values which were conceived to be no part of the material world, and an emphasis upon matter in its spatial, mechanistic and mathematical aspects. This culminated in the view that the real world was the physical world — the world of physics. The thoughts of humans, concepts and values, were regarded as accidental by-products of physical forces. Concepts were but subjective constructs. To view them as having objective significance was to be the victim of a pre-scientific metaphysics.

At this time it is not necessary to pursue the problems that arise from Descartes' position. These in fact belong to the whole history of modern philosophy. The important thing is that the modern mind cannot avoid making a distinction between thought and things.

It may be true that at the metaphysical level the object and the thought of that object are one in the sense that both are within the unity of thought. It would seem that there can be no absolute separation of thought from things, or things would remain unknown. Nevertheless, at the level of day by day experience the distinction between them is necessary. Indeed, the capacity to make such a distinction is a criterion of sanity itself.

Despite the evident necessity for a clear separation between thought and things, the history of the past few centuries shows a remarkable confusion to have prevailed. The reason for this becomes clear only upon an analysis of the modes of intellectual inquiry that have dominated the modern world. The mechanistic and quantitative methods of modern science precluded an understanding of anything that was not mechanistic and quantitative. However, thought itself cannot be reduced to quantity and mechanics. Nevertheless, the preoccupation with the mechanistic and quantitative led to a devaluation in the ontological status of the *res cogitans* of the Cartesian dualism. Thought, universals, concepts, values, came to be regarded as somehow less real than *res extensa*. The realm of universals became an empty shadow-land; the authentic world was the world of physical existence.

The failure to view *res cogitans* as truly real had two results: firstly, a tendency to explain the ideal components of a situation in terms of what alone was considered to be real, namely, material determinations; and, secondly, to frequently confuse the ideal and material.

The analysis of individualism in its nominalistic form indicates that from Duns Scotus and Ockam to John Locke; from Hume to J. S. Mill; from Herbert Spencer to Floyd Allport, every important representative of this sociology has insisted that only particular things have real existence. All that is, exists only as a singular in its pure individuality. Only the individuals associated with an institution are real; the institution is but what individuals do in common, or how some individuals are organized to serve the purpose of other individuals. In itself apart from individuals the institution has no objective reality. At the same time the institution is viewed as external, coercive, and restrictive. But the institutional forces impinging on the individual are regarded as the work of other individuals — kings, priests, legal functionaries, etc. — attempting to impose their will in terms of their particular vested interests. From the nominalistic standpoint the institution was supposed to be something unreal. Yet it seems strange how something so unreal could become the object of so much hostility and vituperation. The fact is that individualism often did regard institutions as having the character of particular things, and more often the reverse. Most interesting is the curious feature that institutions and rationality are often regarded as opposites. It is apparent that individualism on some occasions confuses institutions with individuals; at others it insists they are universals, and thus, *vocis flatus*.

An examination of the school of positivism reveals a similar ineptitude in its handling of the two sides of the Cartesian reality. In the work of Comte there is the attempt to overcome the dualism by considering the sequences and coexistents in perception alone to be real, and thus, the only legitimate subject matter of science. Abstractions are unreal and this applies, says Comte, to general notions like gravitation, atom, and cause. In point of fact, the Comtean approach tends to consider the sensory phenomena only to be real and the universal it utterly denies. Here again no insight into the problem of institutions and knowledge is possible because of the denial of the ideal component of institutions.

Further, the positivism of Durkheim explicitly says that social facts are to be treated as things, as *choses*. Thus while the reality of the *res cogitans* is not expressly denied, it is forthwith disposed of in its ideal character, and is viewed as if in fact it were *res extensa*. Now it is true that Durkheim at many points moves in the direction of conceiving the reality of the ideal component of the social situation but the fetter forged by his methodology regarding thought as things could not be transcended. It is the fundamental confusion of these two orders of reality, that not only vitiates, but makes absurd the formal statement of the Durkheimian sociology of knowledge. As has been seen Durkheim seeks to derive the categories from social facts, but the latter continued to be thought of as "things."[11] Indeed, Durkheim included genuine sensory elements such as the distribution of the group in space, etc. among his *choses*. Throughout his work Durkheim refuses to relinquish entirely the notion that reality consists of things, and therefore, sociology must be the science of social things. Always he labors to translate ideal components into pseudo-sensory entities in order that his research shall conform to what he considers to be the predicate of science, namely, that valid knowledge must be knowledge of some segment of the sensible world (*res extensa*).

On turning to Mannheim the very term existential betrays a metaphysical preference. Like individualism and positivism, historical relativism looks upon the existential, the conditions of existence as the real and as the determinant of thought. The theoretic has no autonomy, nor does it proceed by an inner dialectic, but is penetrated at every point by the social process. However, if it is asked what is meant by the social process one discovers only confusion. Mannheim has said that the categories of socio-historical (the stylistic structure) are determined in their emergence by the fundamental existential reality and this latter is external and non-rational. It will be noted that in enumerating the social situation, the individual volitions, and the stylistic structure as the three elements present in all ideological judgments, Mannheim has endeavored to separate in some measure the ideal from other elements since the stylistic structure is clearly ideal. However, at other times in speaking of the social situation he appears to have forgotten his distinction. Class and class interests involve a stylistic structure and Mannheim in emphasizing class strata as important aspects of the existential conditioning of thought has like the individualists and positivists failed to distinguish the sensory datum from the ideal. His inclusion of the stylistic structure as a determinant of the same order as the external, non-rational factors begs the whole question of the non-rational determination of the theoretic for the stylistic structure is plainly itself theoretic.

The schools selected for examination represent dominant and widely accepted viewpoints in sociological theory. Their influence has been enormous, not only in theoretical inquiry, but as sociologies expressing themselves in history. On the one hand each of these views appears to develop in such a way as to correct weaknesses in another sociological frame of reference. For example, Comtean positivism endeavors to remove the fiction of the autonomous and self-sufficient individual and to place him within a context. Just as the motion of a material body is to be explained not by a mysterious nature as such but by its place in the network of a system of bodies, so Comtean positivism would explain individual conduct by the individual's place in a system of individual relationships (society). The Comtean sociology does not proceed beyond this and is no more than a social physics.

In the same way Durkheim carrying on the tradition of his predecessor looks beyond the individual to society in such a way that it ceases to be a complex of individuals. Rather it becomes a set of ideal relationships since the emphasis is upon the categories, concepts, and values which give the relationships. Thus the Durkheimian sociology has lost the crudity of a social physics and carried the analysis of the social to a new level. Likewise the disquieting intuitions of Durkheim that sociology must be a theory of knowledge becomes in the concept of stylistic structure almost an explicit premise in Mannheim.

On the other hand there is a definite presupposition that runs through the three schools. This is the view that the ideal component of a situation has negligible ontological status. In other words the ideal elements of *res cogitans* are viewed as functions of *res extensa*. Deeply imbedded in each of these schools is the idea that a scientific explanation of social phenomena will require the reduction of the social to the level of sensory phenomena. It does not matter what phrase is employed, "observable phenomena," the "individual," *les choses,* or "existential." The final principle of explanation is a concept of a sensory datum, or a datum regarded as if sensory. A final principle of explanation in terms of ideal elements is attempted by Kantian individualism. However, the categories as criteria of validity were intended for use in the validation of knowledge of sensory phenomena. Kant had not envisaged any connection between such criteria and the social process. However, in a broad sense the principle of Kant is not open to criticism as violating the genetic fallacy. It is, in fact, only the Protagorean and nominalistic varieties of individualism which tend to commit this error.

Those who have believed most strongly in the possibility of valid knowledge have been fully conscious of the fact that naïve experiences have to be referred to some standard before becoming a part of the world of knowledge. This standard is always conceptual. The great problem becomes that of determining the conceptual scheme which is to be the yardstick of valid knowledge. In this case it becomes difficult to see in what way the existential can determine the validity of a judgment except as the stylistic structure within a given social situation makes the so-called existential an object of knowledge with the consequent emergence of new knowledge and a new stylistic structure. To point out that the existential may be an object of knowledge and such knowledge may determine judgments is hardly the same thing as stating that existential factors determine the validity of a judgment.

It would seem, then, that no sound objection can be offered to Husserl's dictum that the validity of a concept does not depend upon its genesis but upon the system of concepts of which it is presumably a part. This would appear to be the placing of an idea within a complex totality of ideas. To know anything is to know in a measure the unified whole upon which any given idea is dependent for its validity.

It is clear that the basic presupposition of individualism in its nominalistic form, as also of positivism, and historical relativism, has been that reality is constituted by *res extensa*. Science is regarded as a knowledge of this realm. Further, it has been the express purpose of Durkheim to exhibit the fundamental categories of thought as a product of the social process. However, an analysis of the term social process indicates his basic presupposition that only *choses* are real, or rather that social facts must be regarded as *choses* to be realities for science. His emphasis upon *choses* requires that the categories be explained in terms of existential elements. Yet the most cursory examination of what Durkheim means by "society" makes it abundantly clear that elements are involved that are in no sense existential. This is obvious when Durkheim speaks of institutions as consisting "exclusively of sentiments and values." It is no less so in Mannheim where the "stylistic structure" turns out to be "the constitutive categories of thought in terms of which an individual, or an age, attempts to grasp the nature of the world." In individualism the role of "rationality" affords another parallel. Such ideal elements cannot be discounted as accidental aspects of the social process. Indeed, it is evident that a direct connection is to be found between these ideal elements of the social process and the categories. That "the realm of the theoretic is penetrated at every point by the social process" is only another way of saying that the ideal elements in society determine the formulation of other ideal elements in society. It begins to be apparent that institutions, as understood by Durkheim, are an ideal part of an ideal system. The fact that categories appear to "grow out of institutions" no longer seems strange. The institutions and the so-called theoretic constitute a single system and a single process. Thus, quite contrary to what individualism believed, institutions are not the antithesis of the rational, but are the rational in the process of expression in the sense that they are concepts and categories whose content is translated into patterns of thought and conduct.

It is now clear in what sense Mannheim and Husserl (at first sight so contradictory) can be reconciled. Certainly, the validity of a judgment can be determined only by the implicative system to which the ideas under discussion belong. However, this system includes the ideal elements of the institutional complex (Durkheim), of the "stylistic structure" (Mannheim), of individual "reason" or rationality (individualism). If there is something which functions in the validational procedure in a manner similar to the Kantian valid element in knowledge, it is assuredly not in the purely existential elements, which are properly only objects of knowledge, but in the ideal system of knowledge as a whole. This totality — the conceptual and categorial scheme of an entire society — is at once the product and expression of social existence, and connotes a meaning which approximates that of the current concept of "culture."

CHAPTER SIX

The Conceptual System

Up to this point the consideration of individualism, sociological positivism, and historical relativism has been directed toward showing that each school as a consequence of its inner
development shifts from some existential factor as a basis for
objectivity to a categorial scheme. Incidentally, some effort was
made to free the hypotheses of Durkheim and Mannheim from the
imperfect conceptions which had justified the objection of Husserl.
In performing these tasks it was indicated that at least the meaning
— if not the traits of form and structure — which the objects of
knowledge possess, is to be attributed to the character of the particular categorial scheme employed.[1] It was suggested also that the
three frameworks, "the categories," "society," and "stylistic structure" might be subsumed under the general concept of "conceptual
system," and that this latter framework of abstractions appeared
to be the same as that which in some anthropological circles today
is referred to as "culture."[2] Leaving aside the question of the
positive identification of these two concepts with one another, it
is now in place to consider the significance of the conceptual system as such, and in particular, for the issues with which the inquiry deals.

The use of the term conceptual system to refer to the framework of collective representations, or universals, would appear to
be more convenient than the term "society." It was the dual meaning involved in the employment of the latter that led to the
confusion and misunderstanding of Durkheim's work. At one
period Durkheim evidently used the term society with the usual

empirical reference of a group of individuals; at another he seems to have meant the system of universals, or what his critics have called his world of "eternal objects."[3] As was pointed out, Durkheim's dilemma resulted from his failure to distinguish clearly between thought and things, or perhaps, more accurately, from his insistence upon looking at *res cogitans* as if it were *res extensa.*

In order to grasp the meaning of the conceptual system, there is some point in returning to the constitutive elemental unit of the system, namely, the concept. The concept has fascinated the thinkers of Western culture from the time of Socrates forward. Its importance has been apparent to all, but its nature and function have not always been understood. The failure to see that the concept is never an individual construct has obscured its rightful significance. Durkheim saw clearly the social source of the concept and followed up a few of the implications of this insight. It is of vital importance to observe Durkheim's emphasis upon the concept as the vehicle of rational communication, and its impersonality as the very essence of rationality and logic. Indeed, no intellectual communication is possible except by an exchange of concepts. The obvious form of such exchange is in language — itself a structure of concepts. The concept as a universal embodies an agreement in respect to some aspect of reality about which there is no longer any dispute. The exchange of concepts implies an effort to conceptualize further and to eliminate entirely the area of subjective impression — that is, to reach objective statement in whatever may be under discussion.

Objectively the power of rational thought is not peculiar to any single one in his separate individuality but is common to all in their societal universality. The disjunct, isolated, miscellaneous impressions of individuals through comparison cease to be subjectivities, and at length a system is formed in which objectivity arises. Insofar as impressions cannot be compared or communicated they cannot be knowledge. Such impressions are without meaning, and hence, valueless for a society.

What is held to be true, or good, etc. must be decided by the individual, but insofar as he is a rational thinking being. However, this rationality is not something especially his possession but something common to all men in his society — to all men whose minds are structured by the fundamental conceptual system which underlies the whole. Whenever a number of men fall back on this framework the specialties of each disappear, and they tend to arrive at the same conclusions. Within the maze of particular impressions there is built up a solid core — the conceptual system — the result of collective experience. This is the ultimate possession of a society, its final court of appeal in matters of objectivity, morality, and beauty.

The system of concepts which supports the life of a society is found only in the minds of the persons who make up that society. However, these ideas as pointed out above, are not subjective impressions. They are concepts, universals, objective ideas which like the language and logic have an independence of any single mind. It is a grave mistake to hypostasize these ideas and see them as actually in separation from persons. This would be to make concrete what is actually an abstraction and would end in a barren sociological mysticism indicative of a deficiency of intellectual resource. This is in fact the supreme self-contradiction of the theory of the collective consciousness. It begins by saying that only the collective representation is real and ends by degrading the universal into a particular. It is the cardinal error of Durkheim that, despite his stature, he conceived of society as an individual personality, and thus fell among the stones and brambles of philosophic bathos.

In the system of universals, or collective representations, the society and its persons have their point of coincidence. The inner core of universals, or categories, may be regarded as a network of thought-determinations which forms a foundation for human social life. These categories — although possessing a history, and not constituting a timeless *prius* (as was once assumed) — by their validational function upon thought and conduct assure for the members of a society an ordered and meaningful existence. Underlying all thought and feeling, they are constitutive of the tissue of social reality. For Durkheim the term "society" came to mean a system, and by the term system is implied the manifold of individual thought, feeling, and action in subjection to a single category. This concept is that of Totality, or form of the whole, so far as through this whole the position and meaning of its parts mutually is determined. For Durkheim the whole is, therefore, articulated and not simply amassed. This "society" or culture is presented as a vast system of concepts self-referrent to the unity of a single living pulse.

All phenomena pass and only the intelligible relations and concepts which these phenomena express remain permanent. However, the phenomena alone are ever actual. The relations and concepts have no actuality *per se*. Further, the realization of the concepts takes place only through persons who express them in institutions, religion, philosophy, and science.

The construction brick of the conceptual system is the concept but, unfortunately, the term structure calls up a rigidity which is the opposite of what is meant. In the conceptual structure the foundations are living and active — as G. H. Mead has intimated, the roots of the mind itself.[4]

It seems difficult for investigators of the social to avoid the pitfall of reification, or as Whitehead has called it, the fallacy of "misplaced concreteness." The conceptual system, or ideal aspect of the social process, has an ontological reality but no phenomenal existence. Such a system in itself is no more than the logical presuppositions of a social order. However, this separation of the conceptual system from the concrete social life of individuals is only a logical one, a separation in thought. The conceptual system is that which is logically prior to meaningful activity. The confusion that is to be found in regard to this matter resides in the insistence that the conceptual system be regarded as having existence like phenomenal things. The system of concepts is objectively real in the sense that it is logically prior to all subjective thought. Rational thought is thought in terms of the entire conceptual system, and the core of the system is constituted by categories. The individual is rational to the extent that his subjective thought is in agreement, or identical with the objective concepts of the system. While in theory the objective rationality of the system should coincide with the rationality of the individual, there are contingent factors that make this identification impossible in fact. Among the factors of contingency is the fact that any judgment is made on the basis of some segregated portion of the system — from some particular institution, or position in the latter. In this sense bias, partiality, limitation is in practice a universal condition of thought. Further, it is possible for the concept, or framework of concepts, embodied by an institution to be inconsistent with the conceptual system as a whole. Thus a judgment made on the basis of a conceptual structure which is at variance with the general conceptual structure will give the appearance of non-rationality.

It should be kept in mind also that the conceptual system has its numerous concealed categories — that is, concepts not explicitly present in the consciousness of a given individual, but nevertheless, carried by the society. These concealed categories have formed the subject matter of much research in the study of personality. They are, like all concepts, social in origin and cannot be of an inherited character, nor can they have their source in the life experiences of the individual. It may be that the most fundamental categories of an age are always concealed from the contemporaries of that age, and only when this set of categories is already passing does it become explicitly formulated.[5] This would mean that the further reaches of the conceptual system cannot be subjected to scrutiny until their character as basic determinants in thought already has been superseded. This concealment should not be thought of as remoteness from every day thinking. Indeed, the contrary would seem to be the case. Such categories are, like the light and air to vision and respiration respectively, unperceived because always and universally present. The individual rises to an awareness of these fundamental conditions of existence only upon their removal. Thus it is that the person makes use of the fundamental categories of the system in every meaningful act. They permeate the whole of his every day existence, but their universality blinds him to their presence. If these categories can be known at all by contemporaries it would seem possible only by abstraction and inference from the concrete acts which are their expressions.

It is of importance to note that the conceptual system is first of all a set of statements by a society in its collective experience of the nature of reality. Whether these statements are viewed as constitutive of the nature of reality, or as transformations of it, becomes secondary.

The conceptual system may be regarded as identical with the realm of knowledge. Since the system results from the unique experiences of a given society the conceptual system may take the form of scientific, metaphysical, or religious knowledge. On the other hand these types may be found together in varying degrees. It would seem, then, that science, metaphysics, and religion have this in common — they are all three conceptual frameworks of an ultimate sort, and each seems to be the product of a specific sort of society.[6] What is remarkable is that each is ultimate in the sense that the society to which each corresponds respectively regards that framework as its final premise for all thinking. From this it follows that all three types are rational. The conceptual is the rational but the basis of acceptance or rejection of a particular concept can be only the conceptual system in its totality. Husserl's demonstration that the validity of a concept is neither proved nor disproved by the circumstances of its origin, but only in terms of the conceptual relationships of which it is a part — this means that the conceptual system alone can determine the valid. It follows that the opposition between rationality and religion, is not an opposition between rational and non-rational. The opposition is between two conceptual systems, or two portions of a conceptual system. Each system must be regarded as rational within itself provided it is a system at all.[7]

The failure to see that scientific and religious (and metaphysical) systems are to be classified as species of a generic idea has led to the mistaken notion that scientific and religious thought are different entirely. Even though a great difference in the content of objectivity as between scientific and religious systems is apparent, there is a common denominator insofar as each presumes to be in possession of the "truth," or to be in possession of a method that leads to it.

Where two conceptual systems are presented to an individual, it will be necessary for him to reconcile their "disparities" by some kind of philosophic rationalization, or to reject one or the other. A third alternative is to see each as constituting its own order of truth.[8] This position, since it violates the notion of the unity of knowledge, tends to be unsatisfactory, unless some way is discovered of reconciling these orders on some more ultimate metaphysical ground.

In view of the fact that each conceptual system has its objectivity and rationality within itself, it becomes necessary to revise the usual notions of the sacred and the secular. Durkheim has shown that where reality is viewed from the standpoint of the social, there is the sacred. But it has been shown that the final frame of reference is the conceptual system, and hence, it is this latter which is sacred. But it has been demonstrated that the conceptual system is also rational. Indeed, the rational is no more than the conceptual system in its totality. The conclusion that must be drawn from this is that the rational and sacred are one. This should not be difficult to accept, since in every society, it has been acknowledged that the sacred is the ultimate "truth." At least there can be no doubt that for the member of the preliterate society the sacred and the rational coincide.

Frequently, the sacred has been thought to be a "higher" order of truth. If a lower order of truth, for example, positive science, comes to be considered as the highest and only valid truth, or approach to it, then the truth of positive science has become sacred. The latter is that knowledge upon which the society conceives itself to depend; the system of concepts to which every problem in a final sense must be referred. Certainly, most societies will see fit to separate the "higher" from the "lower." It may well be that economic activity may be the expression of concepts placed by a society at a lower level in its conceptual hierarchy.[9] However, this would not be true in all societies; concepts expressing themselves in economic activity might be sufficiently ultimate in some societies to be viewed as sacred. Similarly, the social definition of sex, military prowess, age, skin color, or anything else will have sacred or profane connotations according to the place of these definitions in the system of definitions — that is, in the conceptual system.

The question arises as to how Western civilization has succeeded in driving a wedge between the rational and the sacred. This can be only because of the presence of two theoretic orders — two conceptual and categorial schemes. These two orders, or schemes, have been those of the Medieval framework on the one hand, and that of individualism and natural science on the other. Insofar as these two major orders have not been metaphysically integrated they have remained relative. The tendency has been to accept the epistemology of the classical theory of knowledge (individualism) and the methods of the natural sciences as constituting the only valid framework for rational knowledge. Using the term sacred in the sense of a society's ultimate statement about reality, this epistemology and method are sacred. However, the name "sacred" has remained the name attached to a former, and in some measure, still effective, framework. This latter is the traditional religious institutional complex which upon dissolution left great fragments of the older "sacredness" to continue in the form of churches and sects. Unfortunately, the term "institution" tended to become associated with the traditional — the established — and not at all with the "reason" of the new conceptual order. Indeed, the rationality of Cartesianism and individualism generally came to be regarded as antithetical to institutional structures.

The difference between objectivity and illusion, between true and false, between good and evil, is never self-evident. Neither objectivity, nor the ideals of human life, are obvious. They can be determined only by rational thought — by the system of universals (concepts) which the society has built up in its collective experience. Indeed, the reconciliation of the reality of these universals with the reality of empirical particulars is ever the goal of thought. One over-all value of such a system of concepts is that it transmits from generation to generation certain ideas about the universe together with the solutions to the problems which these ideas regarding the universe raise, and thus relieve individuals from the task of discovering for themselves what they wish, and to some extent, must know.

The conceptual system conquers as it were the extensive and intensive multiplicity of things. Whether the system is positive science, or revealed religion, there is a bringing together in reflection of the manifold of the external world. Moreover, concepts never exist independently of the individuals in a social process. In the language of G. H. Mead this would indicate that the symbols men use are never merely particulars; they are universals. They must be universal in order to be meaningful at all, and they must refer to an experiential content. Once again, in Mead's terms the significant symbol is always part of the social act. Even in such an abstract field as mathematics the meaning of the problem is present within it, even though the rational process is carried on without a knowledge of what that meaning is. Insofar as the individual is able to incorporate those meanings of the social group to which he belongs and which are universal — that is, which bring out the same response in all individuals of the community — he has incorporated the mind of that social group. The universal is not necessarily universal through time, and universals must be continually revised.[10] The process of communication limits universality in that everyone cannot speak the same language. Any group of individuals who speak the same language may have different universes of discourse, but by virtue of their speaking the same language there is a potential universality to all their meanings as they are contained within that language. Meaning is always the same to the person who is indicating the meaning as it is to the person who responds to it; otherwise it is not meaning; it must have a universality to be meaningful.

The universal is not to be confused with the means by which men conceive it, but it is still not necessary to suppose that there are in existence "essences" which exist in the mind, although it does not have to be presumed either that when one thinks of this universal he thinks of a particular instance.

Thus the universality of thought and meaning is the result of the relationship which obtains in the social act,[11] in which the individual takes the attitude of the others — the "generalized other" — which is the crystallization of all the particular attitudes of others toward him. That the person, as distinguished from the biological individual, is a resultant of society, and that he is dependent upon society for his existence (that there is a common dependence of all individuals upon one another), forms the basis for the development of both logical and ethical norms.[12] These norms exist in the consciousness of individuals as a recognition of this common social dependence. The individual in taking over the institutions of the society in which he lives is internalizing the basic structure of the conceptual system. These institutions represent the common response of all individuals (in the society in which they are found) to given situations. This organization of attitudes which are common to all members of the society is the basis for the order of society; it is in the institutions that the organization of a society is represented.

That the conceptual system arises in the social act and is re-translated back into empirical form in the on-going activity of the individuals making up class and institutional groupings — this point of view appears to have dominated the thought of G. H. Mead. A somewhat similar position is taken up by John Dewey. The epistemology of both thinkers has its source in the Darwinian theory of evolution and sets up as fundamental premises for each respectively that mind wholly emerges within conduct (Mead), and action (Dewey). Dewey declares that human beings find it necessary to act in order to satisfy needs, and that the function of thought is to serve as an instrument in the process of need satisfaction. This adherence to certain biological tenets is not of significance for the present study, but Dewey's general insistence upon the practical character of knowledge — that all science is applied science — is of first importance. In this connection Dewey points out, "It is a strict truism that no one would care about *any* exclusively theoretical uncertainty or certainty. For by definition in being *exclusively* theoretical it is one which makes no difference anywhere."[13] Thus Dewey contends that valid segments of the conceptual system are made up of ideas "which when they are referred back to ordinary life experience and their predicaments, render them more significant, more luminous to us, and make our dealings with them more fruitful."[14] The conceptual system as a framework of abstractions is for Dewey not a set of ideas in any static sense but, "Ideas are statements not of what is, or has been, but of acts to be performed."[15] Thus the conceptual system is knowledge only to the extent that it is acted upon, tested, and used as the basis of experimentation in the solution of actual problematic situations. Indeed, concepts as instruments arise from the ambiguities of experience, from the problem solving activity of the organism in its attempt as a part of nature to adjust to another part of nature, that is, to the environment. At the human level the very recognition of a problematic situation by a subject involves conceptual elements, and hence implies an antecedent conceptual system. Dewey attempts to analyze the partial discontinuity in nature of organism and environment at all levels, but he concludes that *reflective* intelligence emerges solely in the confrontation of a problem situation by the human animal.

Both Mead and Dewey prefer to discuss the problem of conceptual thought and of validation of experience in terms of the symbolic process. Mead's "significant symbol" comes into being for the subject with the development of the social self. As an internalized language symbol, the significant symbol conveys a meaning that is wholly social; it refers to the self and to others. Since the symbol is a *substitute stimulus,* symbol systems allow the control of present behavior and the manipulation of the environment by absent stimuli. In the language of symbols this means that the conceptual system in its variety of symbolic forms, as so many substitute stimuli, constitutes a power over the social and physical environment of enormous complexity. The society's success in handling the problematic situations of the past is carried forward in the conceptual system as "acts to be performed" in the problematic situations of the future.

For Dewey, then, formal validation consists in elaborating clearly the relations that obtain between symbols, but "truth" resides in the successful application of the symbolic process to the non-symbolic aspect of experience. Here again, as with Mannheim, truth and error do not flow from considerations of internal consistency, or formal logic, but from the success or failure of ideas in some concrete setting.

The conceptual system begins to dissolve when it questions its own foundations. The ultimate concepts of the system must remain sacred which is to say that they must remain unquestioned if they are to remain ultimate. Medieval Christianity was already on the point of fragmentation when the Scholastics began to question its premises; Greek theology was gone even before the individualism of the Sophists; and now positive science begins to examine its own fundamental assumptions. Institutional structures, whether marriage and the family, economic, educational, or state can remain sacred only so long as they are not open to question. To question is in a sense to profane, and indicates that another conceptual framework is in process of formation. It is from this new predicate that questions regarding the old sacred system arise. Thus the conceptual system as the basis of objectivity carries its validity within itself — not in some transcendent absolute realm, nor even in empirical reality as such — but as the self consistency of its concepts. Empirical knowledge is objective insofar as the concepts which constitute it are consistent with the conceptual system.[16]

Every definition of a segment of reality by a society in its collective experience prepares the individual of that society to respond to that segment as so defined. The entire system of definitions preparing the individuals of a society to respond accordingly is the conceptual system. The actual response is an interpretation of the meaning of the object, or situation, as defined by the system. In this sense individual conduct is a rational expression, rational in terms of what concepts are presently the premises of the individual's thought. The non-rationality, or illogicality of human conduct, quite apart from irrational drives, is a consequence of action in terms of a limited number of concepts, instead of in terms of the inferential whole that constitutes the conceptual system. Almost any action is meaningful to the man whose action it is at the time it takes place. Viewed from another perspective in the conceptual system, the limited rationality of the action may become apparent. The rationality involved in any action is never absolute; the degree of rationality present is determined by the conceptual system in its totality. Since the system contains categories which at any specific time remain concealed, it means that any final judgment on the rationality of a given action is impossible.

Although many lower animal collectivities are called societies, it is apparent that human beings act together in ways different from lower animal association. At the merely animal level constraint and obligation — in Durkheim's words, the unique properties of social facts — are not to be found. Moreover, there is no mediation of interaction by significant symbols. The collectivities of ants, bees, etc., can be explained by the biological structure of the individual members. The complex patterns that these collectivities exhibit appear to be a consequence of the way the organism is made. No interpretation of a stimulus in terms of a conceptual scheme is evident.

In human societies interaction takes on another form. Human personalities do not co-operate as a result of coerced responses merely. Their co-operation is not a direct result of their biological make up, or else their co-operative pattern would be the same throughout the world. The patterns of human co-operation, unlike those of other species, have a limited fixity only. Such universally and definitely fixed patterns as do exist are limited in number and may well be called drives or instincts to indicate their biological nature. But the kind of patterns that are the basis of most human co-operation are called institutions and have a fixity that is limited to a particular society, and often to a given stage of the history of that society.

No one who seriously studies the work of the cultural anthropologists can fail to be impressed with the diversity of institutional forms which the societies of the world present. In comparison with the fixed, co-operative patterns that characterize insect and lower animal societies, each human society, and even segments of such, has its own distinctive pattern. This indefinite plasticity of man's nature, the wide range of artificial environments which man has created have enabled him to supersede the natural selective limits of other species and to dominate the earth.

As an empirical phenomenon the institution appears as one of these fixed patterns peculiar to man as over against the fixed biological patterns of both men and animals. To see the institution as a symmetry in a series of social items in this strictly empirical way is to overlook the ideal aspect of the institution which is constituted by the concept, or value, which it embodies. Although the conceptual system arises in the social process (institutions, class groupings, etc.), the system is objectified or expressed again in the institutional structure. The conceptual system is the logic as well as the religion, metaphysic and science of a society, and the institutional structure exhibits that logic. Thus the institutions of a society appear as a system, or as interconnected behavior patterns. The objective interrelationships of a social order in some measure manifest the inner connection of concepts. The institutions form an external actuality which unlike the externality of the objects of physical science displays a degree of rationality that is the embodiment of conceptual thought.[17] The institution always bears the mark of universality as opposed to individuality, of the collective as opposed to the private. That same universality, impersonality, and relative permanence — features which are the distinguishing marks of the concept are also the distinguishing marks of the institution. Just as social life removes the disparities of individual perception and from these experiences constructs concepts, so too, the institution translates back into empirical form the logic of the concept. In the same way the dysfunctional elements of a social order are readily explained by the inconsistencies, contradictions, of the conceptual system.

Since institutions express the conceptual system, and the latter is a society's final statement of the world and its meaning, it follows that basic institutions are held to be sacred. For as shown above the sacred is but the fundamental concepts of the conceptual system. Finality is always sacred. A further corollary is that institutional behavior of a basic kind as opposed to merely instrumental, is originally sacred, or religious behavior. This characteristic sacredness is seen clearly in the older institutions such as marriage, the family, the monarchy, etc. However, these institutions tend to lose their older sacredness as they are recast in terms of new knowledge discovered in scientific research. This sacredness — the cement of a former social order is removed from the institutional structure by research and is replaced by ideas which this research discloses.[18] But this research is premised not on a theological or metaphysical system, but on the conceptual scheme of positive science.

CHAPTER SEVEN

Recapitulation and Conclusion

The study was initiated in an endeavor to contribute to the problem raised by the indeterminate epistemological status of social elements in knowledge as exhibited in the contrary validational procedures employed by the classical theory of knowledge and the sociology of knowledge respectively. On the one hand the classical theory, anchoring objectivity in the cognitive act of a rational subject, separated him from the institutional structure which it tended to regard as vestigial, non-rational, and a source of bias and error. On the other hand the sociology of knowledge taking up an inverse position to the classical theory made the institutional structure the source and warrant for the logical categories' operating in individual thought. This issue was seen to involve the major problem — namely, what constitutes the nature of the relationship between institutions and knowledge?

Insofar as this study has approached these questions its method has been indirectional, and its immediate concern has been the nature of the relationships between certain conceptions in regard to institutions and corresponding formulations of the theory of knowledge.

First, it was shown how among conceptions of institutions three situational types are distinguishable, and how there is related to each conception a theory of knowledge that implies a guarantee of objectivity of a unique and particular kind.[1]

Methodologically, it was possible to take the three conceptions of institutions with their corresponding notions of objectivity as constructions similar to the kind formulated by Max Weber as ideal-types. Like the latter, the situational types are in no respect metaphysical entities, but devices intended to stylize certain structures of mentality. Making use of the types in this manner, it seemed relevant to examine certain schools of thought in which the thinking seemed to be infused, permeated, and dominated by these situational types respectively. The schools selected for examination were: (a) individualism, (b) sociological positivism (Comte, Durkheim), (c) historical relativism (Mannheim).

The primary object of the analysis and comparison of viewpoints was to bring to light the basic presuppositions involved. By this procedure it seemed possible to seek out the causes of their inadequacy in order to move forward with some assurance toward a more satisfactory formulation and solution of the question.

The first school examined was individualism.

For the most part individualism looks upon institutions as having no reality in themselves and deems them to consist of the behavior of autonomous individuals acting in common. As social organization, institutions are viewed as instruments of vested interests and the products of non-rational tradition — coercive, restrictive, and frequently an obstacle to progress. The "reason" of the individual and the unreasonableness of institutions are depicted in terms of the sharpest contrast. The sacred element in institutions is felt to be mere irrationality, and the rational individual sets himself the task of transforming these institutions into contracts. In this way the supporting brace of the moral order is dissolved and society becomes a collocation of discrete forces.

The varieties of individualism form a continuum. At the singularistic pole is the kind, which in opposition to institutional standards, definitions, and rules, interprets both thinking and acting in terms of the individual in his separateness and discreteness. At the other — the universalistic pole — is the type, which while emphasizing the limitations imposed upon thinking and acting by institutions, classes, etc., insists that thought and conduct be based upon universal predicates common to all men, and inderivative from any conceivable kind of social structure.

Since practical considerations precluded a discussion of any large number of types of individualism, it seemed desirable to select for analysis the polar opposites, as represented by Protagoras and Kant respectively, and one important form of the mixed, or middle, variety — utilitarianism.

In respect to modern individualism some attempt was made to show how the theoretical problems involved in the validation of thought compelled a transition from an outlook at once nominalistic and singularistic to one idealistic and universalistic. On the whole this is to be observed in the development of the classical theory of knowledge from Locke to Hume; from Locke to the French *philosophes* and *idéologues;* and from Hume to Kant.

The most radical form of individualism is sometimes called subjectivism, and is exhibited in the dictum of Protagoras that "man is the measure of all things." The context of this phrase reveals that it means man as individual and his renunciation of all universally valid standards.

The Protagorean theory of knowledge reduces to a theory of perception, and insists that there is no other knowledge than perception. It is seen quite readily that perception as such cannot be regarded as knowledge. To possess knowledge it is necessary not to perceive merely, but to relate the disparities in perception by concepts. Now it is possible to furnish, and take account of, conceptual and categorial elements in three ways: Firstly, to indicate their presence in the institutional structure (e.g., the sacred society); secondly, to introduce them in the form of a metaphysic (Kant); thirdly, by an empirical mode of explanation to attempt a demonstration of their emergence in the socio-historical process (Durkheim, Mannheim, and Mead). However, Protagoras separates the individual from the social structure, and yet establishes no other ground between perceptions. Hence, epistemologically, this form of individualism collapses in relativism; and sociologically, in anarchism.

Modern individualism also as expressed in the classical theory of knowledge began its development with an epistemological recourse to the subject. Since institutions came to be regarded as intellectually bankrupt, the ontological orders, whose reality the institutions purported to express, were felt to be the chimera of ancient ignorance and superstition. In this situation the tendency was to search for objectivity, either in the things observed in ordinary experience, or in the cognitive act of the subject. For nominalism, until its climax in Hume, these two sources remained the basis of objective knowledge. Institutions, class groupings, and social existence in general, came to be viewed as sources of error, bias, and contingency. Men, it was held, are impelled to prejudice and distortion by their respective positions in the social structure, and the problem is one of "freeing" thought from its anchorage in classes and institutions. However, as with the individualism of Protagoras, it became increasingly apparent that empirical observation could not accomplish its own validation. It cannot distinguish clearly between truth and error, objectivity and illusion. Yet since the meaning of individualism is inserted in the metaphysical finality of the individual as opposed to society, individualism in view of this premise could not return to social structure for a validational base. Renouncing its nominalistic emphasis upon things, but still clinging to the cognitive act as the basis of objectivity, it was led to a consideration of what, in a strictly logical sense, are the indispensable prerequisites of that act, and hence to the question of the categories.

Now the categories may be viewed in two ways. On the one hand they may be regarded as constitutive of the world in an ontological sense. When the categories are predicated of reality in this manner, the institutions through which they are expressed carry also an ontological meaning. On the other hand the categories may be viewed as immanent laws of the intellect, necessary principles that are essential to any experience, but not arising within experience. In this case the basis of validation does not rest on the conception of some ontological order, but in the logical requirements, or fundamental determinations, of thought. Such is the position of individualism as developed in the philosophy of Kant.

Durkheim first comes to the problem of institutions through a concern with the anarchic tendencies of utilitarian thought. For him society is a moral order and institutions are its structural constant. Making no serious attempt in his earlier work to define in a precise way what he means by an institution, he proceeds in his *Le suicide* to prove to the satisfaction of most students of the subject of suicide that a relationship exists between institutional structure and the act of self-destruction. Feeling that the moral life of individuals had its source and center in institutions, Durkheim comes to suspect that the fundamental categories of thought also are socially determined — that individual thinking is a function of institutional structure. If this could be shown, then the concept of institution would have become the predicate of sociology, or the fundamental principle to which any aspect of the social would be reducible. Indeed, the final stage of Durkheim's work is an intensive struggle to verify this thesis.

Moreover, Durkheim observed that the theory of rationality assumed by the utilitarians was invalidated by the presence of varying frameworks of fundamental categories in the societies of the world. Research did not appear to have shown that the thinking process, like the blood stream, was the same in all times and places. Durkheim's projected solution to the problem of the categories was to show that they "grow out of the institutional structure." However, his attempt to explain the categories in this fashion placed him in a dilemma from which he was quite unable to extricate himself.

On the one hand, the basis of Durkheim's position was to be found in his ideal interpretation of the principal elements of society which he came to think of as consisting "exclusively of ideas and sentiments." On the other hand, he tried to account for the change and development of the fundamental categories of thought by making the elements of society concrete entities. At first this conversion of that which he considers to be intrinsically ideal into *choses* was a methodological device employed by him to bring the study of society into line with the empirical sciences generally. However, on other occasions he commits the error of treating genuinely empirical components of the situation as if they were cultural (abstract), or in his terms, social.

Thus Durkheim was driven by his research findings to delimit the field of the social to ideal categories, but his anchorage to Comtean empirical positivism compelled him to speak of these ideal categories as "things." In other words, Durkheim endeavored to guarantee the objectivity of his account by an appeal to something with which, in view of his ideal definition of the social, he should not have been concerned. There is, of course, no possibility of deriving ideas from things, and Durkheim's attempt, which was aimed at showing the social determination of the theoretic, broke down in a hopeless confusion of thought with things.

The sociology of Mannheim consists of a rigorous thinking through of all that is implied in the concept of ideology. Mannheim tried to demonstrate that all socio-cultural thinking is ideological — is tied to an existential base conceived to consist of a social situation of which an essential component is the stylistic structure of a historical epoch, or social class. The goal which Mannheim sets himself, although exhibiting many differences in detail, fundamentally is defined in the same way as that of Durkheim. This being the case it is not surprising to find that he falls into the same dilemma. Like Durkheim, he appeals to the reality of the existential as the determining factor in thought, not as a condition of genesis only, but as entering into the validity of judgment. Here he comes into conflict with Husserl's dictum that the validity of a judgment is in no sense dependent upon its origin. It may be said without reservation that Mannheim never grapples seriously with the "genetic fallacy" on a logical plane. In refutation of it he merely points to the facts of history in order to demonstrate empirically that existential factors can be relevant to the validity of a judgment. Despite indisputable historical evidence that he adduces, Mannheim continually exceeds the limits of his argument and thus fails to meet the objection of Husserl. So much Scheler and others admit. As with Durkheim, the confusion of the existential with the ideal undermines the logic of his standpoint and Mannheim is compelled to fall back into simple arbitrary opposition.

The failure in turn of individualism, sociological positivism, and historical relativism to determine the nature of the relation between social structures and the processes of thought is more clearly understood when the basic presupposition upon which all three schools erect their intellectual constructions is isolated. This presupposition appears to consist in a deep-seated belief in the reality of the existential and counterwise in the non-reality of the ideal. Individualism, in its nominalistic form, has always insisted that universals are *flatus vocis* and that only particular existences are real. The emphasis upon the sensory fact is an essential part of the Lockean sociology, and it is not to be wondered at, that in areas where that sociology has expressed itself in history, the belief that existential factors are the only real ones should be taken for granted.

Similarly, Durkheim, in the concept of *chose*, explicitly selects the existential as the foundation for a science of society. The conversion of the ideal social fact into a *chose* is felt to be necessary for the application of scientific method to society. Ontologically, Durkheim always considers social facts to be ideal. However, his methodology gives them an entirely different significance since they become pseudo-empirical entities.

Likewise with Mannheim there is the endeavor to interpret the ideal components of the social situation in terms of a non-theoretical factor — the existential.

Now it is precisely here that the three schools break down — the first, individualism, in its denial of the reality of the institutional; the two remaining in their failure to bridge the gap between the emphasis on the existentiality of the institutional and the ideality of the theoretic.

Yet the most cursory examination of what Durkheim means by "society" makes it abundantly clear that elements are involved that are in no sense existential. This is obvious when Durkheim speaks of institutions as consisting "exclusively of sentiments and values." It is no less so in Mannheim where the "stylistic structure" turns out to be "the constitutive categories of thought in terms of which an individual, or an age, attempts to grasp the nature of the world." Similarly, in individualism the role of "rationality" affords another parallel. Such ideal elements cannot be discounted as accidental aspects of the social process. Indeed, it is evident that a direct connection is to be found between these ideal elements of the social process and the categories. That "the realm of the theoretic is penetrated at every point by the social process" is only another way of saying that the ideal elements in society determine the formulation of other ideal elements in society. It begins to be apparent that institutions, as understood by Durkheim, are an ideal part of an ideal system. The fact that categories appear to "grow out of institutions" no longer seems strange. The institutions and the so-called theoretic constitute a single system and a single process. Thus, quite contrary to what individualism believed, institutions are not simply factors of distortion and bias — although they may be this due to the extent that such institutions do not express the meaning of the system in its totality — but are for a given society the latter's expression of its conception of objectivity.

It is now clear in what sense Mannheim and Husserl (at first sight so contradictory) can be reconciled. Certainly, the validity of a judgment can be determined only by the implicative system to which the ideas under discussion belong. However, this system includes the ideal elements of the institutional complex (Durkheim), of the "stylistic structure" (Mannheim), of individual "reason" or rationality (individualism). If there is an *a priori* valid element

in knowledge — or something which is to function in the process of
validation in a manner similar to the way in which Kant conceived
of this element — it is assuredly not in the existential elements,
which are properly only objects of knowledge, but in the ideal system of knowledge as a whole. This totality — the conceptual system
— is not to be set over against the social, but is identical with that
of which the social is both creator and the expression, an ideal
entity referred to by Durkheim as "society" but which approximates closely to what is connoted by the current concept of "culture."

The above resolution of very complex sociological viewpoints
into elements has meant the discovery of a principle that permits
a more unified whole to emerge. However, the new position is
liable to many misunderstandings and hence possible repudiation.
Before proceeding to its implications it will not be amiss to review
briefly the fundamental points of the argument.

It was demonstrated that each of the three major schools
selected for analysis contained a basic presupposition and a corollary — namely, that the existential alone is real and that the ideal
has negligible ontological status. However, the effort to reduce
to existential terms a manifest theoretical order as constituted
by the fundamental categories of thought, led to the dilemma that,
despite the existential predicate, each explanatory formulation of
the problem pointed unmistakably to an ideal reference. This is
clearly evidenced in the "rationality" of individualism, the "stylistic structure" of Mannheim and the "society" of Durkheim. Now
one way out of this seemingly unavoidable contradiction is to challenge the main assumption. In effect this was done by Durkheim in
Le suicide and *Les formes élémentaires de la vie religieuse.* Thus,
when the major premise of the three schools is reversed, and the
ideal is explicitly taken as principle in the validation of thought,
the difficulties that presented themselves are soon surmounted.
For example, the logical demand of Husserl as to the necessary
autonomy of the theoretic; the insistence of Mannheim that "the
subject's whole mode of conceiving things is determined by his historical and social setting"; and Durkheim's institutional determination of the categories — these very disparate claims and research
findings become capable of reconciliation in the notion of "conceptual system."

If then the three schools have been compelled to introduce

an ideal principle in explanation of the theoretic, it is to be observed that this is no less so in the interpretation of social action. In individualism there is the flat contradiction of its presupposition of physical necessity in the assumption of freedom derived from a metaphysically given rationality. Similarly, in Mannheim the emphasis shifts from a social reality conceived of in existential terms to that form of the "stylistic structure" designated as a "relative utopia." Thus Mannheim declares, ". . . our first task is to discover the point at which situationally transcendent ideas for the first time become active, i.e., become forces leading to the transformation of existing reality." Likewise Durkheim increasingly exhibits an idealistic position. This is evident when the *conscience collective* becomes the *representation collective*. In other words, the collective conscience has been replaced by a system of concepts. In the later Durkheim the emphasis is upon the conceptual system and its basic categorial structure. Hence he was brought close to a conclusion not quite reached — that obligation and constraint, the unique properties of social facts, are determinations by a system of universals. In this way the institutional framework with its moral determinations becomes the translation of the content of the abstract "society" into observable patterns of conduct. This means that obligation and constraint which earlier appeared to Durkheim as fundamental to the concept of the social, indeed, as the constitutive principle of society, have now become secondary to the primary role of the conceptual system and its inner framework — the categories.

An effort was made to show that the "objectivity" of each school examined rests ultimately upon a categorial framework, i.e., ideal criteria of validity. Further, the concept of "category" as used by individualism; the concept of "society" as set forth in the final work of Durkheim; and the concept of "stylistic structure" of Mannheim — all connote a meaning which makes possible their subsumption under the general concept of "conceptual system." The implication is that the conceptual system is the validational base of all experience.

However, the content of the objectivity of the three schools was not found to be the same. The "society" of Durkheim may be regarded as identical in meaning with the concept of conceptual system, and thus both concepts connote the same order of objectivity. In this type of objectivity, which is characteristic of the sacred society and expressed in its institutional structure, there is a complete interpenetration of the category of Value with the more strictly cognitive categories of the system. Hence, the nature of this objectivity involves for the subject a rationality where "ends" are given in any knowledge he may possess of the objects of his world. Further, at one and the same time this objectivity validates values and empirical knowledge.

Turning to Mannheim it was of importance to note that the knowledge he discusses is political knowledge. An analysis of political knowledge indicates that values are bound up with it in an almost inseparable fashion. The objectivity which Mannheim envisages is a synthesis that gives agreement at the level of values quite as much as at the level of existential facts. While the question of values enters into political knowledge in the form of policy, the validation of values in a strict sense is a philosophical problem. Thus Mannheim's objectivity of synthesis while limited to socio-political phenomena is very similar, if not the same, as the kind of objectivity exhibited in the sacred society. In both these types of objectivity the categories include Value, and the existential knowledge of a situation, or a thing, is infused with a valuation imposed by a society, class, or institution.

In the case of individualism it was shown that objectivity was transferred from the institutional structure, and thus from an ontology of Divine origin, to the cognitive act of the subject. Institutions continued to have a role in the validation of thought, but negatively — as factors of distortion, bias, and error. In effecting the separation of the thinking subject from the institutional structure, it separated him from many of the values which the institutions embodied, and which as valuations the latter had imposed upon the external world. Individualism ceased to emphasize the sacred and profane aspects of things. Objects were no longer regarded in terms of the holy and the unholy, the sinful and taboo, the evil and the good, the beautiful and the perfect, etc. It became possible to think about objects in detachment from values. Thus, there developed a clear distinction between the object as a part of nature and the value that was presumed to inhere within the object. The moral, aesthetic, and religious attributes assigned to nature by the institutional complex began to disappear, and moral, political, aesthetic judgments, etc. were confined to the relation between observer and things. They were allowed no dominion in universal nature, that is, in the relation between things, or context of existential facts.

In this connection it was deemed significant that Kant, who reflects and expounds the individualistic mode of thought, excludes Value from the framework of the categories.

The objectivity of the epistemology of individualism bears the closest possible relationship to the objectivity of the natural sciences. It connotes the usual meaning in which objectivity is understood as referring to objects and their relationship which retain their recognizable identity at different instances of reference, in contrast to the changing nature of objects and their relationships due to the entrance of subjectivity. For the individualism of Kant this subjectivity leading to the changing nature of the object is removed on the application of the universal categories as over against the particular categories of historical social groupings and institutions. In addition, with the exclusion of the category of Value from the framework validating experience, there is for the subject a rationality, which in contrast to the rationality provided by the objectivity of Durkheim's "society," involves what Parsons has called a "randomness of ends."

Despite the seeming differences of content in the respective notions of objectivity in the three schools, the latters' reconciliation in the notion of conceptual system is by no means a formal one. Since the concept of conceptual system refers to "society," or to the entire system of universals, which according to Durkheim is built up in the collective experience of the group, this system in its totality — and for Durkheim, Totality is its principle category — necessarily gives the form of objectivity under which the remaining types of objectivity must be subsumed. It is apparent that the forms of objectivity exemplified in the sociologies of knowledge of Durkheim and Mannheim have application to conceptions of a religious, moral, and political order. However, the objectivity of the conceptual system is one that has application to both the physical and social universe, but without the physical universe having been separated in any distinct way from the social. The objectivity of Mannheim's synthesis has application only to the social. In turn the objectivity of individualism is one that has application to physical phenomena in its separation from the social, and to the latter insofar as the social are also physical.

It seems, then, that the categorial frameworks which constitute the validational bases in the Mannheimian sociology of knowledge, and the individualistic theory of knowledge, are each constructions of selected categories, or concepts, of that total conceptual system which Durkheim has referred to as "society." The framework of categories that make up the individualistic scheme excludes Value; the framework that makes up Mannheim's scheme includes Value. Further, while individualism in the epistemology of Kant regarded the categories as fixed and *a priori*, the Durkheimian form of the sociology of knowledge regards all categories as arising in the social process. Hence, the conceptual system of a given period is but a cross-section of the ideal aspect of that process.

The mediation of the individualistic and sociological approaches to the problem of knowledge requires an acceptance on the part of the classical theory of (a) the historical and social genesis of all concepts and categories, and (b) that the specific categories of the Kantian framework are a selection from a more general conceptual system, and (c) that this conceptual system is expressed, as it was produced, in the forms of social existence — institutions, classes, etc. In turn the sociology of knowledge must recognize that its own validational bases are not existential facts in the sense of empirical phenomena, or *choses,* but categorial structures. In this recognition both the classical and sociological procedures for achieving objectivity set up as fundamental, a principle of ideal reference.

It has been shown that a leading characteristic of all forms of individualism was its repudiation of institutional structure as a validational base for either thought or conduct. Yet this institutional structure was but the product of an earlier stage of the social process, and expressed an earlier form of the conceptual system. Individualism in denying the reality of institutions did not recognize that the object of its denial was in fact an outworn categorial order. Moreover, individualism did not at first view itself as an institution, or as the matrix of a new institutional complex. In its assertion of the profound nature and finality of the individual as opposed to society in the ontological conception of the world, it failed to recognize that this, too, was a socially formulated "perspective."

Having recapitulated the general argument of the inquiry it may be well to summarize more precisely its principal findings.

Reduced to minimal dimensions these are:

1. The categories are basic concepts, or structural beams of an implicative, conceptual system. All concepts are developed in the social process. As rational thought is the subsumption of particulars under universals, the rationality of the individual is both defined and limited by the character of the conceptual system of the society of which he is a member.

2. The concept of "category" as employed by individualism; the concept of "society" as set forth in the final work of Durkheim; and the concept of "stylistic structure" of Mannheim refer to specific types of categorial framework. Each type functions as a validational base for individual experience and yields its own distinct content, or kind, of objectivity.

3. The relation between the forms of thought and institutions is that between a concept and the process by which it is produced and expressed. The process has an ideal aspect, and this latter constitutes the conceptual system. Thus there is a logical nexus between the forms of thought and institutions, for at one level both are sets of abstractions, and together, make up the conceptual system. The relation, then, turns out to be that which certain basic concepts — the structural beams of thought — bear to the totality of the conceptual system.

In addition to the express problem which this inquiry has sought to illuminate, it has aimed also at overcoming the widely evident distrust of rational thought. Insofar as the twentieth century disclaims the authority of rationality as the supreme guide in human affairs, just so much does it return to the standpoint of Schopenhauer that the universe is in its very essence irrational. Certainly, in recent decades rationality has maintained itself only with difficulty. Not only in literary, philosophic, and political areas has this pervasive misology been apparent, but within science itself. In particular the sciences of human behavior have moved ever further in the direction of interpreting their phenomena in terms of irrational and non-rational motivations. On the one hand the influence of the natural sciences with their mechanistic determinism; and on the other the biological sciences with their instincts and drives have influenced only too strongly both psychology and sociology. Freud, Pareto, and even Durkheim, display a common tendency in the emphasis upon what they believed to be the non-rational components of human action. Moreover, the kind

of use that has been made of the concepts of institution and culture respectively has been to stress non-rationality rather than
otherwise. This has been because the essential rationality of the
ontological reference of these concepts either was not seen at all, or
not clearly understood. Indeed, most sociology has been a sharp
polemic against the belief that human conduct is in any large
degree rational. Few have been prepared to concede that human
conduct could be comprehended to a marked extent in purely
intellectual terms. So far as the present work is concerned it has
sought to show that this current metaphysic on the nature of man
is not inevitable, and the re-establishment of human action on the
foundation of the almost discarded faith in rationality may be one
of the outstanding achievements of the science of sociology.

Notes

Chapter I: INTRODUCTION

1 For the present work the designation "classical" or "traditional" theory of knowledge is used primarily to refer to a negative, critical conception in regard to the relationship between institutions and objectivity — a conception which is common to that series of theories of knowledge having its origin in the individualism of Locke and tending to culminate in the Kantian Critique of Pure Reason.

2 ". . . the older method of intellectual history, which was oriented to the *a priori* conception that changes in ideas were to be understood on the level of ideas (immanent intellectual history), blocked recognition of the penetration of the social process into the intellectual sphere. With the growing evidence of the flaws in this *a priori* assumption, an increasing number of concrete cases makes it evident that (a) every formulation of a problem is made possible only by a previous actual human experience which involves such a problem; (b) in selection from the multiplicity of data there is involved an act of will on the part of the knower; and (c) forces arising out of living experience are significant in the direction which the treatment of the problem follows. In connection with these investigations, it will become more and more clear that the living forces and actual attitudes which underlie the theoretical ones are by no means merely of an individual nature, i.e. they do not have their origin in the first place in the individual's becoming aware of his interests in the course of his thinking. Rather, they arise out of the collective purposes of a group which underlie the thought of the individual, and in the prescribed outlook of which he merely participates." (K. Mannheim, *Ideology and Utopia,* trans. L. Wirth and E. Shils [New York: Harcourt Brace and Co., 1949], pp. 240 f.)

3 In regard to the import of the sociology of knowledge, and the issues with which it must deal, note the following: "Of

these [the issues] the first and basic one is the elaboration of the theory of knowledge itself, which has hitherto found a place in philosophy in the form of epistemology. . . . But it no longer is the exclusive concern of the professional philosopher. . . . Such a task requires more than the application of well-established logical rules to the materials at hand, for the accepted rules of logic themselves are here called into question and are seen, in common with the rest of our intellectual tools, as parts and products of the whole of our social life." (Louis Wirth, "Preface," Mannheim's *Ideology and Utopia,* trans. L. Wirth and E. Shils [New York: Harcourt Brace and Co., 1949], p. xxix.)

4 In this connection, besides the men specifically discussed below, of particular importance are Descartes, Hume, and Nietzsche. Emphasizing the role in thought of non-rational determinants of a somewhat different order are Schopenhauer, von Hartmann, and Freud. In each of these, and in many other writers, the social and psychological elements are viewed as factors of contingency in the attainment of valid knowledge.

5 For an excellent account of the contribution of Bacon, the *philosophes* and Nietzsche, etc. to the theory of ideology see, Hans Barth, *Wahrheit und Ideologie* (Zurich: Manesse Verlag, 1945). On the place of Bacon, the *philosophes,* Nietzsche and Freud in the problem of bias see also the admirable essay by Reinhard Bendix: *Social Science and the Distrust of Reason* (Berkeley and Los Angeles: University of California Press, 1951).

6 "In this connection Bacon finds opportunity to direct a most violent polemic against the word-wisdom of Scholasticism, against the rule of authority, against the anthropomorphism of earlier philosophy, and to demand a personal examination of things themselves, an unprejudiced reception of reality." (W. Windelband, *A History of Philosophy,* trans. J. H. Tufts [2d ed.; New York: Macmillan Co., 1926], p. 384.)

7 "The human understanding is no dry light, but receives an infusion from the will and affections; whence proceed sciences which may be called 'sciences as one would.' For what a man had rather were true he more readily believes." (Francis Bacon, "Novum Organum," *The English Philosophers from Bacon to Mill,* ed. E. A. Burtt [New York: The Modern Library, 1939], p. 37.)

8 "There are four classes of idols which beset men's minds. To these for distinction's sake I have assigned names,— calling the first class Idols of the Tribe; the second, Idols of the Cave; the third, Idols of the Market Place; the fourth, Idols of the Theater." (*Ibid.,* p. 34.) "There are idols formed by the intercourse and association of men with each other, which I call Idols of the Market Place, on account of the commerce and con-

sort of men there." (*Ibid.,* p. 35.) Also: "But the Idols of the Market Place are the most troublesome of all." (*Ibid.,* p. 40.) Although Bacon's classification of the idols is obviously a rhetorical one, a close examination quickly reveals that the idols are premised on two aspects of man, namely, his biological nature and his social existence.

9 "Every-day perception — he [Bacon] confesses, admitting the well-known sceptical arguments — offers, indeed, no sure basis for a true knowledge of Nature; in order to become an experience that can be used by science it must be purified from all erroneous additions which have grown together with it in our involuntary way of regarding things." (Windelband, *op. cit.,* p. 383.)

10 ". . . in nature nothing really exists beside individual bodies, performing pure individual acts according to a fixed law . . ." (Bacon, "Novum Organum," *op. cit.,* p. 89.)

11 "Although the roads to human power and to human knowledge lie close together, and are nearly the same, nevertheless on account of the pernicious and inveterate habits of dwelling on abstractions, it is safer to begin and raise the sciences from those foundations which have relation to practice, and let the active part itself be as the seal which prints and determines the contemplative counterpart." (*Ibid.,* p. 89.)

12 Cf. "At the same time, the profound respect for method, which had been the original inspiration of Bacon's work, becomes more and more pronounced. Any mode of procedure which is to make sure of progress in its deportment and to fuse together the scattered energies of many minds must be independent of subjective accidents and be necessitated by the facts themselves. It will reduce differing capacities to the same level and increase the effectiveness of the less talented. For 'gifts in themselves poor and unpromising become of importance when employed in the right way and order' . . . . Method seems here to have cut itself loose from persons, and to work with the unvarying accuracy of a machine. This is the beginning of that overvaluing of method and undervaluing of personality which has been the cause of much error in modern life . . . . So already at this early date, we have that fundamentally false identification of 'nature' with 'world,' of natural science with science generally, which has set up so much error and confusion." (Rudolph Eucken, *The Problem of Human Life,* trans. W. S. Hough and W. Boyce Gibson [New York: Scribner's, 1916], pp. 341 f.)

13 See: F. Picavet, *Les Idéologues, Essai sur l'histoire des idées et des théories scientifique, philosophique, religieuses, en France depuis 1789* (Paris: Alcan, 1891); also E. Cailliet, *La Tradition*

littéraire des idéologues (Philadelphia: The American Philosophical Society, 1943).

14 "But surely there is a great distinction between matters of state and the arts [science]; for the danger from new motion and from new light is not the same. In matters of state a change even for the better is distrusted, because it unsettles what is established; these things resting on authority, consent, fame and opinion, not on demonstration." (Bacon, "Novum Organum," *op. cit.*, p. 64.)

15 This search for the universal and necessary as opposed to the institutionally, or historical-social conditioned, is especially characteristic of individualism in its most powerful form as e.g. in the *Critique of Pure Reason*. The reader should note that while the term "ideology" has come to be associated with the sociology of knowledge, the original "ideologists" were exponents of an extreme individualism.

16 The present usage of the term ideology with its strong connotation of mistrust and disparagement expresses a meaning quite different from that originally intended. For Destutt de Tracy and the school to which he belonged ideology was simply the analytical study of human thought processes. See: A. L. C. Destutt de Tracy, *Projet d'élements d'idéologie à l'usage des écoles centralies de la Republique Francaise* (Paris: P. Didot, 1801); also, by the same author, *Élements d'idéologie* (Paris: Chez Madame Levi, 1825-1827).

17 The degree of loathing which the *illuminati* felt for the institutions of the Church and state in particular is well-shown in the characteristic exclamation of Diderot: "Men will never be free until the last king is strangled in the entrails of the last priest!" Quoted by Will Durant, *The Story of Philosophy* (New York: Simon and Schuster, 1926), p. 253.

18 The unhistorical, anti-institutional character of ideologistic thought was bitterly assailed by Napoleon. It is largely due to the contempt thrown upon the *idéologues* by the French Emperor that the use of the term ideology in a pejorative sense arose. Note: "All the misfortunes that our beautiful France has been experiencing have to be ascribed to 'ideology,' to that cloudy metaphysics which goes ingeniously seeking first causes and would ground legislation of the peoples upon them, instead of adapting laws to what we know of the human heart and the lessons of history. Such errors could only lead to a regime of men of blood and have in fact done so. Who cajoled the people by thrusting upon it a sovereignty it was unable to exercise? Who destroyed the sacredness of laws and respect for the laws by basing them not on the sacred principles of justice, on the nature of things and the nature of civil justice, but

simply on the will of an assembly made up of individuals who
are strangers to any knowledge of law, whether civil adminis-
trative, political, or military? When a man is called upon to
reorganize a state, he must follow principles that are forever in
conflict. The advantages and disadvantages of the different systems of legislation have to be sought in history." Reply by
Napoleon to the Council of State at its session of December
20, 1812, quoted by Pareto (*Mind and Society*, III, 1244) from
the *Moniteur universal*, Paris, December 21st, 1812 and requoted
by F. A. Hayek, *The Counter Revolution of Science* (Glencoe:
The Free Press, 1952), n., p. 225.

19 It is of some importance to note that the image for
Bacon is a mechanical one. "Bacon counted the teleological mode
of regarding Nature as one of the idols, and, indeed, as one
of the dangerous idols of the tribe, — the fundamental errors
which become a source of illusion to man through his very
nature: he taught that philosophy has to do only with formal
or efficient causes, and expressed his restriction of philosophy to
physics and his rejection of metaphysics precisely by saying that the
explanation of Nature is physics if it concerns *causae efficientes,*
metaphysics if it concerns *causae finales*." (Windelband, *op. cit.,*
p. 401.)

20 "Altogether too frequently we are inclined to accept as objective those categorical structures and ultimate postulates which
we ourselves have unconsciously read into our experience, and
which for the sociologist of knowledge, are revealed only sub-
sequently as the partial, historically, and socially conditioned
axioms of a particular current of thought. Nothing is more self-
evident than that precisely the forms in which we ourselves think
are those whose limited nature is most difficult for us to perceive, and that only further historical and social development
gives us the perspective from which we realize their particularity."
(Mannheim, *op. cit.*, p. 167.)

21 The *idéologues* refer to their quest as the search for
"pure perception" (after Locke) rather than "reason" — a feature
which should make for no difficulty in understanding the objective of their researches. Their belief in progress, their intense
confidence in education and the perfectibility of man are predicated upon the reality of reason. To make the thinking process
in any final sense a derivative of emotional patterns, or of institutional and class affiliation would have seemed to the *idéologues* a surrender to that irrationality they strove to combat,
and indeed, the abandonment of any further hope for the future
of man.

22 It is the belief in an absolute sphere of truth that
accounts for the optimism of the *idéologues*. Despite their in-

sistence upon the distorting and corrupting character of the institutions of their age, they have complete faith in the power of knowledge and in the reformative potentialities of education. This emphasis upon ideas — an attitude that made ideas an independent variable in history — contrasts strongly in some respects with the emphasis upon socio-economic structures in the Marxism of the following period.

23   Note: "Dans son *Cours de Philosophie Positive,* Auguste Comte présupposes en rapport intime entre les phases du dévelopement de la société et les genres du savoir. Il attache même une importance exagérée à ce rapport, auquel il accorde presque toute son attention. La célèbre loi comtienne 'de trois états' (d'ailleurs plus que discutable): l'état théologique correspond à une structure sociale archaique, la forme de connaissance métaphysique à la structure sociales féodale et, enfin, la forme de connaissance positive à la structure sociales industrielle. Auguste Comte, qui au fond est un idéaliste, a une tendance secrete à attribuer la causalité plutôt aux genres du savoir qu'aux types de la société. Ceci devient particulièrement claire pour la phase positive. En effet si on lit attentivement Comte, on voit, qu'il croit qu'au moment où l'humanite arrivera definitivement à la phase positive de la connaissance (identique à la philosophie positiviste de Comte), elle trouvera tous les moyens pour diriger la société, la dominer et la transformer. Par conséquent, si dans la phase théologique et dans la phase métaphysique subsiste une certaine dépendance réciproque de la société par rapport à la connaissance et de la connaissance par rapport a la société, dans la phase positive, c'est nettement la société qui devient dépendante de la connaissance." (G. Gurvitch, *Initiation aux recherches sur la sociologie de la connaisance* [Paris: Centres d'études sociologiques, 1948], pp. 5 f.)

24   This acceptance of an absolute rationality and its incompatibility with the ideological doctrine placed Marx in a logical dilemma of which opponents like Werner Sombart and Max Weber were quick to take advantage. Marx's discussion and attempt to escape from the difficulty appear in widely scattered sections of his work. See particularly: Karl Marx, *A Contribution to the Critique of Political Economy* (Chicago: Charles Kerr, 1904), pp. 10 ff.

25   Mannheim, *op. cit.,* pp. 267 f.

26   In the face of Mannheim's critical scrutiny of "idealistic" and positivistic thought-models; in view of his insistence upon an irreducible residue of evaluation or "purposeful intent" in all knowledge, this passage may seem to the reader like a gross misinterpretation of Mannheim's position. However, it is expected that the sense in which the above characterization is cor-

rect will be clarified by the longer discussion of Mannheim that is given in this study below, Chap. IV.

27 See particularly: Émile Durkheim, *The Elementary Forms of the Religious Life*, trans. J. W. Swain (Glencoe: The Free Press, 1947).

28 See G. H. Mead, *Mind, Self and Society* (Chicago: University of Chicago Press, 1934).

29 Mannheim is chiefly concerned with the inner dimension of reality. Following Dilthey and Rickert, he, like Max Weber declares sociology to be a discipline of interior comprehension (verstehen) in opposition to the goal of explanation (erklarung) sought by the natural sciences.

30 The Thomas theorem, "If men define situations as real, they will be real in their consequences" seems to have particular application here. If a conception regarding institutions is held that defines them as universals having their ground in an ontology of Divine origin, the actual relationships of men to the institutions in terms of power, obedience, and general normative attributes will be very different than when the institutions are regarded only as associations of individuals and subject to the purposes of individuals. The dissertation hopes to make clear that the conception of the institution is a very real constituent of it.

31 ". . . institutions constitute the logical focus of sociology." (Talcott Parsons, *Essays in Sociological Theory* [Glencoe: The Free Press, 1949], p. 10.)

32 Max Weber, *Gesammelte Aufsatze zur Wissenschaftlehre* (Tubingen: J. C. Mohr, 1922), pp. 190-210.

Cf. also, Mannheim, *op. cit.*, pp. 180-190.

The "ideal-type" of Weber, and the "images" or "mentalities," utopian, ideological, etc. of Mannheim derive from an order of concepts developed by Hegel and which he called "concrete conceptions." By the latter Hegel understood concepts or principles which, in contrast to ordinary abstractions, realize themselves, or constitute the dynamic element in the concrete history of peoples. Certain alterations in regard to the use of such concepts were affected by Weber as a consequence of the inquiries into the problem of scientific and historical method undertaken by Dilthey, Rickert, and Windelband. The Hegelian influence has meant a persisting interest in the variations in the form, in addition to the content of mental life, as witnessed not only by the writers mentioned above, but also by Nietzsche and Spengler with their Dionysian, Apollonian, and Faustian types — the latter making their way into modern anthropology, particularly in the work of Ruth Benedict. However, the classification of the "prelogical," or mystical and "logical" mentalities employed by Lévy-Bruhl derive, through Durkheim, from Comte and the mental types implied in the so-called, "Law of the Three Stages."

In contrast to this German and French preoccupation with styles, mentalities, and types of thinking, British empiricism has tended to view individual minds as varying about a single axis and of human thinking as homogeneous.

Of the attempts to bring the philosophical insights regarding the variability of thinking into the field of scientific research, the most successful have been those of Mannheim, Weber, and the school of Durkheim.

33 Cf. "If the primitive confounds things which we distinguish, he also distinguishes things which we connect together, and he even conceives these distinctions in the form of sharp and clear-cut oppositions. Between two things which are classified in two different phratries there is not only separation, but even antagonism. For this reason, the same Australian who confounds the sun and the white cockatoo, opposes this latter to the black cockatoo as to its contrary. The two seem to him to belong to two separate classes between which there is nothing in common. A still more marked opposition is that existing between sacred things and profane things. They repel and contradict each other with so much force that the mind refuses to think of them at the same time. They mutually expel each other from consciousness." (Durkheim, *op. cit.*, pp.238-239.)

34 Talcott Parsons in discussing the intuitionism of Max Weber points out that even intuitions, insights, etc. require validation by theoretical, conceptual criticism, and that the quality of immediate certainty, of direct assurance in the perception of meaning cannot in itself be trusted and accepted. He remarks: "Our immediate intuitions of meaning may be real and, as such, correct. But their interpretation cannot dispense with a rationally consistent system of theoretical concepts." (*Structure of Social Action* [Glencoe: The Free Press, 1949], p. 589.)

35 Cf. ". . . we can say generally that whatever is regarded as a truth functions as a *norm of thinking*, imposes upon the conscious agent who recognizes it a distinctive selection and organization of some data of his experience. The data acquire thereby the character of object matter of knowledge. The 'truth' itself — and even more so the whole system of which it is an element — possesses in the active experience of all those who recognize it an 'objective' significance which makes its validity seem to them independent of their 'subjective' emotions, wishes, representations. They *participate* in a system of knowledge, just as a leader or a member participates in a social group, a manager or a workman in that technical system which is called a factory or a workshop."

(Florian Znaniecki, *The Social Role of the Man of Knowledge* [New York: Columbia University Press, 1940], p. 8.)

36 The sociology of knowledge is that branch of sociology which has knowledge as its object. In this connection the word knowledge is to be understood in the broadest possible sense as including all manner of mental productions, e.g. a religious myth, a political doctrine, etc. Of the various definitions two may be selected as showing the different consequences that follow according to what definition is allowed. The first is that the sociology of knowledge is "the study of the relationship between society and mental productions." Conceived in this way the study may assume ideas to influence social facts or vice versa; it permits also the assumption of some kind of reciprocal influence. The system of Sorokin — largely idealistic — requires this definition. Those who have been influenced by Sorokin tend to emphasize the role of ideas — that is, they declare that the structural beams of a society's culture consist of philosophical presuppositions which determine social life. Further, they insist that a society can be understood only to the extent that these presuppositions can be made explicit.

The second definition is that "the sociology of knowledge is the study of mental productions insofar as they are influenced by social factors." The phrasing implies a one way process, and in the system of ideas and social facts the latter becomes the independent variable. This way of approaching the study of knowledge — often called the existential conditioning, or determination, of thought — is that of the school of Mannheim. (See Chapter V of the present work.)

37 The general concept developed in the course of the study, and which can be employed for the subsumption of the specific concepts of objectivity of all three schools mentioned above, is that of "conceptual system." (See Chapter VI.)

Chapter II: INDIVIDUALISM

1 The literature dealing with individualism is vast. The present account owes much to the following three authors and their respective works: Albert Schatz, *L'individualisme économique et social* (Paris: A. Conlin, 1907); Karl Pribram, *Die Enstehung der Individualistichen Socialphilosophie* (Leipzig: C. L. Hirshfeld, 1912); Alexander Rüstow, *Das Versagen des Wirtschaftsliberalismus als Religiongeschichtliche Problem* (Istanbul: Europa Verlag, 1945).

2 In the case of modern individualism one should not forget its close association with the Augustinian and revolutionary traditions.

3 From the modern standpoint contract is itself an institution. The numerous obligations, duties, expectations, that underlie the possibility of contract were not seen by Mill, Spencer, etc. and for many years the sub-contractual level of sacredness remained unexplored. For a discussion of these conditions — the mechanical solidarity — that must support the organic solidarity of the individualistic society see: Émile Durkheim, *The Division of Labor in Society*, trans. G. Simpson (Glencoe: The Free Press, 1947), chap. vii.

4 In modern individualism the contractual attitude toward marriage and the family appears as early as the Reformation. Each of the great revolutions since that time have insisted that marriage is but a civil contract and sets up instruments of divorce whereby persons might be released from the irksome obligations of the institution. Much of the spurious liberty permitted by these revolutions was soon afterwards recalled in the interests of statism, but not before a separating out of many of the sacred values in marriage and the family had taken place.

5 "To use terminology which applies equally to Rousseau, Paine, Hegel, and Marx, all social institutions were to be dissolved in order to 'free the individual'. . . ." (C. C. Zimmerman, *Family and Civilization* [New York: Harper & Co., 1947], p. 569.) Cf., also: "In America the eighteenth century was one of struggle for political freedom. The nineteenth century was to be a struggle for the freedom of the individual from the family." (*Ibid.*, p. 546.)

6 While individualism tended to ascribe this negative character to institutions many of its representatives, anticipating the conception of a planned society, held that the irrational aspects of many existing institutions could be eliminated, and that an institutional structure wholly rational could be constructed. See especially, the *philosophes*.

7 Cf. Rudolph Eucken, *The Problem of Human Life*, trans. W. S. Hough and W. B. Gibson (revised ed.; New York: Scribner's 1916), p. 415. "The French Enlightenment . . . . It is a period in which the Subject reaches a maximal degree of independence and practices the most outspoken criticism. All rigid distinctions are melted down; even the hardest, dryest material is stirred and freshened, but at the same time broken up."

8 Rene Descartes, "Meditations," *The Method, Meditations, and Selections from the Principles of Descartes*, trans. John Veitch (7th ed.; Edinburgh and London: Blackwood and Sons, 1880), p. 97.

That Descartes carefully separates reason from the social process and regards the latter as a source of error, even though he does recognize the fact that man must be influenced in his thinking by one or another milieu, is clear from the following passage: "But I had become aware, even so early as during my college life, that no opinion, however absurd and incredible can be imagined, which has not been maintained by some one of the philosophers; and afterwards in the course of my travels I remarked that all those whose opinions are decidedly repugnant to ours are not on that account barbarians and savages, but on the contrary many of these nations make an equally good, if not better use of their Reason than we do. I took into account also the very different character which a person brought up from infancy in France or Germany exhibits, from that which, with the same mind originally, this individual would have possessed had he lived always among the Chinese or with savages, and the circumstance that in dress itself the fashion which pleased us ten years ago, and which may again, perhaps, be received into favour before ten years have gone, appears to us at the moment extravagant and ridiculous. I was thus lead to infer that the ground of our opinions is far more custom and example than any certain knowledge, and, finally, although such be ground of our opinions, I remarked that a plurality of suffrages is no guarantee of truth where it is all of difficult discovery, as in such cases it is much more likely that it will be found by one than by many. I could, however, select from the crowd no one whose opinions seemed worthy of preference, and thus I found myself constrained, as it were, to use my own Reason in the conduct of my life." *Ibid.*, pp. 1 ff.)

9   Mannheim, *op. cit.*, p. 56.

10   R. A. P. Rogers, *A Short History of Ethics* (London: Macmillan and Co., 1921), p. 34.

11   "The fundamental thought, which the philosophy of the Enlightenment would hold as to the great institutions of human society . . . was to see in these institutions the products of the activities of individuals; and from this followed the tendency to single out those interests whose satisfaction the individual may expect from such general social connections when once these exist, and to treat them in a genetic mode of explanation as the motives and sufficient causes for the *origin* of the institutions in question, while at the same time regarding them from a critical point of view, as the standard for estimating the *value* of the same. Whatever was regarded as having been intentionally created by men should show also whether it was then really fulfilling their purposes." (Windelband, *op. cit.*, p. 518.)

12   In its initial stages individualism seeks to validate knowledge only by experience denying the reality of innate ideas (Locke). However, the radical, nominalistic form of empiricism finds itself incapable of handling the problems of error, relativism, and illusory perception. Thus it is driven to skepticism as

in Hume, or to the erection of *a priori* criteria of validity as in Kant.

13 "And here the weakness of the Enlightenment at once appears side by side with its strength. As always, it takes the standards of its criticism for existing institutions, and of its proposals for their change, from the universal eternal nature of man or of things; thus it loses from sight the authorization and vital force of historical reality, and believes that it is only needed to make a *tabula rasa* of the existing conditions wherever they show themselves contrary to reason, in order to build up society entire in accordance with the principles of philosophy. In this spirit the literature of the Enlightenment especially in France, prepared for the actual *break with history*, the Revolution." (Windelband, *op. cit.*, p. 521.)

14 Strictly speaking the philosophy of Kant is the completion of the critical, reflective movement inaugurated by Locke. Yet it seems correct to say that Kant's work also belongs to the period of metaphysical reconstruction (Fichte, Hegel) insofar as in the theory of knowledge *a priori* elements are taken as criteria of validity. In this culmination of the classical theory of knowledge, individualism in fact points beyond itself.

15 "Proceeding from the Heraclitic hypothesis of perpetual flux, and specially applying it to the individual subject, he taught that man is the measure of all things, of those things that exist, that they are, and of those things that do not exist, that they are not. That, namely, is true for the percipient subject, whatever, in the perpetual flux of things and himself, he at any moment perceives and feels. . . . But now, as perception and sensation are with countless people countlessly diverse, and excessively various even in one and the same person, there resulted from this the further consequence, that there are in general no such things as any objective affirmations or determinations whatever; that opposed assertions in regard to the same object are to be received as equally true; that we may dispute *pro* and *contra* on all things and everything with equal authority; and that neither error nor refutation of error can possibly take place." (Albert Schwegler, *Handbook of the History of Philosophy*, trans. J. H. Stirling [4th ed.; Edinburgh: Edmonston and Douglas, 1872], p. 35.)

16 The Protagorean theory contains the important discovery that the perception is not to be identified with the perceiving subject, nor with that which is perceived. The theory is, then, a form of phenomenalism. For a discussion of the technical philosophical aspects of the theory, with which the present work does not concern itself, consult: Windelband, *op. cit.*, pp. 91-94.

17 "Perception . . . is indeed the *completely adequate knowledge of what is perceived* but no knowledge of the thing. . . . This is the meaning of the Protagorean *relativism,* according to which things are for every individual such as they appear to him; and this is expressed in the famous proposition that *man is the measure of all things."* (Windelband, *op. cit.,* p. 92.)

18 Just as subjectivism makes objective knowledge impossible, so in the moral sphere the foundations of authority are denied. All forms of individualism are anti-social in principle, and the radical subjectivist type, whether of ancient or modern times, would reduce society to a hopeless anarchism of thought and conduct. Such considerations reveal the interrelated character of the problem of moral (institutional) conformity and the problem of knowledge.

19 Immanent laws in a purely logical, not psychological, sense.

20 David Hume, "Appendix," *A Treatise of Human Nature,* 2 vols. (Everyman ed.; London: J. M. Dent and Sons, Ltd., 1911), p. 319. Hume's italics.

21 An examination of the philosophy of Locke had made it apparent to Hume that a self-consistent empiricism could not allow the concept of substance any exceptional place among concepts. Substance was seen to have no more objective validity than any other concept, and all the others were in the last analysis derived from sensory perception. The concepts of universality and necessity, associated with the category of "cause," Hume did not find in experience as such. If all knowledge arises in experience (the nominalistic premise) then these concepts become mere chimera of the mind. To recapitulate: Because we are accustomed to see that one thing follows another in time, we conceive the idea that it must follow, and from it — that is from a relation of succession, we make a relation of causality. In this concept we exceed experience and proceed to formulate concepts for which we have no authority. Hume is, in effect, arguing for the variability of cause — not for the invariability that Comte, J. S. Mill, and other positivists have stressed. In other words Hume is saying that we are in the habit of seeing things together, but this invariability is of our own expectation. It is subjective. However, this subjectivity is not for Hume an *a priori* element.

22 The twelve categories of Kant are as follows: Unity, Plurality, Totality; Reality, Negation, Limitation; Inherence and Subsistence, Causality and Dependence, Community or Reciprocity; Possibility and Impossibility, Existence and Non-existence, Necessity and Contingency.

23 I. Kant, *Critique of Pure Reason,* trans. Norman Kemp Smith (New York: Humanities Press, 1950), p. 389.

24 "It is reason which prescribes its laws to the sensible universe; it is reason which makes the cosmos." (I. Kant, *Prolegomena to Any Future Metaphysic* [New York: Liberal Arts Press, 1951], pp. 44, 51.)

25 There are various difficulties in Kant of an important character, but which are not discussed in this study. Among these is the highly artificial "deduction" of the categories from the twelve types of judgment. Again, the antithesis between sense and thought, on which it is based, is very questionable. Further, his attempt to bridge the gulf between percept and concept by means of the "constructive imagination" is not altogether satisfactory. His inherent subjectivism breaks out in his treatment of the categories and gives the impression that they belong to the peculiar structure of human intelligence, and thus not possessing thorough objective validity. Moreover, Kant makes it clear that the order which is apprehended in respect to objects is not the real order but only a phenomenal one. There is no way of telling just what reality does belong to this mediate form of apprehension. It constitutes the only world we know.

26 It is this fictitious "consciousness-in-itself," or universal ego, of Kant that is seized upon by Hegel in the notion that the unity of the world is possible only with reference to a knowing subject. But Hegel insists that this unity "is a process of continual historical transformations and tends to constant restoration of its equilibrium on still higher levels." The "world spirit" is the integration of these various historical transformations. However, the important development coming from Hegel is the sharpening of the concept of consciousness-in-itself into a flow of definite historical differentiations or "mentalities." Thus there is a conceptual or categorial structure for each of these "mentalities." However, this vague conception of a definite "mentality" belonging to a given historical epoch gives way in the work of Marx, Mannheim, and others, to the conception of a "stylistic structure" which is the possession of a social grouping such as a class, and which provides the constitutive categories of thought for the members of that class. In this way the formless philosophical concept of Kant has been transformed into, and identified with, a basic conception of the sociology of knowledge.

27 *Supra*, p. 41.

28 See p. 143, n. 22.

29 *The Critique of Practical Reason* and *The Critique of Judgment* discuss certain of these fundamental determinations of experience as conceptions, but not as categories.

30 Floyd H. Allport, *Institutional Behavior* (Chapel Hill: University of North Carolina Press, 1933) quoted by Talcott Par-

sons, *The Structure of Social Action* (Glencoe: The Free Press, 1949), p. 408 n.

See also: Floyd H. Allport, "The Nature of Institutions," *Journal of Social Forces*, VI (1927), 167-179.

31   The distinction is sometimes made between metaphysical universals and logical universals, i.e., between the specific type which really exists in individuals composing the species and the general notion, an abstraction of thought. Allport accepts only the latter which he calls a "logical (or hypothetical) construct." This radical individualism is, of course, pure nominalism, for nominalism is the absolute negation of the metaphysical universal as an objective reality.

32   The influence of Rousseau has tended to be strongly individualistic for the most part. Nevertheless, Rousseau's problem was the rendering of a consciousness of community compatible with individuality. Rousseau thought that he had solved the problem by postulating a community freely established by means of a voluntary compact entered into by men enjoying the primitive State of Nature, and by supposing that in a community thus spontaneously generated the individual is so completely identified with the whole of which he forms a part that there is no conflict whatsoever between the personal will and the general will of the community. The terms of the general will he states thus: "Each of us puts his person and all his power in common under the supreme direction of the general will, and in our corporate capacity we receive each member as an indivisible part of the whole." Evidently, the general will of Rousseau is Hobbes' Leviathan with his head chopped off.

What will happen asks Rousseau if, through some perversity of human nature the individual should manifest "a particular will contrary to the general will"? In that case, says Rousseau, he will be coerced. What, then, becomes of his primitive and inalienable liberty? It remains undiminished says Rousseau; the man's perversity simply shows that he does not know what his real will is; coercion is in accordance with his real will; the community in coercing him is merely forcing him to be free! Being forced to be free seems identical with being compelled to obey. Perhaps, Rousseau was close to an answer to his problem but in his terms it remains unsolved.

33   It may seem strange to find Kant classified as revolutionary. Mild and placid he was morbidly anxious to avoid giving offense to the powers that were. But revolutionary thought does not necessarily connote violence, and revolutionary thought may be stated in language displaying little or no passion. There can be no doubt that Kant's individualism as shown in his conception of the categorical imperative, his idealism, his cosmopolitanism,

his humanitarianism, his pacifism were radically incompatible with the more rigid aspects of the social structure of his day — particularly with its belligerent nationalism. He formulated the principles of an utopian order whose realization would imply a moral revolution.

34   Opinions disseminated by Richard Carlile (1790-1843) in his journal, *The Republican*.

35   (1745-1832). Bentham is famous for the "greatest happiness principle" used by the Philosophical Radicals of the early nineteenth century to carry through numerous reforms — electoral, parliamentary, constitutional, and legal. "Nature," says Bentham, "has placed man under the governance of two sovereign masters, pain and pleasure. It is for them alone to point out what we ought to do, as well as to determine what we shall do." Such is the "principle of utility," which "approves or disproves of every action whatsoever according to the tendency which it appears to have to augment or diminish the happiness of the party whose interest is in question." The strong individualism of Bentham is seen in his statement regarding the distribution of pleasure in the community, "every one is to count for one, and no one for more than one."

   See: J. Bentham, Introduction to the *Principles of Morals and Legislation* (Edinburgh: Ballantyne & Co., 1843), pp. 101, 160, 207.

   "Utilitarianism is the doctrine that the 'greatest happiness of the greatest number' provides the ultimate ethical standard. It attempts to combine the theory that pleasure is the final good with the law of impartiality, according to which all persons have an equal right to a share of the pleasures available. . . . It is peculiarly characteristic of English Ethics, being foreshadowed in Bacon and Hobbes, and appearing in various forms in the eighteenth century." (R. A. P. Rogers, *A Short History of Ethics* [London: Macmillan & Co., 1921], p. 234.)

   "Utilitarianism . . . is characterized for the most part by limiting its care 'for the greatest happiness of the greatest number' to man's earthly welfare; the mental and spiritual goods are not indeed denied, but the measure of all valuation is to be found in the degree of pleasure or pain which a circumstance, a relation, an act, or a disposition may call forth. Theoretically, this doctrine rests on the unfortunate inference of the associational psychology, that because every satisfied desire is accompanied with pleasure, the expectation of the pleasure is, therefore, the ultimate motive of all willing, and every particular object is willed and valued only as a means for gaining this pleasure . . . a general tendency of British theory has been to unite a social standard or criterion of moral value with an individualistic and even egoistic theory of motives. This seemed the more possible to Bentham, because in the individualistic language of his day the community was defined as a fictitious body of individual persons who are considered as constituting as it were, its members. The interest of the community, then, 'is the sum of the interests of the several members who compose it.' Hence it might seem that one way to promote the interest of the community would be for every man to seek his own interest. If, however, it should be necessary to bring pressure to bear upon the individual in order to keep him from interfering with the interests of others, Bentham conceived that the principle reliance should be placed upon what he called the four sanctions, which he specified as the physical, political, moral, and religious, meaning by these pleasures and pains derived from physical sources, from the penalties of law, from public opinion, or from belief in divine rewards and punishments. It is for pain and pleasure alone 'to point out what we ought to do, as well as to determine what we shall do,' and the ambiguity in the terms 'pain' and 'pleasure,' according to which they mean in the one case pleasure or pain of the community, and in the other pleasure or pain of the agent, permits Bentham to suppose that he is maintaining a consistent hedonistic theory." (Windelband, *op. cit.*, pp. 662-64.)

36   (1766-1836.) Godwin's is the most extreme statement of individualism in political literature in existence. His political treatise was first published in 1793. See: William Godwin, *An Enquiry Concerning Political Justice* (New York: A. A. Knopf, 1926.)

37   The history of the term "utilitarian" is given by Mill as follows: "The author of this essay has reason for believing himself to be the first person who brought the word utilitarian into use. He did not invent it, but adopted it from a passing expression in Mr. Galt's *Annals of the Parish*. After using it as a designation for several years, he and others abandoned it from a growing dislike to anything resembling a badge or watchword of sectarian distinction. But as a name for one single opinion, not a set of opinions — to denote the recognition of utility as a standard, not any particular way of applying it — the term supplies a want in the language, and offers in many cases a convenient mode of avoiding tiresome circumlocution." (J. S. Mill, *Utilitarianism* [Everyman ed.; London: J. M. Dent & Sons, Ltd., 1910], p. 6 n.)

In the same work Mill proceeds to define utilitarianism thus: "The creed which accepts as the foundation of morals, Utility, or the Greatest Happiness Principle, holds that actions are right in proportion as they tend to promote happiness, wrong as they tend to produce the reverse of happiness. By happiness is intended pleasure, and the absence of pain; by unhappiness, pain, and the privation of pleasure." (*Ibid.*, p. 6.)

The above definition which is consistent with the way that utilitarianism has been conceived historically is, nevertheless, but an aspect of utilitarianism as understood by Talcott Parsons who defines it thus: "The theoretical system characterized by these four features, atomism, rationality, empiricism, randomness of ends will be called in the present study [*Structure of Social Action*] the utilitarian system of social theory." (Parsons, *Structure of Social Action*, *op. cit.*, p. 60.)

38   Cf., J. S. Mill, *On Liberty* (Everyman ed.; London: J. M. Dent & Sons, Ltd., 1910).

39   "Over himself, over his own body and mind, the individual is sovereign." (*Ibid.*, p. 73.)

40   It should be noted that the voluntarism of certain philosophers is a determinism of ends.

41   "The entire history of social improvement has been a series of transitions by which one custom or institution after another, from being a supposed primary necessity of social existence, has passed into the rank of universally stigmatized injustice and tyranny." (J. S. Mill, *On Liberty, op. cit.*, p. 73.)

42   The view that the institutional structure imposed a coercive control upon the individual had been promulgated by Rousseau and still earlier by Locke. The former had insisted "that human nature is fundamentally good, all social organization is founded upon revocable contracts, and social institutions are merely chains that, even though at first they have utility, later become anchors that keep men from progressing." Human happiness is destroyed by restrictive institutions. Indeed, happiness is a function of freedom and freedom is possible only when the individual has replaced institutional bondage by individual will. Now this position is assuredly individualistic but thus far not rationalistic. Contrary to Rousseau, Locke had declared that man is inherently bad — a modern version of the Medieval doctrine of man's natural depravity — and justified the use of institutional controls such as the military and superstitious terrors of religious faith.

This emphasis upon will in the work of writers like Locke and Rousseau indicates the surviving influence of Nominalism (Duns Scotus, Ockam). What was originally a counter emphasis — that upon rationality, so evident in Descartes and Spinoza, derives from Realism (Anselm, William of Champeaux). In the nineteenth century those emphases have merged into the autonomous, rational, self-sufficient individual.

43   Cf., E. B. Tylor, *Primitive Culture* (7th ed.; New York: Brentano, 1924).

44 Herbert Spencer, *The Data of Ethics* (New York: American Publishers Corp., n. d.), p. 147.

45 Max Stirner, *The Ego and His Own,* trans. S. T. Bynington (Modern Library ed.; New York: Boni and Liveright, Inc., n. d.), *passim.*

Chapter III: POSITIVISM

1 It is customary to label Durkheim a "sociological" positivist in order to distinguish his position from that of empirical positivism. However, at the outset of his career Durkheim wished to extend the empirical positivistic method (as outlined by Comte) to that segment of reality referred to as the "social." He felt that only in terms of empirical positivism could any approach be adjudged scientific, or knowledge, science. Thus the movement of Durkheim's thought is not from empirical to sociological positivism for Durkheim's position is at first both empirical and sociological. His works reveal a steady and constant shedding of nominalistic elements and a growing realism in the medieval sense, a realism already present in his very conception of sociology as such. It is for this reason that observers, particularly Talcott Parsons, often regard Durkheim in the final phases of his thought as, indeed, an idealist, but one who refuses to admit that fact.

2 References to Comte with two exceptions are based on the following: Auguste Comte, *Cours de Philosophie positive,* ed. E. Littre, 6 vols. (2d ed.; Paris: L. Hachette et Cie., 1864).

3 In respect to psychology Comte followed Kant in his *Metaphysical Elements of Natural Science,* that a science of psychology is impossible. For Kant the "I think" is neither perception nor concept; but a mere consciousness, an act of mind which attends, unites, supports all perceptions and concepts. This act of thought is in psychology falsely converted into a thing and what applies to the former analytically is transferred to the latter synthetically. To be able to treat the ego, or personality, as an object and apply categories in its regard, it would have required to have been empirically given in perception, which is impossible. For Kant only that which is phenomenal — noumena to which categories have been applied — can be made the subject matter of a science. For Comte, too, the observable must be external to the observer. The intelligence cannot contemplate or observe itself. (Comte, *op cit.,* I, 30 and VI, 402-403.)

4 Contrary to general opinion, Comte did not believe that mathematical methods could be used successfully in the study of

society. He vehemently scorns Quetelet's fruitful suggestion as to the employment of statistics and mathematics of probability in social analysis. His insistence was that method had to be altered with the level of complexity of the phenomena, e.g., astronomy (mathematical); physics and chemistry (mathematical and experimental); biology (comparative); sociology (historical). (Cf., *Ibid.*, III, 29, 291; IV, 365-7.)

5   Ortega y Gasset has said that nothing exhibits our intellectual descent from the Greeks more surely than the continued search for ultimate principles. This is the substance of his statement that "Western thought is forever imprisoned in the grip of Greek ontology." See: Jose Ortega y Gasset, *Toward a Philosophy of History*, trans. H. Weyl (New York: W. W. Norton & Co., 1941), p. 71.

6   Auguste Comte, *Early Essays on Social Philosophy*, trans. H. D. Hutton (New Universal Library; London: Routledge & Sons, 1911), p. 223.

7   Comte's method in one respect may be said to undergo an inversion on reaching sociology. He points out that the more complex functions become the less possible is a detached measurement of them. It happens that at the social level the character of the phenomena in a total way are better known to us than its component functions. We already know society and history through participation in them. It would be a mistake to place the achievements of the previous sciences, e.g., biology, physics, etc., first in our research on human affairs. The laws of society can be learned from the variations of their own phenomena. Thus while the same empirical axis runs through the classification, in sociology the results of the biological sciences are not a springboard for jumping off into the problems of the former.

8   At this point Kant and Comte are on common ground. Of the former's four groups of fundamental categories, quantity, quality, relation, and modality, it is the category of relation that subsumes the rest. It is the principal category since every judgment expresses a relation.

The close relationship between empirical positivism and Kantianism is expressed by Comte himself in a letter to Gustave d'Eichthal, dated Dec. 10th, 1824: "I have always considered Kant not only as a very powerful thinker, but also as the metaphysician who most closely approximates the positive philosophy." See: P. Lafitte, "Materiaux pour servir à la Biographie d'Auguste Comte: Correspondance d'Auguste Comte avec Gustave d'Eichthal," *La Revue Occidentale,* second series, XII, 19 année, 1891, Part II, 186 ff.

9   Comte formally divides the history of thought into three stages, viz., the theological, metaphysical, and positive. However, he regards the metaphysical as one of transition only, and basically the same as the theological. Thus, there are two species of thought — the theological, or that in which volitions and values are attributed to objects; and the positive, or that which refuses to attribute volitions and values to the nature of objects, but seeks only to establish invariable relationships between the objects. Comte allows for a larger cognitive element in the metaphysical than in the theological stages. However, he says: "L'etat metaphysique, qui n'est au fond qu'une simple modification general du premier." (Comte, Cours de Philosophie positive, op. cit., I, 9; also, IV, 213.)

10   In respect to the question of what constitutes a fact, whether social or not, Comte shows a marked naiveté. There is no principle in his methodology which permits the reclassification of sensory data. His refusal to be "metaphysical" has prevented him from setting up a conceptual scheme such as is necessary to establish "invariable relations" or "laws." Apparently, he expected to find these at the level of common sense.

11   Comte's absurd Religion of Humanity with its stupid rituals and ceremonies is his belated recognition that a social physics constitutes no answer to the problem of human affairs. This development in Comte's thinking is most certainly not without significance but it has no place in his Positive Philosophy.

12   The adverse character of the critical remarks made regarding Comte are not intended to obscure his importance in the continuity of Western thought. For decades his sun was rising with undeniable evidence. The book which will re-interpret and point out the significance of Comte in a monumental manner has yet to be written. Until Comte much of the work in the human studies was a helpless and uncertain groping. Comte opens up sources to which much of the essentially modern can be traced. The French dogmatist threading the way of a defiant warrior could not have foreseen the new enemies of science that his work would have to combat in the decades to come. In the background of a century he stands out as one of those rare figures who mark out the crossroads. However, only the fruits of another century will serve to establish the legitimacy of these eulogies. The story of thought in the twentieth century centers in the interrelated problems of social knowledge and social action. The stubborn fact of human defeats have dimmed the vision with which Comte and his sociology began. But in the rising tide of irrationalism of the present century the achievement of Comte remains a citadel against the upholders of non-logical and irrational action — upholders who if successful would convert the Western world into

a vast intellectual desert. The historical role of undermining in a fatal manner a purely philosophical treatment of human affairs was Comte's. His work may play the same role in preserving a rational approach to the same study. In insisting upon rationality as the very rock of knowledge, as the surety to guarantee the solidity of civilization, he has extended support to every rational interest and raised a bulwark for all the future against the flood of misological theory that ever threatens to engulf mankind.

13   (1858-1917.)

14   In his later years Comte had tended toward a sociological theory of knowledge and a humanistic view of nature. Implicit in Comte is the view that the unification of the sciences is possible only if man is taken as center. Durkheim's concept of society, which contains far reaching implications for the theory of knowledge, is derivative in part from this notion of Comte.

15   E. Durkheim, *Les formes élémentaires de la vie religieuse* (Bibliotheque de philosophie contemporaine; Paris: F. Alcan, 1912), *passim*.

16   The most distinguished representative of the above point of view on the philosophical, as against the strictly sociological, is Lucien Lévy-Bruhl.

17   The view that society is a moral entity is scattered throughout the early part of Durkheim's work. In particular, see: E. Durkheim, "Determination du fait moral," *Sociologie et philosophie* (Paris: F. Alcan, 1924).

18   "This body of rules governing action in pursuit of immediate ends insofar as they exercise moral authority derivable from a common value system may be called social institutions." (Talcott Parsons, *The Structure of Social Action* [2d ed.; Glencoe: The Free Press, 1949].)

19   "Up to this point having rejected utilitarian teleology Durkheim still thinks of the actor passively on the analogy of a scientist studying the conditions of his situation." (*Ibid.*, p. 709.)

20   It should be observed that the empirical positivism of Comte and Mill is abandoned by Durkheim by mid-career. Even his sociological positivism wears thin and his idealism (not a Hegelian dialectic but Medieval realism) implicit in his work from the beginning becomes increasingly evident.

21   See E. Durkheim, *Le suicide* (Paris: F. Alcan, 1897), *passim;* see also, *Les formes élémentaires de la vie religieuse, op. cit., passim*.

22   Compare Durkheim's *Le suicide* with his *Les formes élémentaires*.

23 Durkheim, *Les formes élémentaires*, etc., *op. cit.*, p. 521.

24 *Ibid.*, p. 321.

25 Durkheim, "Preface," *Les règles de la méthode sociologique* (Paris: Alcan, 1895), p. XXIII; also *Les formes élémentaires*, p. 523 n.

26 Parsons, *Structure of Social Action*, *op. cit.*, p. 389.

27 ". . . Durkheim in escaping from the toils of positivism has overshot the mark and gone clean over to idealism." (Parsons, *Structure of Social Action*, *op. cit.*, p. 445).

28 Durkheim's epistemology has inspired the five works of Lévy-Bruhl on preliterate mentality; Halbwachs on the social frames of memory; Francis Cornford, Jane Harrison, Pierre-Maxime Schul, all on the thought structure of Ancient Greece; Alexander Moret on Egypt; and Marcel Granet on the language and ideas of Ancient China. In addition, Mauss, Hertz, and Bouglé not only felt the impact of Durkheim's theory of knowledge, but in a large measure contributed to its development.

In considering the magnitude of Durkheim's achievement it should be remembered that the tradition of De Bonald, De Maistre, and Comte did much to make it possible.

29 Durkheim, *Régles, op cit.*, pp. xi ff.

30 "La présente étude, en dehors de ses resultats immediats peut donc servir a montrer, par un exemple topique l'erreur radicale de la méthode qui considere, les faits sociaux comme le développement logique et téléologique de concepts détermines." (E. Durkheim, ed., *L'Année sociologique*, 12 vols. (Paris: F. Alcan, 1896-1912), I, 69.

The above passage is part of a study of the Australian primitives. It is pointed out that the Australians are organized into sib systems with totemism. Each sib has its totemistic animal or bird as well as its human members. Durkheim endeavors to show that around this central social axis the world of the Australian primitive is built. Animals and birds are related to the totemic complex and the other objects are local in the system. At last all known objects are brought under the social system of classification. The Australian primitive classifies and organizes his universe by the same system that he relates himself to his social order.

31 "Sans doute, à mesure que le jugement collectif se développe et vient éclairer davantage la volonte sociale, celle-ci devient aussi plus apte à diriger le cours des evenements et à leur imprimer une marche rationnelle. Mais les fonctions intellectuelles supérieures sont encore beaucoup plus rudimentaires dans la société que dans l'individu, et les cas où leur influence est preponderante n'ont été jusqu'à présent qu'une infini exception." (*Ibid.*, I, 70.)

32 "Ce n'est pas en vue de régler sa conduite ni même pour justifier sa pratique que l'Australian répartit le monde entre les totems de sa tribu; mais c'est que, la notion du totem étant pour lui cardinales, il est une nécessité a situer par rapport a elle toutes ses autres connaissances. On peut donc penser que les conditions dont dependent ces classifications, très anciennes ne sont pas sans avoir joué un rôle important dans, la genese de la fonction classificatrice en général." (*Ibid.*, VI, 66-67.)

33 "En résumé, si nous ne sommes pas fondés à dire que cette manière de classer les choses est nécessairement impliqué dans le totemisme, il est, en tout cas, certain qu'elle se recontre très fréquement dans les sociétés qui sont organisées sur un base totemique. Il y a donc un lien étroit, et non pas accidentel, entre ce système social et ce système logique. Nous allons voir maintenant comment, a cette forme primitive de la classification, d'autres peuvent être rattachées qui présentent un plus haut degré de complexité." (*Ibid.*, VI, 33-34.)

34 "Si donc la mentalité humaine a varié avec les siècles et les sociétés, si elle a évolue, les différents types qu'elle a successivement présentés ont été la source les uns des autres. Les formes les plus hautes et les plus récentes ne s'opposent pas aux formes les plus primitives et les plus inférieures, mais sont nées de ces dernières." (*Ibid.*, XII, 37.)

35 "Ce que nous avons essayé de faire pour la classification pourrait être egalement tenté pour les autres fonctions au notions fondamentales de l'entendement. Déjà nous avons eu l'occasion d'indiquer chemin faisant, comment même des idées aussi abstraites que celles de temps et d'espace sont, à chaque moment de leur histoire, en rapport étroit avec l'organisation sociale corréspondante. Le méme méthode pourrait aider également à comprendré la maniére dont se sont formees des idées de cause, de substance, les différentes formes du raissonement, etc." (*Ibid.*, VI, 72.)

36 "Les premières catégories logiques ont été des catégories sociales; les premières classes de choses ont été classes d'hommes dans lesquelles ces choses ont été integrées. C'est parce que les hommes étaient groupés et se pensaient sous forme de groupes qu'ils ont groupé idéalement les autres êtres, et les deux modes de groupement ont commencé par se confondre au point d'être indistincts. . . . Les choses étaient censees faire partie intégrante de la société et c'est leur place dans la société qui déterminait leur place dans la nature." (*Ibid.*, VI, 67.)

37 "Non seulement la forme extérieure des classes, mais les rapports qui les unissent les unes aux autres sont d'origine sociale. C'est parce que les groupes humains s'emboîtent les uns dans les autres, le sous-clan dans le clan, le clan dans la phratrie, la phratrie dans la tribu, que les groupes de choses se disposent suivant le

même ordre . . . . Ainsi la hiérarchie logique n'est qu'un autre aspect de la hiérarchie sociale et l'unite de la connaissance n'est autre chose que l'unité même de la collectivité, étendue à l'univers." (*Ibid.*, VI, 68.)

38 "Les choses sont, avant tout, sacrees ou profanes, pures ou impures, amies ou ennemies, favorables ou defavorables; c'est a dire que leurs caracteres les plus fondamentaux ne font qu'exprimer la maniere dont elles affectent la sensibilite sociale." (*Ibid.*, VI, 70.)

39 Talcott Parson's criticism of Durkheim's epistemology is as follows: "now his epistemology has brought the basis of human reason itself into the same relativistic circle, so as to make the previous relativism itself relative, since the relativism of social types is itself a product of a system of categories which are valid only for the particular social type. This is a doctrine which may be called 'social solipsism.' It involves all the skeptical consequences which are so well known in the case of individual solipsism. It is, in short, a *reductio ad absurdum.*" (Parsons, *Structure of Social Action, op. cit.*, p. 447.)

40 Durkheim expressly says that social facts are to be treated *"comme des choses."* Durkheim recognizes that his "social facts" are not sensory phenomena but concludes that since they exhibit "exteriority" or "resistance" to the subject, then they "can be considered amenable to the natural science approach." However, at other times he includes sensory phenomena among his social facts.

41 With his usual acumen Talcott Parsons points out that the concept of the "social" is with Durkheim rather a statement of what the individual is not. "It is to be noted that the category 'social' is arrived at by a process of elimination, is thus a residual category." (Parsons, *Structure of Social Action, op. cit.*, p. 351.)

42 "Society has become the thing the idealist philosophers are talking about. It consists as he [Durkheim] says 'exclusively of ideas and sentiments,' and not it may be further said, merely of 'ideas' but of the *Idea* for the categories are the very matrix out of which particular ideas are formed . . . . Society becomes not a part of nature at all, but in Professor Whitehead's phrase, of the world of 'eternal objects' . . . . For the effect of identifying society with the world of eternal objects is to eliminate the creative element of action altogether . . . . Their defining characteristic is that the categories of neither time nor space apply to them." (*Ibid.*, p. 444.)

Chapter IV: HISTORICAL RELATIVISM

1 "Until recently knowledge and thinking, while recognized as the proper subject matter of logic and psychology, were viewed as lying outside of social science because they were not considered social processes." (Wirth, *op. cit.,* p. xxvii.)

2 Mannheim, *op. cit.,* p. 71.

3 See the present work, pp. 38-40.

4 G. H. Lewes, *Problems of Life and Mind* (Boston: Houghton-Mifflin Co., 1891).

5 T. Buckle, *History of Civilization in England* (New York: D. Appleton, Century Co., 1934).

6 The Protagorean relativism should be distinguished carefully from the relativism that is a consequence of what Mannheim calls the "aged," or "idealistic" theory of knowledge. *Infra,* pp. 75-77.

7 Mannheim, *op. cit.,* p. 275.

8 *Ibid.,* p. 71.

9 M. F. Scheler, "Probleme einer Sociologie des Wissens," *Die Wissensformen und die Gesellschaft* (Leipzig: Der Neue-Geist Verlag, 1926), pp. 55, 127.

10 "These categories of social and historical knowledge are to be understood only by relating them to the fundamental existential reality which determined their emergence; they are to be understood as an expression (Ausdruck) of the inter-relation of thought and the external, non-rational, existential factors which determined it. For Mannheim this inter-relation is to be conceived in terms of valuations and will. These valuations and volitional elements have, naturally, no transcendent (non-existential) referents. Thus the categories of social and historical understanding which emerge in the historico-social process have their whole basis in the fact that an active, valuing subject (of somewhat indeterminate metaphysical nature) 'lives into' an external world. In this thought and action are not wholly disparate; thought and modes of thinking, are brought within a larger activistic framework." (M. Mandelbaum, *The Problem of Historical Knowledge* [New York: Liveright Pub. Corp., 1938], p. 73.)

11 "Perspective [stylistic structure] in this sense signifies the manner in which one views an object, what one perceives in it, and how one construes it in his thinking. Perspective, therefore, is something more than a formal determination of thinking. It refers also to qualitative elements in the structure of thought, elements which must necessarily be overlooked by a purely formal logic." (Mannheim, *op. cit.,* p. 244.)

12   "The existential determination of thought may be regarded as demonstrated in those realms of thought in which we can
show   (a) that the process of knowing does not actually develop
historically in accordance with immanent laws, or that it does
not follow from 'the nature of things' or from 'pure logical possibilities,' and that it is not driven by an 'inner dialectic.'   On
the contrary, the emergence and crystallization of actual thought
is influenced in many decisive points by extra-theoretical factors
of the most diverse sort.   These may be called, in contradistinc-
tion to purely theoretical factors, existential factors.   This existential determination of thought will also have to be regarded
as a fact   (b) if the influence of these existential factors on the
concrete content of knowledge is of more than mere peripheral
importance, if they are relevant not only to the genesis of ideas,
but penetrate into their form and content and if, furthermore,
they decisively determine the scope and intensity of our experience and observation, i.e., that which we formerly referred to as
the perspective (stylistic structure) of the subject." (Mannheim,
op. cit., p. 240.)

13   "The social situation . . . is not to be considered as a
single entity but as the integration of many diverse factors. Mannheim views it as the analogy of the term 'constellation' as used
in astrology, meaning thereby the co-presence of many diverse elements all of which have bearing on the life of the individual
involved. Further, the social situation so-conceived is ever changing." (Mandelbaum, *op. cit.,* pp. 73-74.)

14   Mannheim, *op. cit.,* p. 264.

15   "The question whether objective truth can be attributed
to human thinking is not a question of theory but is a practical
question. In practice man must prove the truth, i.e., the reality
and power, the 'this-sidedness' of his thinking. The dispute over
the reality or non-reality of thinking which is isolated from
practice is a purely scholastic question, wrote Marx." (Karl Marx,
"Theses on Feuerbach," *Selected Works* [Moscow and New York:
International Publishers, n.d.], I, 471, quoted in J. J. Maquet,
The Sociology of Knowledge, trans. J. F. Locke [Boston: The Beacon Press, 1951], p. 88.)

16   Mannheim's contention that existence is never existence
as such but is always a concrete form of social existence implies
a determination of individual existence by the social order itself,
not as something existing only in the imagination of man, but
as something according to which he really responds. He assumes
a reality which is concretely determined by socio-historical processes.

This view appears to be basically the same as that of G. H.
Mead. "Truth" is not regarded as something which can be dis-

covered by an introspective procedure, nor something which appears only when the student separates himself from the facts of nature; on the contrary the very mode of perceiving these facts of nature is bound up with the socio-historical position of the observer. The facts cannot be separated from the person who perceives them and the cultural situation which determines the manner in which he views them.

It is the responses to certain situations which have become common, and from which have been derived common responses, that have given rise to thought. The individual carries on these common responses; he finds patterns of thought existent in the social group which provides means of adjusting to his particular situation and utilizes them. Such patterns are the foundation for logical thought. This view is implicit in Mead's description of the internalization of the institutions of the social group of which he is a member as determining the thought of the individual.

When the individual becomes a member of two or more social groups which are divergent in their interests, and which claim divergent responses from him, he begins to doubt that objectivity is not ambiguous, and to be skeptical of the value of thought. It is the problem which thus arises that Mannheim's sociology of knowledge attempts to clarify. It becomes necessary for the individual who seeks to understand the alternatives of action and of thought to understand the socio-historical situation out of which these alternatives have developed. This is necessary before any agreement, even a provisional one, is possible between two or more individuals, or groups, which have divergent interests. In Mead's terminology, it becomes impossible for communication to exist under conditions of opposing interests because the person cannot take the attitude of the other — he cannot become an object to himself from the viewpoint of the other.

Mannheim points out that these mutually opposing views, by having been identified with the social situations out of which they have developed, are found not to be infinite and totally divergent, but finite in number and complementary to one another. This implies the possibility of their integration into a comprehensive whole. However, social situations are constantly changing and new ones are arising, and new knowledge will develop from these situations. The integration, or synthesis, would have to be a dynamic one. The synthesis, Mannheim thinks, would be brought about by the "intellectuals," a relatively classless stratum which is capable of subsuming under itself the varied points of view of a heterogeneous society. In Mead's terms the intellectuals are those who could take the attitudes of the others who represent mutually divergent views and synthesize them into a "generalized other" to which they would respond. It is a society of such individuals which Mead represents as the ideal human society. However,

Mead is more concerned with the specific manner in which social action gives rise to the development of significant symbols, communication, and thought than with the problems of political decision in a world in which political tenets are determined by social interests and the conditions of social life.

17   The Marxist theory of ideology is developed directly from the position of the *idéologues* — Destutt de Tracy, Cabanis, Maine de Biran, J. B. Say, Condillac, and Degérando.

The *idéologues* point out that with reference to institutions they find a knowledge *"engagée,"* but that they seek a knowledge *"detachée et desintéressée."*

Chapter V: SUMMARY AND INTERPRETATION

1   Bakunin. The indeterminism of the liberal utilitarian position as exhibited in the autonomous individual is a limited expression of the passionate anarchism of Bakunin and Landauer: "The will to destroy is a creative will . . . . I do not believe in constitutions or laws. The best constitution would leave me dissatisfied. We need something different. Storm and vitality and a new lawless and consequently free world." (Bakunin, cited by Mannheim, *op. cit.,* p. 196.)

Note also: "The possibility and the necessity of the social process as it fluctuates from stability, to decay, and then to reconstruction is based on the fact that there is no organism that has grown up that stands above the individual, but rather a complex relationship of reason, love, and authority. Thus again and again there comes a time in the history of a social structure, which is a structure only as long as individuals nourish it with their vitality, when those living shy away from it as a strange ghost from the past, and create new groupings instead. Thus I have withdrawn my love, reason, obedience, and my will from that which I call the 'state.' That I am able to do this depends on my will. That you are not able to do this does not alter the decisive fact that this particular inability is inseparably bound up with your own personality and not with the nature of the state." (From a letter of Gustav Landauer to Margarete Susmann, reprinted in *Landauer, G., Sein Lebensgang in Briefen,* ed. Martin Buber [1929], II, 122; quoted by Mannheim, *op. cit.,* p. 235.)

Speaking of Chiliastic utopianism (anarchism) Mannheim says: "We perceive in Landauer what is characteristic of all anarchists, namely the antithesis between the 'authoritarian' and the 'libertarian'— a contrast which simplifies everything and blurs all partial differences . . . . From this point of view every historical event is an ever-renewed deliverance from a topia (existing order) by a utopia, which arises out of it. Only in utopia and revolution is there true life, the institutional order is always only the evil residue which remains from ebbing utopias and revolutions." (*Ibid.*, p. 178.)

2 J. J. Rousseau.

3 Friedrich Nietzsche, *Thus Spake Zarathustra* (Modern Library; New York: Boni and Liveright, Inc., n.d.); note also: ". . . we find as the ripest fruit . . . the *sovereign individual*, that resembles only himself, that has got loose from the morality of custom, the autonomous 'supermoral' individual (for 'autonomous' and 'moral' are mutually exclusive terms) — in short, the man of the personal, long, and independent will, competent to promise — and we find in him a proud consciousness (vibrating in every fibre), of what has been at last achieved and become vivified in him; a genuine consciousness of power and freedom." (Friedrich Nietzsche, *The Genealogy of Morals* [Modern Library; New York: Boni and Liveright, n.d.], pp. 42-43.)

4 Max Stirner, *The Ego and His Own* (Modern Library; New York: Boni and Liveright, n.d.), *passim*.

5 Thomas Carlyle. The "Great Man" theory of Carlyle is associated with Romanticism. Superficially, it appears to run counter to the individualism of the nineteenth century. However, both types have their roots in the Augustinian tradition.

6 John Dewey points out that "We are, for example, only just beginning to recognize the extent in which the whole British empiricistic philosophy was developed as a method of criticism of institutions, political, and ecclesiastical. It became the working creed of the 'liberal' school, because it was originated by Locke in order to provide an analytic method of attack upon beliefs connected with institutions he desired to abolish or to reform. Then there is the use made by the utilitarian school of an individualistic and introspective psychology to establish a scientific basis for economics and politics." (John Dewey, "Philosophy," *Research in the Social Sciences,* ed. Wilson Gee [New York: Macmillan Co., 1929], p. 260.)

7 The concept of "survival" together with those of "animism" and "adhesion" were proposed by E. B. Tylor in 1871.

8 Ortega y Gasset, *The Modern Theme*, trans. J. Cleugh (London: C. W. Daniel Co., 1931), *passim*.

9 "The fiction of the isolated and self-sufficient individual underlies in various forms the individualistic epistemology and genetic psychology." (Mannheim, *op. cit.*, p. 25.)

10 "Durkheim introduces an explicit criticism of the radical empiricist position which comes to the conclusion that valid knowledge cannot be accounted for on an empiricist basis. The *a priorist*

school has been essentially right in its critical attack upon empiricism and in its insistence that valid knowledge involves something beyond the empirical element, namely, the 'categories which are equally essential to knowledge, but are qualitatively distinct from, and not derivable from the empirical.' " (Parsons, *Structure of Social Action, op. cit.*, p. 442.)

11 E. Durkheim, *Les règles de la méthode sociologique* (Paris: F. Alcan, 1895), pp. xi ff.

Chapter VI: THE CONCEPTUAL SYSTEM

1 Here again the ontological status of concepts might well be raised. While all thinkers recognize the concept as the fundamental characteristic of the theoretic, not all are agreed upon its objective reality, or that it corresponds to any reality. Since the time of Kant, the emphasis has been upon the mind creating knowledge through its own activity. Both Simmel and Rickert regard experience as formless, but declare that the categories are implicit within experience and provide the means for ordering its content. It is undetermined as yet to what extent data undergo a transformation in arriving at intelligible form.

2 Cf., "The culture of a society is an *abstract*. It cannot be seen. However, it can be deduced by observing the ways in which people act, the thoughts they express and the tools they use. In the words of Kluckhohn and Kelly: '. . . Culture is like a map. Just as a map isn't the territory but an abstract description toward uniformity in the words, acts, and artifacts of human groups.' " (C. A. Dawson and W. E. Gettys, *An introduction to Sociology* [3d ed.; New York: Ronald Press, 1948], p. 30.)

3 A close examination of the opening and concluding chapters of Durkheim's *Les formes élémentaires de la vie religieuse* indicates that Durkheim understood by a category, or concept, when considered in its impersonality as a universal, precisely what Whitehead understands by an "eternal object." However, while Durkheim admits that universals are not meant to be subject to change, since they enable the thinker to overcome the flux of phenomena, nevertheless, these universals are not eternal, and their possibility of genesis and disappearance resides in the social process.

Cf., "I am maintaining that the understanding of actuality requires a reference to ideality . . . these transcendent entities have been called 'universals.' I prefer to use the term 'eternal objects,' . . . . Eternal objects are thus in their nature, abstract. By 'abstract' I mean that an eternal object is in itself — that is to say, its essence — is comprehensible without reference to some one particular occasion of experience. To be abstract is to transcend particular concrete occasions of actual happening. But to transcend on actual occasion does not mean being disconnected from it. On the contrary, I hold that each eternal object has its own proper connection with each other such occasion, which I term its mode of ingression into that occasion . . . thus the metaphysical status of an eternal object is that of a possibility for actuality." (Alfred North Whitehead, *Science and the Modern World* [Mentor Books ed.; New York: The New American Library, 1948], pp. 159-160.)

4 "It is absurd to look at the mind simply from the standpoint of the individual human organism; for although it has its focus there, it is essentially a social phenomena." (George Herbert Mead, *Mind, Self, and Society* [Chicago: University of Chicago Press, 1934], p. 133.)

It should be noted that Mead is not talking of the conceptual system as the ground of mind, but of the social process. However, this study has taken the view throughout that the conceptual system is the ideal aspect of the social process.

5 ". . . it is the nature of contemporary categories to remain concealed." (Mandelbaum, *op. cit.*, p. 72.)

6 When Comte declared that "religion embraces the whole of existence and the history of religion resumes the entire history of human development," he is in effect stating that the activities of human existence are directed by the culture (conceptual system). In his much maligned, "Law of the Three Stages," Comte explicitly recognizes the non-homogeneity of human thought. However, Comte's positivistic emphasis makes him declare for scientific thought as the only rational thought. However, if as indicated above, the conceptual system constitutes its own rationality, then scientific thought is not the only rational thought. The "Three Stages" are at least two, if not three, separate conceptual systems, and today are to be found telescoped within one another.

In the same way the distinction made by Lévy-Bruhl between civilized and preliterate mentality has a validity (although not just as he supposed) insofar as two general species of conceptual system can be recognized.

Likewise, in a smaller way, the "ideology" of Marx and the "stylistic structure" of Mannheim point to the conceptual structures that determine the meaning and form of the individual's thought and activities. Of course, the "ideology," or "stylistic structure," is but a partial and sub-system within the larger conceptual system.

7 The identification of religion with the ultimate conceptual system was seen by Durkheim. Yet Durkheim recognizes that

there is some difference between religion and science but cannot render clear just what the distinction is. It has been pointed out above that the distinction is to be found partly in the presence, or absence, of the category of Value in the system.

8 This also raises the problem of the "false consciousness" which appears in various forms throughout history. See: Mannheim, *op. cit.*, pp. 62-63, 66, 68, 84, 87.

9 "Le travail est la forme eminente de l'activite profane." (E. Durkheim, *Les formes élémentaires de la vie religieuse* [Bibliothèque de philosophie contemporaine, 2d ed.; Paris: F. Alcan, 1912], p. 439.)

10 All the enduring relations have been subject to revision. There remain the logical constants, and the deductions from logical implications. To the same category belong the so-called universals or concepts. They are the elements and structure of a universe of discourse. Insofar as in social conduct and with others we indicate the characters that endure in the perspective of the group to which we belong and out of which we belong only to the wider character which the problem in reflection assumes, and never transcends the social conduct within which the method arises. Mead, *op. cit.*, p. 90 n.

11 *Ibid.*, p. 76.

12 *Ibid.*, p. 310.

13 John Dewey, *The Quest for Certainty* (New York: Minton, Balch & Co., 1929), p. 38.

14 John Dewey, *Experience and Nature* (Chicago and London: Open Court Publishing Co., 1929), p. 7.

15 John Dewey, *Essays in Experimental Logic* (Chicago: University of Chicago Press, 1916), p. 138.

16 Cf., "My contention is, that this world of science is a world of ideas, and that its internal relations are relations between concepts, and that the elucidation of the precise connection between this world and the feeling of actual experience is the fundamental question of scientific philosophy." (A. N. Whitehead, *The Organization of Thought* [London: Routledge and Kegan Paul, 1917], p. 109.)

17 Most writers on institutions have been struck by the nonrational aspect of institutions as witness the following: "Are the great institutions, then, the product of men's intellect, ideas, interests, purposes, ideals? This does not seem to be the case, if for no other reason that there is so much which is utterly unintelligible and devoid of reason in institutions." (G. Panunzio, *Major Social Institutions* [New York, 1949], p. 144.)

18 "This unavoidable implicit ontology which is at the basis of our actions, even when we do not want to believe it, is not

something arrived at by romantic yearning and which we impose upon reality at will. It marks the horizon within which lies our world of reality . . . . Thus it may be asked whether under certain circumstances, while we are destroying the validity of certain ideas by means of ideological analysis, we are not, at the same time, erecting a new construction — whether in the very way we call old beliefs into question is not unconsciously implied the new decision." (Mannheim, *op. cit.*, p. 79 n.)

Chapter VII: RECAPITULATION AND CONCLUSIONS

1 *Supra,* Chap. I, pp. 25-26

Afterword: Knowing as Narration; Stanley Taylor's Unpublished Papers, with Commentary by Elwin H. Powell

> ... *Only through narrative can we represent "lived time." Life imitates narrative; narrative imitates life.*
> —Jerome Bruner
> "Life as Narrative"
> *Social Research,* 1987

For those with an epistemological eye, *Conceptions of Institutions and the Theory of Knowledge* is a work of art. Hear the words of Mark Kennedy: "My copy of Taylor's book is about used up. What do you do with a book when all the lines are underscored ... I get new knowledge with each rereading. It's like the fable of the Rhine's treasure. The more you take from it the more there is to take" (personal letter, December 1, 1987).

What is this new knowledge that Stan Taylor offers? What, after all, does it mean to know?

For Taylor to know is to classify. All reasoning is a process of subsuming particulars (percepts) by universals (concepts). Not sensation but social cognition is the source of knowledge. Consider the question, How big is the moon? To the child or the primitive the moon might look like a large silver platter, certainly bigger than the background specks we call the stars. But in reality the stars are gigantic burning suns and the moon only a small, dead rock. So, whose perception do we choose as valid, the primitive's or the scientist's? Inevitably, says Taylor: "The experiences of everyday life are reclassified according to the concept of objectivity obtaining in the institutional structure ... The thingness or objective aspect of the world is not given by its ontological status... but by the conceptual system" (*Conceptions of Institutions and the Theory of Knowledge,* pp. 36–37).

A conceptual system is a map, a root-metaphor, a narrative. The verb "narrate" means "to recount," and it derives from the Latin "gnarus" out of the Greek "gnoses," "to know" (*Oxford English Dictionary*). Literature, art, science, history, and even jurisprudence are forms of narration. Says Jim Elkins: "The codes that relate our normative system to our social construction of reality and to our visions of what the world might be are narrative."[1] And Bruner observes that in even the simplest chronicle the events will be seen to be "events chosen with a view to their place in an implicit narrative."[2]

Narration emerges to deal with choice; stories are a way of organizing information into knowledge to use as power in the decision making process. Perhaps five hundred thousand years ago the narrative intelligence may have arisen out of fire use, a thesis recently put forth by Alexander Marschark and years ago by the Greek dramatist Aeschylus.[3]

Narration is dialogue, not only an informing but a transforming process. Real discourse is a simultaneous replication and paraphrase, where you resay the words of others as if they are your own. This we do in speech: I replicate your words in my mind, translate them into my language, and feed them back to you as a paraphrase. You said X, but don't you mean Y, and then together we reach Z: thesis, antithesis, synthesis. This seems easy to do "out loud."

Scholarship is dialectical narration on paper—and it is very difficult to do. Scholars who only replicate are pedants; scholars who are all paraphrase are mere babblers. Like Durkheim and Mannheim before him, Stan Taylor mastered the difficult art of replication and paraphrase, of incorporating the written work of others into his own creations. A text of 130 pages, *Conceptions of Institutions and the Theory of Knowledge* has fifty pages of footnotes: Every assertion is grounded in previous scholarship. Not merely reiterating the words of others, Taylor is reformulating them in his own theory of the conceptual system.

Buried treasure lies in Stan Taylor's footnotes. Appearing on pages 51 and 153 is a remarkable text-footnote dialogue on Hume. And the five pages and twelve footnotes (pp. 65–70 and pp. 159–62) could stand as a veritable book on Comte, the "inspired madman," as Ortega y Gasset called him, who created sociology.

But the essence of Taylor is contained in the following passages on pages 26 and 143 of *Conceptions of Institutions*:

> Like all nominalists [Francis Bacon] tends to subordinate reason to the primacy of will, as if knowledge followed from what is done rather than from what is thought.[11] Hence the emphasis on method.[12] Indeed that distrust of reason which was to reach its culmination in the twentieth century is present already in Bacon.

Taylor's footnote 11 is a direct quotation from Novum Organum, showing the reader he accurately represents Bacon's position. Footnote 12 quotes Rudolf Eucken in 1916 saying

> Method seems here [in Bacon] to have cut itself loose from persons and to work with the unvarying accuracy of a machine. This is the beginning of that overvaluing of method and undervaluing of personality which has been the cause of much error in modern life.... So already at this early date [16th century] we have that fundamentally false identification of "nature" with "world," of natural science with science generally, which has set up so much ... confusion.

Libraries classify *Conceptions of Institutions* as a study in the methodology. But Taylor himself had no method except patient narration, like Willard Waller, who said scientific method was only a matter of "Looking at events until they become luminous." For Kenneth Hoover, "science is the art of reality-testing."[4]

Searching for a "scientific" understanding of "world," Stanley Taylor wrote three papers I have only recently come to comprehend:

1. "To Create History: Reflections on the Power of the Written Word" (circa 1947) explores the interplay of ideas and the media of their expression and senses the exhaustion of the Cartesian narrative. Through excerpting I have reduced the manuscript from twenty-five to twelve pages, and I have added footnotes as a way of updating the paper without altering Taylor's text.

2. "Choosing as Interpretation: Constructing Objects, Making Decisions" is my condensation and restructuring of a twenty-one-page manuscript Taylor had sketched out in 1963. I have added footnotes to facilitate dialogue on the paper.

3. "Against the Dark Ocean of the Unknown: The Conceptual System and the Sociology of Art" argues for the unity of art and science. This paper was finished by Taylor in 1964; I have not added to or altered a word of it.

Between 1959 and 1962 Stan Taylor and I were colleagues at the University of Buffalo, before he settled into a professorship at the University of Alberta in Canada. He was admired by Buffalo students—Fred Clifton, a young philosopher, said Stan Taylor was "stoned on ontology." Glenn Goodwin remembers Taylor as a man of "warmth, dignity and understanding."

On a September day in 1964 Stan left his unpublished papers with me. A marvelous afternoon on the verge of autumn we walked in Buffalo talking of "everyone":

...of Theodore Drieser and Max Weber: who is the artist; who is the scientist? Both personify their data in order to understand an institution—capitalism. Or look at Sinclair Lewis's *Main Street* (1920) and the Lynds' *Middletown* (1925): Lewis's fiction shows the facts of life; the Lynds' facts reveal the fictions people live by—both are simultaneously works of art, works of science.

...of Louis Leakey and his patient labor in establishing man's 2 million year (2 myr) presence on earth and Raymond Dart's recent (1961) report of stored femurs, which implied a collective use of implements by *Australopithecenes*. Our Austin circle in 1951 had argued out the Durkheimian proposition "One fact is no fact." How many bones do you need for a scientific generalization? It was hardly more than one piece of charcoal that enabled Teilhard de Chardin in the 1920s to establish the reality of fire use in the Peking cave at 500,000 B.P. (before the present).

...talked of the role of choice in evolution, with Stan urging me to read Franklin Giddings and of course Kropotkin (does cooperation imply more choice than competition?)... We said we would someday do a paper on "paleosociology."

We walked around Delaware Park Lake and back to my house on Jewett Parkway in late afternoon for tea, while I explained that the fate of humanity depended on reelecting President Lyndon Johnson. Laughing, Stan said the election had no more significance than Pope Leo running against Pope Urban (or whatever their names were) in the thirteenth century. In good spirits, as always, Taylor left for the long drive back to Edmonton Alberta. (At age fifty-seven he had gone to driving school and acquired an automobile.) We exchanged Christmas cards but not letters.

Then, on May 18, 1965, I was called to the phone and before I picked up the receiver I said to myself, *Stan Taylor's dead.* Or so I thought I thought twenty years ago. His death was unanticipated— he was in good health, and his life had gone well in Alberta. Two days after the phone call, I received a postcard from him written only hours before his fatal heart attack in Minneapolis; he was then en route to Buffalo for summer teaching.

On May 20 came the last rites in Barrie, Ontario. The service, done with terse good taste, took place in the Anglican church of Stan's boyhood. He had left Barrie and the church forty years ago, so there were only a handful of us at the graveside—Stan's wife, Susan, two of his brothers and a sister, Mark Kennedy, my wife, Nita, and I. Buried in a country churchyard, on a hill.... I gazed into a sea of green and listened to clods bouncing off a metal casket.

So now only the concept of Stan Taylor remains—and it never leaves me. Nothing mystical or sentimental in that: Stan is a functional presence in my daily life: every course I teach begins with his definitions, and all my research departs from his instruction to seek the connection between Concept and Institution. It's like a religion, sociology—a shared narrative. In the beginning is the word. Alvin Gouldner says the Greek logos can be rendered narrative.[5]

Every noun is a condensed story—and a kind of seed. Julian Jaynes says that "language is an organ of perception, not simply a means of communication."[6] We see through the words in our mind, not with our eyes only. So on August 18, 1981—16 years after his death—new words from Stan Taylor began to germinate in my consciousness, to alter my perception. I retrieved his papers from my attic file and began to struggle with the question of choice and the construction of objects. Out of two chapters of Taylor's projected book on social theory I made a six page class handout, which I also passed on to friends and colleagues. Attempting to replicate his words in my paraphrase, I was led into an nth reading of *Conceptions of Institutions and the Theory of Knowledge* and a reexamination of notes I had in his course in 1951. Eventually a paper emerged as "Fragments for a Sociology of Knowledge: From the Lectures and Unpublished Papers of Stanley Taylor," in *Catalyst,* 1985.

Thanks to the miracle of xerox I was able to circulate *Conceptions of Institutions* and the *Catalyst* piece to my seminar in the sociology of knowledge in Spring 1987. From Taylor's writings came the organizing question of the seminar: How is the natural environment transformed into a social world? Acknowledging his debt to Dewey and Mead, Taylor observes that "the epistemology of both thinkers has its source in the Darwinian theory of evolution" *(Conceptions,* p. 121).

So in the seminar we looked for the evolutionary origins of the concept and came upon a new question: does the concept emerge to resolve the stress of choice? We were choosing animals before we became thinking animals. Around 2–4 myr we started using physical objects—stones, bones, sticks—for food getting and defense, and so voluntarism was built into our bio-social being. To pick up and use objects requires a quality of decision not known to the animal that relies on tooth and claw for survival.[7] A protoconceptualization is implied by the act of throwing stones—the "first denotative gesture, i.e. a pointing out of an object, an act not performed by any other animal," says E. S. Ferguson.[8] To throw a rock—not merely toss it, as do chimpanzees—requires the forethought of taking aim. The technology of rocking opened up a new food supply of small animals, who literally did not know what hit them.

From 2 myr onward existential choices becomes more complex and demanding as physical objects were being used to reconstruct a world. For instance, stones were used to designate areas—home bases, territories—as early as 1.7 myr at Olduvai Gorge; red ocher used for paint making dates from the same time. Fire use may date from 1.5 myr. Fire enabled hominids to frighten away predators and turn the environment of the cave into a world. Without fire the cave is a death trap. Fire enabled people to move out of the tropics and into cold northern climates; dealing with winter imposed the need for planning and new choices—groups that learned to anticipate the change of seasons increased their chances of survival. Fire use requires a quality of narratization, says Marschark, which lays the foundation for conceptualization. Through conceptualization—the capacity to organize information into knowledge to use as power—man prevailed in the evolutionary struggle.

Class handouts were distributed at each meeting of the seminar, so by the end of the semester a sheath of paper surrounded Taylor's *Conceptions,* and in June 1987 I mailed it to Irving Louis Horowitz of Transaction Publishers. Interested in reissuing Taylor's book, Horowitz asked me to write an introduction to the book.

Researching the introduction, I returned to my attic files and had to conjure with myself at twenty-six, in the void of anomie—an ordeal. But in my files I also discovered lost papers of Stan Taylor's—a joy.

The lost papers—on history, on art—show Taylor's unusual capacity for "interpretive reliving," as Dilthey would call it.[9] In the paper on history (1947) we glimpse the end of the Cartesian epoch, in the paper on art (1964) the dawn of a new day. Aesthetics is reintroduced to sociology, and Taylor solves his own dilemma, saving both the unique and the universal, feeling and thought: " ...in art the rationality of man reaches perception of itself, and what seems like the essence of eternal things is translated into the language of the present."

Thus the life of Stanley Taylor finds its fulfillment.

"Without Beauty truth sinks to triviality," said Whitehead. "Truth matters because of Beauty."[10]

Notes

Afterword: KNOWING AS NARRATION: STANLEY TAYLOR'S UNPUBLISHED PAPERS, WITH COMMENTARY BY ELWIN H. POWELL

1. James R. Elkins, "On the Emergence of Narrative Jurisprudence: The Humanistic Perspective Finds a New Path," *Legal Studies Forum*, IX (1985), pp. 123–156. For two days of conversation on narrative sociology at the annual meeting of the Association of Humanist Sociology in Atlanta in 1985 I am much indebted to Jim Elkin, B Wardlaw, Barton Parks, and Glenn Goodwin.

2. Jerome Bruner, "Life as Narrative," *Social Research*, LIV (Spring 1987), pp. 11–29.

3. Alexander Marschark, *The Roots of Civilization: The Cognitive Beginnings of Man's First Art, Symbol and Notation* (New York: McGraw Hill, 1972), pp. 113–20.

4. Willard Waller, "Insight and Scientific Method," *American Journal of Sociology* 40 (1934), pp. 285–97. cf. Kenneth Hoover, *The Elements of Social Scientific Thinking* (New York: St. Martin's Press, 1984), p. 12.

5. Alvin Gouldner, *Enter Plato: Classical Greece and the Origin of Social Theory* (New York: Basic Books, 1965), p. 390.

6. Julian Jaynes, *The Origin of Consciousness in the Breakdown of the Bicameral Mind* (Boston: Houghton Mifflin, 1976).

7. Jin Yuan, "The Origins of Human Consciousness," *Journal of Social and Biological Structures* (1987), pp. 301–24.

8. E. S. Ferguson, *The Singularity of Man: The Origins and Evolution of Consciousness* (Boynton Beach, Fl.: Star Publishing Company, 1974), p. 110, et passim.

9. Hajo Holborn, "Wilhelm Dilthey and the Critique of Historical Reason," *Journal of the History of Ideas,* XI January, 1950), pp. 93–118, says: "History is more than a presentation of a phenomenal world, or a mere visualization of the dead past. It is the living experience of the student of history as well... a way of understanding the world." Cf. Elwin H. Powell, "The Limitations of Sociological Positivism (Austin: Unpublished M.A. thesis at the University of Texas, 1951), chapter 5, "Meaning and the Social Process: Mead, Cooley and Dilthey" pp. 77–94.

10. Alfred North Whitehead, *Adventures of Ideas* (New York: Macmillan, 1933), p. 344.

To Create History:
Reflections on the Power of
the Written Word

The magic of words depends not only on the infinite resources of the spirit but is conditioned also by the nature of the page upon which the mind impresses the stamp of thought, of feeling and of will.... And what appears to be physically insignificant—a few sheets of paper—may alter the destiny of a people and revolutionize the consciousness of all mankind.

The printed word has unique power.... We read life into the printed text and so it leads us to a dimension beyond itself to an inwardness answering to our own.

There is a connection between the printed word and the tissue of events, ideas and beliefs which make up a given historical epoch.... The rigidity of law among the early peoples of the Mediterranean is in a measure a reflection of the stone tables upon which the laws were inscribed; parchment embodies the permanence and narrowness of the Middle Ages; paper, cheap in cost and light in weight, characterizes the modern age with its ceaseless flux of ideas, the instability of its mental life, ...its inability to secure an anchorage.

Ultimately history is shaped by public opinion, by an evolving collective consciousness, and the media for the communication of ideas influences the course of the political process. In folk society the formation of opinion is an almost unconscious process. But in Greece we see the beginnings of deliberation. In the Greek city states people reached joint decisions; and second only to the rhetoric of the agora in shaping Athenian opinion were the theatres. In the later Hellenistic period speeches were passed around in manuscript form.[1]

For the Romans, as long as they were a scattered peasantry, there was little scope for publicity, but with the coming of Greek culture, oratory acquired a preponderant influence. Theatre also assumed importance.

The urban culture of the later Roman Empire gave a fairly wide scope for the opinion process: pamphlet literature was assuming sizeable proportions by the time of Caesar. Above all, there developed in the highly organized and centralized Roman Empire a sense of the importance of news as a factor in the creation and direction of an enlightened public opinion. As transportation and communication improve, the supplying of news became a specialized profession: Caesar had news sheets published in 59 B.C. —and these news sheets became an appreciable factor in shaping the general pattern of public opinion.[2]

With the fall of the Roman Empire (circa 500 A.D.), urban society gave way to an agrarian system of diverse and scattered groups and a culture blanketed under a common religious ideology. Illiteracy and the breakup of the population into small groups eliminated the prerequisite of an articulate and dynamic public opinion. Not until the controversy between the German emperors and the Papacy (circa 1500) reached a head was any coherent attempt made to arouse the sympathy of a scattered population.[3]

Then came printing—with Gutenberg's press (1440) printing made economical the multiplication of texts on a large scale, and therefore permitted an expansion of the range of influence of published works. It brought an increase in tracts, and thus revivified the role of debate in the opinion forming process. Leaders of the Reformation attempted by books and pamphlets to extend the influence of their doctrines and to arouse groups previously apathetic—thus printing became a menace to the older religious authority.

With the written word comes new possibilities for vicarious experience and by the 17th century the individual was deluged with a welter of novel ideas. Reason itself was undergoing reconstruction.

The belief in the rationality of the universe; the assumption that truth is one, absolute, and invariable; the overwhelming confidence in the constructions of reason; the disregard of all but pure intellection—these are an attitude of mind created by Scholasticism, a product of centuries of logic chopping and fine distinctions. Since Paris was the center of Scholasticism it seems but natural that the man who detached this mental attitude from its

historical residue and separated the living nucleus from the
mountainous piles of dead metaphysics should be a Frenchman—
Rene Descartes. It was he who converted reason into a new
intoxicating revelation. Henceforward, reason becomes the touch-
stone not only of mathematics and natural science but even political
philosophy. Tradition, history and concrete vital reality assume a
marked negligibility in the face of intellectual perfection. Past,
present and future fuse into geometrical order. Indeed, future
institutions and states will begin from unquestionable principles,
from mathematical bases. The foundations of the American,
French and Russian revolutions were laid with the writing of the
Meditations of Descartes... the specifically modern is a consequence of this metaphysical root.[4]

Now for the first time the "idea" comes into its own; no longer
in the shadow of divine revelation, it is itself a revelation. In politics
constitutions will be preferred to mere institutions, and principles
to princes. In science mathematics will take precedence over the
senses—"In natural philosophy we must abstract our senses," said
Newton.

Printing coincided with the rise of rationalist philosophy in
Europe. As technology printing existed in China, and also among
the Moslems, but its full development required a certain climate of
thought, a cultural soil where it could thrive and flourish.

Printing meant in a measure the annihilation of time and
space.... While other organisms react directly to the environment
man interposes a tissue of values between his biological nature and
the outer universe. The technological structure we know today has
its roots deep in the values of Renaissance man. The longing for
the infinite which characterized the Renaissance man (e.g. Bruno)
found concrete expression in the conquest of finite space—by the
adventurers who trod the last mile of the earth's surface and by the
technicians who fashioned the machines of flight which conquer
space and time together. And the time the engineer thus over-
comes is not time as lived but mathematical time—a concept
originating in the abstract reason of Descartes and Newton. Speed
alone can master a reality so conceived; that is, reduce it to the a
priori form imposed upon reality at the beginning of the modern
era. In the realm of intellectual intercommunication the speed
necessary for shattering the barriers of time and space was found
in the modern newspaper.[5]

Men of the older tradition of the 15th and 16th century looked askance at the printing press, and in a way their worst fears have been realized. For the press has been the "action in distans" applied to communication. The edifice raised by tradition, law, politics, and art seemed to crumble steadily before the ceaseless pulverization of rationalist thought whose explosive force was centered in the pure reason, in the "geometric" concept (e.g., Descartes' Fourth Meditation: "Everything that reason conceives it conceives rightly and there is no possibility of error").

In the West the destructive power of ideas increased with the printing press—authority and tradition has waned in strength to our own time. But is printing always a disruptive, revolutionary force? Printing may also be a brake, a conservative and retarding factor in civilization. A study of communication in ancient times would support such a contention. Once a law was chiseled in stone, written in papyrus or velium it required a concerted effort to delete or even amend such a law. This unalterability of the written law has presented a baffling problem to students of law and has been a stone wall to both reformers and revolutionaries. The fixity of all written things prevents life passing beyond that point in history. The written word obstructs like a huge boulder in the stream of life whilst the waters eddy and swirl, spreading thinly and unevenly over the shores.

We have seen that printing first appeared in the far east among the Buddhists who utilized the invention for the stamping of images; to fix in visible form the religious symbol on the minds of the masses. In Europe too printing was at first essentially imitation and preservation. It gave the manuscripts of the church a new life for the content of the past was thus preserved and permitted to dominate the future. So the present becomes prisoner to the past, enclosed between the covers of a book.

But if printing is conservative it is also revolutionary. Few would deny that the printing and wide circulation of the Bible helped to destroy the authority of the church; that in some degree the Encyclopaedists prepared the French Revolution; that "Das Kapital" was the handbook of Lenin. The solution to this enigma can be found by looking at the history of printing and the history of ideas respectively.

The Gothic period raised the manuscript to a high level. The expensive, durable parchment was extremely scarce, as were also writers and came to be looked upon as almost sacred. When the book appeared it carried an aura of mysticism created by centuries of copying monks. Indeed, to our own time the written word has been more heavily weighted than speech; a strange power, a curious penumbra attaches to the book, a finality, an inevitability is generated by its own backgroud. "It is written... " is sufficient to arrest attention; to detract from speech; to cast a spell. Thus it was that when the men of the 15th and 16th centuries wrote their thoughts in books their words carried a conviction that no printed matter could convey today. The awe with which men beheld the Bible was transferred to other books—to the literature of the Greeks, but also to the new writers that flooded Europe. For many generations the thoughts and attitudes of that period prevailed and penetrated into all corners of the world.[6]

So it was that the book, at first a copy of the manuscript, a mere tool of imitation, became converted into a hammer for smashing of past idols—a hammer weighted with Cartesian rationalism. But as it goes about its work of destruction it sets up new idols and by its fundamentally conservative nature preserves these against future changes. But as books multiply they cheapen and the power of the book declines. Yet literature obstructs rather than hastens change. New ideas, new styles, new expression make their way ever more slowly—spontaneity becomes a usage, a custom, a tradition.

Very often our fathers saw a body of irrefragable truth where there was only tedious absurdity, or prolix, pedantic scholarship. In the 16th and 17th centuries a printed word could stir a million hearts and the counter-stimulation enabled the writers to rise to great heights. The impulses of the Renaissance spread throughout Western Europe; an intellectual curiosity seized upon all literature available. In some countries as late as the 17th century the Bible was the only book accessible to all. It became the center and substance of thought; its imagery; its symbols; the stern terrifying fierceness of the Hebrew prophets—in striking contrast to the sophistication of the Royal Courts—sank into the tissue of culture to produce an almost epic atmosphere, rich, dark and sombre. Especially was this true of England. Perhaps Milton alone was able to express this deep religious passion, and to provide the largeness of idiom, to invent an immortal rhythm, attaining in exalted moments the sublime.

But today the book no longer decides the destiny of Empires. Only the newspaper headline, the journalistic article, vitally affect public opinion. In the future it may be that revolutionary developments will follow the spoken word. It has been said that all

profound prophets come from the desert. Great religous move-
ments are essentially "country" as distinguised from "town" phenomena. Early Christianity, Mohammedanism, etc. are reactions
against the lush life of the urban community. Puritanism and
Calvinism were based on the Bible but it is the hard, fierce
smouldering desert intensity that grips through the pages of the
Old Testament. This moral fervor never quite passes from rural
areas; only the prophet is required for the religious passion to
break forth. Fascism declared itself to be a rural movement.
Although hardly typical of what we have just discussed, Fascism
bears many of its outward signs. These were shown in the burning
of books in Berlin; the increased importance of the spoken as
against the written, word (in a nation Germany which once
surpassed all others in its consumption of printed matter this is
significant); the emphasis upon the will and upon feeling rather
than upon reason; its fanatical adherence to a prophet. The
follower of the prophet possessed a clear vision of the self to be
realized compared to the blurred, confused image of his opponent.

It is clear now that as those ancient spiritual forces which
constituted the government of man fast disappeared with the rise
of the modern age the printed word fell heir to their spiritual
strength. All such power to continue must strike roots deep into
reality for it was the abandonment of reality which destroyed the
institutions of the Middle Ages. The sensational, the momentary,
cannot provide substantial foundation for the conduct of life. In
conclusion it must be said that man no longer finds revelation in
the printed word. The ideas which books convey fail to carry us
into the domain of reality. Even natural science—once a revelation—seems to have become the mere interplay of ideas. The
feeling that man is in contact with cosmic reality is fast fading.
Nonetheless, a sublime restlessness manifests itself; the ultimate
and decisive questions still press in upon us. To rise to the
challenge of these problems is to create history—to find and to be,
a mission and a destiny.

Notes

TO CREATE HISTORY: REFLECTIONS ON THE POWER OF THE WRITTEN WORD

Stan Taylor cited as the main references for this paper, H. A. Innis, *On the Economic Significance of Culture* (1946); William Albig, *Public Opinion* (1939); Walter Lippman, *Public Opinion* (1922); N. Angell, *The Press and the Organization of Society; B. Bernays, Crystallizing Public Opinion;* and Q. Wright, *A Study of War* (1939). But the sources are not specifically cited in the text. The paper is not dated, but it was written after World War II and before Taylor moved on to the University of Chicago. I have added endnotes to suggest further explorations of the relationship between consciousness and the written word (E.H.P.).

1. "The Athenian Equivalent of a Free Press Was the Theater," I. F. Stone, *The Trial of Socrates* (Boston: Little Brown, 1988), p. 134. For a glimpse of the role of the manuscript in later Greco-Roman life, see Gore Vidal, *Julian* (New York: Modern Library, 1962) p. i.

2. Leaflets played a role in politics. Tacitus reports the execution of "a certain Titus Curtisius" in 24 A.D. who had published leaflets calling for slaves to rise up in revolt. D. R. Dudley, *The Annals of Tacitus, a New Translation* (New York: Mentor, 1966), p. 155.

3. Not till the 18th century did Europe again attain the level of literacy that the ancient world achieved by 100 B.C., says Ramsay. In the seventh century B.C. Greek soldiers on expedition in Egypt left written accounts of their lives carved in cliffs which, says Ramsay, show a much higher level of literacy and of civilization than the Christian crusaders 1,700 years later. W. M. Ramsay, *The Letters to the Seven Churches of Asia and Their Place in the Plan of the Apocalypse* (New York: A. C. Armstrong, 1905), (pp. 1–4). Paper was in full use in Egypt by the fourth millennium and according to Herodotus was in ordinary use in Greece by the fifth century B.C.

4. Cf. Bernard Williams, *Descartes: The Project of Pure Enquiry* (Atlantic Highlands, N.J.: Humanities Press, 1978).

5. In 1981 when President Reagan was wounded by a would be assassin the Washington ABC headquarters—only blocks away—

learned about the attempt from an electronic inquiry from its London office—an ocean away.

6. Cf. Walter Ong, *The Presence of the Word: Some Prolegomena for Cultural and Religious History* (Minneapolis: University of Minnesota Press, 1967); and *Orality and Literacy: The Technologizing of the Word* (New York: Methuen, 1981).

Choosing as Interpretation: Constructing Objects, Conjuring with the Self as Actor

> ...a living being acts. Its reason for movement lies within itself, and in that action...the living being determines its environment...selects its own time system and the space that this involves. It thus determines the world within which it lives. Its determination, however, is a selection, and a creation only in the sense of reconstruction.
> —George H. Mead,
> *The Philosophy of the Act*, 1938, p. 417

For three centuries psychology, political science, and economics all operated with an image of the individual as a self-contained entity, thus obscuring the role of association in human affairs. The simple facts of human experience, that it occurs in a network of relationships, involves the exchange of information and reciprocal decision making—these were matters ignored by professional scholars.

But by the turn of the century the idea of the individual was giving way to the notion of social self, a phrase first used by James Mark Baldwin (1890), elaborated by Franklin Giddings (1896), deepened by Charles Horton Cooley (1902) and perfected by George Herbert Mead (1930).

As we move up the scale from animal to human society, said Giddings. "Concourse develops into intercourse, the chief aspect of which is the interchange of thought and feeling by means of language and the chief consequences of which are the evolution of a consciousness of kind and of a nature that is intellectually and morally fitted for social life."[1]

Concourse proceeds by a "conversation of gestures" but inter-course involves the use of symbols which become significant through the process of "taking the role of the other" as Mead called it[2] Interaction involves reading the meaning of the gesture of the other person and then responding to the intention behind it. Hence evaluation, assessment, judgment and decision always enter into the determination of meaning. Our interpretation of the act of the other becomes the stimulus for our response to the other.[3]

So participants in a social act must interpret, not simply respond to the acts of one another. Each one follows the act of the other, trying to conceive what is called for, fitting his own conduct to the behavior of the other. Interaction then becomes an evolving, developing affair, not merely a calling out of what is already lodged in the actors. Interaction becomes transaction (Dewey's word), not a routine stimulus-response affair, and requires being acutely aware of the content of the mind of the other. From this sizing up, interpretation, and re-orientation there emerges the unity called "society."

According to Mead, every society consists of individuals whose lines of activity must fit together. Indeed, a group means an aggregation of people acting concertedly. For Mead, insect and lower animal societies are vastly different from human societies. In the insect society an alignment is laid down in the genetic make-up of the species; the behavior of the insect is pre-determined by its biology. Insect and lower animal societies retain a certain fixity over vast periods of geological time. But human society as we know it is relatively new—10,000 years since the agricultural revolution of the neolithic; 500,000 since the taming of fire and the occupation of caves in the Middle Paleolithic, 4.5 myr since the descent from the trees and the assumption of upright posture. The apparent size and structure of the brain has been constant for 300,000 years but society has changed enormously since then. Indeed, our society has changed greatly in only a few generations. The alignments of human society are built up in an interactional process through a process of collective discernment, judgment and redirection. In a word, human society is made by man.

Mead points out that the human infant begins his life with an unformed make-up—a repertoire of reflexes, of fixed, stereotyped modes of action. The infant is able to wiggle, twist, and squirm but not to act concertedly.... The infant's organization, however, is plastic, and he is placed in a structured, social setting. Those who surround the child have defined ways of behaving towards it, and the child begins to transform its unorganized, undirected activity into organized ways of behavior. What essentially happens is that the associates of the child act as a set of defining agents, indicating to the child how it should act. In the beginning significant others "choose" the child; in time the child comes to choose the other....[4]

Socialization is a defining process. Through active association we discover the meaning of our world, construct the objects which direct our conduct. *Webster's,* gives as the definition "object" "something mental or physical toward which thought, feeling, or action is directed." The object is never pre-established for the human; it is constructed out of social experience. Each object is a plan of action, says Mead, one which embodies the actions of others in it. Objects are a group creation.

Things are given in nature but objects are defined through interaction. For instance, a chair as a thing is transformed into an object by the process of sitting. A group not organized for sitting would not view the chair as a chair. Conceivably the "thing" chair might be viewed as a weapon or a sacred object, but it would not be chair unless it served as a seat. The objects of our world are fashioned out of social experience—paved streets, engines, stones, trees, etc.—are things which we turn into objects through the use we make of them.

People can be physically adjacent and live in quite different object worlds.... The physical anthropologist, the physician, the beauty operator, the racketeer, all see something different in the same human objects. Perceptions are shaped by social roles. "Does the broker see the ding-an-sich as real estate?" asks W. H. Auden.[5]

Human beings then live in a constructed world, not an environment in the biological meaning of the word. This world is made up of physical objects (things), social objects (other people) and abstract objects—ideas like Liberty, Justice, Truth, Progress, etc. An object is anything the actor can designate and respond to. All kinds of fictions can also be objects. The world of objects of any actor is obviously subject to being formed and changed through the very course of interaction with others; in primitive society the meaning of objects is relatively fixed; in modern civilization all definitions are now flux.

To be a social self is to become an object to oneself. The subject becomes an object by approaching itself through the roles of others. The self can and does take a mutiplicity of roles simultaneously, but there is a general role which represents the whole community and embraces the specific roles of individuals. This general role, or generalized other as Mead called it, enables the person to engage in consistent behavior in varying situations. Through the generalized other the person emancipates himself from particularized situations. By restructuring perception through the general role people are able to nullify, modify and redefine the objects of their constructed social world.

By virtue of possessing a self the human being is able to introduce an order of selection—of choice—among the objects of its world. Thus the actor begins to exercise direction and control over his conduct. This control is accomplished by the individual acting back upon itself, indicating to itself what it seeks. Persons consist of the flow of such indications to themselves. Hence the restraint of impulse, the overcoming of temptation, etc. as the individual acts back upon himself. Self control exists because the person becomes a small society., the i.e. becomes the subject and the object of his own act.

For Mead, the "I" and the "me" are polar aspects of the self in action. The "I" initiates the act and then a "me" is called forth: in effect the person asks, "how does my gesture look to the other?" And of course I am also asking what does his gesture look like to me, what is his intention? For instance, I am hungry and have food: do I eat it all myself or share it with my friends, who are also hungry? Consciousness of the needs of other members of my own community enables me to transcend biological impulse. In addition there is the power of the generalized other which compels me to subordinate my wish to communal demands. In fact, food sharing is the first activity that differentiates the human from the ape society. Thus humans are compelled to choose between satisfying selfish and altruistic impulses.[6]

Human life, then, becomes a running interaction between the "I" (the subject) and the "me" (the object) of the self, always operating in a social world. The "me" is defined by the response of significant others; the "I" interprets the meaning of the "me," decides what "me" to present for judgement by the generalized other. This decision is made through a conjuring process.

To conjure, says the *Oxford English Dictionary*, is: "to swear together, to band, combine, or make a compact by oath... to

conspire... to entreat... summon invocation... imagine... con-
trive... juggle."

So the person conjures with himself as actor, guided by the me
as defined by the other. In the process the actor counsels the self,
advises the self, talks to the self. This is a building up of an action,
not an unrolling of something already organized. Always in the
process of reconstruction, the act emerges through the continuous
interplay of self and other and the outcome is never known until it
is over.... The actor brings in many thoughts of anxiety and guilt
and reflects upon the judiciousness of the action. There are always
possibilities for rearrangement within the act as the process of
assessing, judging, planning, rationalizing, etc. goes on.... Once in
motion the act may be checked or stimulated but always human life
remains a case of making decisions and weighing alternatives.[7]

Thinking—Reason itself—is an inter-personal process, and
can never be understood as the cogitation of a biological individual.
Plato defined thought as "the unuttered conversation of the soul
with herself." External discourse is internalized as reflection;
thought, says Mead, is a telescoped act. Circumspection, obedience
to law and custom, the use of intelligence mold the direction and
character of the act. Images brought to bear on the arena of
impulse shape the career of the act. Thus, Reason and Will come
together in a single system.

Association is a defining process and as such the source of
decision in human affairs; as developed selves we choose our
associates—and are chosen by them. Significant others—who may
exist for us as live perceptual beings, or only imaginary concepts—
are the constructed objects of our social world.... Association is
also an evolutionary process, extending into a distant past, project-
ing into a far future.[8]

Notes

CHOOSING AS INTERPRETATION: CONSTRUCTING
OBJECTS, CONJURING WITH THE SELF AS ACTOR

This paper is extracted from a 21 page text called "Sociological
Theory and Problems," with ch. I entitled "The Social Dimension
of Human Behavior: Its Belated Recognition" and Chapter II
"The Construction of a World (Objects): The Symbolic Interac-

tionist Theory of George Herbert Mead." Occasionally I have inserted facts and figures and dictionary definitions to help the reader through the abstractions of Mead and Taylor, and for the same reason I have reshaped especially cumbersome constructions. I would of course be happy to share the original Taylor with anyone who requested a XEROX of it. The footnotes are also my addition—there were none in the original draft, which is hardly more than a sketch (E.H.P.).

1. Franklin Giddings, *Principles of Sociology: An Analysis of the Phenomena of Association and of Social Organization* (New York: Macmillan, 1896), p. 71.

2. Stanley Taylor draws the main Meadian ideas in this paper from G. H. Mead, *The Philosophy of the Act* (Chicago: University of Chicago Press, 1938), pp. 37, 546–47, 655. And from G. H. Mead, *Mind, Self and Society* (Chicago: University of Chicago Press, 1934), pp. 77–100, 227–81, et passim.

3. For ramifications of the idea of interpretation, see Samuel Weber, *Institution and Interpretation* (Minneapolis: University of Minnesota Press, 1987); Howard Becker, "Interpretive Sociology," in G. Gurvitch and W. Moore, eds., *Twentieth Century Sociology* (New York: The Philosophical Library, 1945), pp. 70–95.

4. From the moment of birth the organism is acting on its environment, trying to evoke a response from it. In his 1914 lectures in Social Psychology, Mead said: "We found in the individual's own stimulation of others the beginnings of self-consciousness and with that the consciousness of meaning. *The Individual and the Social Self: The Unpublished Work of George Herbert Mead*, ed. David Miller (Chicago: University of Chicago Press, 1982), p. 51. To stimulate another implies a decision, albeit unconscious. Cf. L. L. Stone, H. Smith, L. Murphy, *The Social Infant* (New York: Basic Books, 1974). In highlighting the plasticity of the infant, Taylor, in this paragraph, enshadows the choosing process which is also underway. Infants suffering from maramus—a traumatizing isolation—may be unconsciously choosing not to respond to a world which has refused to respond to them. If the infant's cries go unanswered, the organism loses the will to stimulate the world.

5. As quoted by Robert Merton, *Social Theory and Social Structure* (New York: The Free Press of Glencoe, 1964), p. 152.

6. Jerome Barkow, "Attention Structure and the Evolution of Human Psychological Characteristics," in M. Chance and R. Larsen, eds., *The Social Structure of Attention,* (New York: John Wiley and Sons, 1976), pp. 203–19, notes that individuals derive standards of moral evaluation from paying attention to internalized representations of others—after the fashion described by Mead and Freud. Barkow sees this process operating with primates "as far back as *Ramapithecus*—10 myr—and certainly by the Homo erectus level [1.5 to .2 myr] these representations were sufficiently powerful to be attended to even in the absence of the originals themselves" (p. 207). That is, hominids carried in their heads a picture of the mother and the dominant male which would undoubtedly shape subsequent choices, as it does with us their descendants. Cf. also James Chisoholm, "On the Evolution of Rules," *ibid.,* pp. 223–51, saying: "Human exchange and human rules are part of the process of evolution and may have their beginnings in the non-human capacities to evaluate and decide" (p. 250).

7. Albert Schuntz says: "The whole distinction between the real and the unreal is always grounded in two mental facts: first that we are liable to think differently of the same object; and secondly, that when we have done so, we can choose which way of thinking to adhere to and which to disregard" in "Don Quixote and the Problem of Reality" (1964) in E. T. Burns, ed. *Sociology of Literature and Drama,* (Baltimore: Penguin, 1973) pp. 251–59.

8. Giddings, op. cit., pp. 202–206, observes that "for thousands of years before man existed natural selection was everywhere supplemented by conscious choice. Indeed choice is a main differentiation of the animal from the plant world: locomotion necessitates choice and the nervous system and brain of the animal organism arose to deal with it." Giddings argued that as locomotive animals lost the protection provided by adaptation to a stable environment and turn to association for protection, association brings variation, and develops intelligence which eventually becomes more important in the evolutionary struggle than brute strength. The fittest survive but it is co-operation and mutual aid and association which confers fitness, says Giddings, drawing on Kropotkin.

Against the Dark Ocean of the Unknown: The Conceptual System and the Sociology of Art

> The imagination of the artist does not arbitrarily invent the forms of things. The artist chooses a certain aspect of reality, but this process of selection is at the same time a process of objectification.
>
> —Ernst Cassirer,
> *An Essay on Man*, 1954

I

Although the artistic has long been the subject matter of that branch of philosophical inquiry known as "aesthetic," no serious attempt has been made to investigate this important aspect of human experience in terms of a single, systematic theory which is not evaluative, or normative, but descriptive and general. Such neglect is itself significant. Reflection indicates that the field of art[1] has remained free from scientific exploration for reasons similar to those which for centuries left the interpretation of religious facts to the theologian, and the moral facts to the ethicist. The changed viewpoint that takes the scientific attitude toward moral and religious facts for granted is due in part to the whole progress of the social sciences over the past century, but more especially to the cultural anthropologists. However, the sociologist who first pierced the circle that shut out the scientist from holy things was Emile Durkheim.[2] It may be suggested that if the artistic is to be understood, and not merely wondered at, an approach to the problem may well be similar to that employed by Durkheim in the adjacent area of the moral.

199

II

Just as it has been stated by some that the essence of the moral, and the sacred, are not amenable to the scientific approach, it will be objected that the innermost nature of art lies outside the methodology of science. Certainly an evaluation of art forms would constitute an unwarrantable trespassing and a depreciation of the subject matter.

The flower that grows out of the trash heap insofar as it is an object of beauty must be evaluated in terms of aesthetic concepts and not in terms of its physical genesis. Its place in the hierarchy of aesthetic values is not dependent upon the existential factors and conditions of its origin.[3] However, there is a set of conditions without which the flower would have no beauty, and these are ideal elements of the conceptual system. It is in terms of this cultural context that either an evaluation, or explanation, is made.

III

The difference between art and science has been held to consist in the mode of approach to the object, or in the standpoint from which the object is viewed. It has been customary to regard the unique, the particular, the different, the unusual as the proper subject matter of the artist; the scientist, it is presumed, will focus his attention upon the recurring features of the object, the usual, the like, the general, the universal, the conceptual. The artist must "uniquize," must emphasize the unlike as significant; the scientist, the like.[4] The artist will exhibit the principle of contrast; the scientist, that of comparison. For the scientist cannot do anything with that which is held to be unique. The latter may excite feelings of wonder, ecstasy, love, or awe, but insofar as it does so, it is not an object of scientific investigation. Indeed, the scientist must refuse to treat the instance as unique; he must strip the instance of its falsifying nimbus of particularity; he must show it to be the member of a class, or as part of a system of relationships, which system will determine the existence of the phenomenon. Such a procedure deprives the object of its isolated and exceptional character; it becomes no longer an object of wonder—it is as it were reduced to size; it is shown to be but a specimen in a given series. Its meaning is no longer grounded in itself but in some deeper unity.

From this it would seem that the artist views the object in its totality. His knowledge appears like deeply penetrating, intuitive vision. On the other hand, the scientist must abstract from the particular that which it has in common with other particulars—in brief, he must conceptualize. So much at variance do these approaches appear—that of intuitive vision and conceptualization—that any reduction of one to the other has seemed impossible.[5] Thus it has been stated frequently that science and art are separate orders, and are utterly incapable of any kind of reciprocal subsumption. Perhaps, it has been the sense of hopelessness felt by the social scientist in the face of the gulf between science and art that has deterred him from investigating the field of the aesthetic. Nevertheless, many observers casually have noted the marked correlation between science and art in given historical epochs. These correlations lead to belief that there is some common ground of explanation for these two endeavors of the human spirit.

The disparity of approach and viewpoint just outlined is, apparently, one of those antitheses, like that of matter and form or sacred and secular that have obtained in the world so long that they are held to be ultimate. There is, however, a common ground so obvious that it is in danger of being overlooked. While it remains true that the scientist is concerned with the conceptual—that is, with universals or abstractions—it should be noted that the concrete particular itself is known to us only as an intersection of universals. If this unique object is transfixed by logical categories, it resolves itself into a cluster of concepts—, that is, e.g., greenness, hardness, transparency, etc. Nothing beyond the universals can be found. This is most clearly seen in the art of music where there is no material medium, as in architecture, sculpture and painting, but only structured sound.

IV

The concept has fascinated the thinkers of Western culture from the time of Socrates forward. Its importance has been apparent to all, but its nature and function have not always been understood. The failure to see that the concept is never an individual construct has obscured its rightful significance. Durkheim saw clearly the social source of the concept but followed up only a few of the implications of this insight. It is of vital importance to observe that the concept is the vehicle of rational communication; indeed, no intellectual communication is possible except by an exchange of concepts. The obvious form of such exchange is in language—itself a structure of concepts.[6] As has been pointed out above, such communication through the medium of concepts is possible only because the latter embodies an agreement in respect to some aspect of reality about which there is no dispute. The exchange of concepts implies an effort to conceptualize further and to eliminate (at least in theory) the area of subjective impression, which means to reach objective statement in whatever may be under discussion.

Objectively the power of rational thought is not a characteristic of the person in his separate individuality. It is what is common to all persons in their societal universality. The impressions of the individual are a chaos of differences, miscellaneous, disjunct, and isolated. When these subjectivities of individuals become susceptible of comparison, objectivity arises. At length a system is formed in which these individual units meet. What is incapable of comparison and communication cannot be knowledge, and is, so far as society is concerned, valueless.

What is to be held right, and good, or beautiful, must be decided doubtless by the individual, but by him so far as he is a rational, thinking being. But his thinking, his reason, is not something specially belonging to him, but something common to all men in his society—to all those whose minds are structured by the fundamental conceptual framework that underlies the whole. Whenever a number of men fall back on this framework the specialities of each disappear, and they arrive at the same conclusions. The daily life of individuals in society passes in a mist and maze of particular impressions—one impression clashes with another, individual with individual, and the tangle and confusion seems hopeless. Nevertheless, there is within the maze a solid core—the conceptual system built by individuals in their collective experience. This is the ultimate possession of a society; its final court of appeal in matters of rightness, knowledge, and beauty.

The system of concepts which underlies and supports the life of a society is found only in the minds of the persons who make up that society. But these ideas are not subjective impressions. They are concepts, universals, objective ideas, which like language and logic have an independence of any single mind. But it is a grave mistake to hypostasize these ideas and see them as actually in separation from persons. This would be to make concrete what is actually an abstraction and would end in a barren sociological mysticism indicative of a deficiency of intellectual resource. This is in fact the supreme self-contradiction of the theory of the collective consciousness. It begins by saying that only the collective representation is real and ends by degrading the universal into a particular. It is the cardinal error of Durkheim that, despite his stature, he conceived of society as an individual personality and thus fell among the stones and brambles of philosophic bathos.

V

The major task of sociology is the scientific exposition and development of those concepts and values which underlie all thought and conduct—which are the fundamental factors in the person's thinking, feeling, and acting, as well as constituting the tissue of cultural reality. In these universals, or collective representations, society and its persons, have their point of coincidence. They may be regarded as the simple ultimate principles into the network of which the entire culture is built, and through and by which, a society, and the members of a society, exist. They are the structural beams of a cultural system. By the term here is meant the manifold of individual cultural items in subjection to a single concept. That concept is the form of the whole, so far as through this whole the position and meaning of its parts mutually is *a priori* determined. The whole is, therefore, articulated and not simply amassed. Thus a culture is presented as a vast system of concepts self-referent to the unity of a single, living pulse.

All existences pass and what alone is permanent are the intelligible relationships and concepts which these existences express. Persons are the necessary singulars for the realization of the concepts which are ever expressed in the arts, in the sciences, in institutions, in religions and philosophies of man.

The ultimate element of structure is the concept. It is the construction brick of all cultural systems. Unfortunately, the term structure calls up a rigidity which is the opposite of what is meant. In the conceptual structure the foundations are living and active—

not dead, crystallized relics—but, as G. H. Mead has intimated, the roots of the mind itself.[7]

Since the conceptual structure is realized only in persons, the totality—the deposit of society's collective experience—becomes a living system determining the individual life in innumerable ways. From this reservoir flows all that is creative. The mind of the individual and his achievements are but an aspect of these creative potentialities—a tiny outcropping in the vast hinterland of culture.

VI

Having discussed at length the place of the concept as the ultimate element in culture, it is time to return to an examination of the concept in the field of art. It is necessary to unite in a common ground the two branches that isolated from each other have seemed on the point of being lost in the sands, to conjoin into unity and totality these two conceptual endeavors.

Whence comes the idea of beauty? There is nothing in the outer world that directly corresponds to it. There are only objects, or more generally, phenomena which are adjudged to be more or less beautiful in terms of this idea. Obviously, the idea of beauty is a concept which has been incorporated into the thought content of the person from his culture. One's idea of beauty is representative as it were of the conceptualization of the sensory experience regarding given segments of reality by a society in its collective experience. This concept, like all concepts, is independent of the individual mind in the same sense that language is independent of the speaker. Such a concept becomes the means whereby the beautiful object is recognized and the standard which determines the extent to which it is beautiful. Since the concept of beauty varies from society to society it follows that what is beautiful for one society may be quite otherwise for another.[8] Indeed, the concept of the beautiful may change radically in various historical epochs of the same society. Nature has not always been regarded as beautiful. The recognition of the beauty of nature is an application of the concept of beauty by Western Culture at a certain stage of its development. Such a Wordsworthian attitude was alien to men like Socrates who said that he never went for walks outside the city since there was nothing to be learned from fields and trees.[9] On the other hand the capacity of the Greek to recognize beauty in the human form and to express this in his culture quite surpasses that of other peoples. Yet this capacity does not pass from the human form to the human face. This last achievement was reserved for the great painters of the Italian Renaissance. Whether the distinction between sensuous and spiritual beauty be valid or not the real determinant in the creation and recognition of beauty is the social concept of it. There is no more erroneous view than that which would regard art as individual expression, and that it is subject to no standard save the individuality of the artist.[10] This would mean the exhibition of mere oddities and eccentricities. It is precisely the individual peculiarities that are worthless, or in other words, meaningless. They are only the tendency toward random, unstructured, goalless behavior that characterizes the biological organism that is as yet unsocialized. That alone which entitles the individual to be termed a person is the presence of the conceptual framework in him. This is his mind and his capacity to think.[11]

VII

The problem of the artistic genius is part of the problem of personality but can only be touched upon here. It is evident that the artist reaches the ultimate concept and value system of a society, but can communicate its essence only in the form of art. Observers have noted that the conscious, deliberate, intentional work of art is usually weak; it is in the unconscious, unintentional that we discover pieces of supreme artistry. This is because the genius acts as a catalyzing force upon the deeper, and consequently more concealed, elements of the conceptual system. But he precipitates only what is already implicit in the structure.

The great artist feels always that it is not he that writes, but that something writes through him. Even when he regards his work as consciously opposed to creations stemming from the fine frenzy he often says more than he is aware of. It was this that led Plato to remark that poets voice great truths but do not understand their own truths. Thus it is that the creative element is viewed, and in a sense correctly, as supra-personal. It is as if the depths of the conceptual system imposed itself arbitrarily on consciousness. When the work of art is completed, not infrequently, it means more than it seems to mean—that is, the symbolism is not read correctly or fully—possibly because the limited conscious individual perception prevents a full appreciation of the concept that the work of art objectifies and expresses.[12]

VIII

The contradiction of the conscious and the unconscious which ceaselessly perpetuates itself in the history of thought finds conscious resolution in the work of art. Here at last intelligence (rationality) reaches a perception of itself. The feeling that accompanies this perception is one of peculiar emotional intensity, of extraordinary release, of almost infinite satisfaction; all contradictions are removed, all mysteries revealed. The unknown something which brings the objective, actual world into harmony with conscious action is nothing else but the ultimate conceptual and value system which supports the life of any given society. The veil with which it obscures itself for others it lays aside for the artist and impels him involuntarily to the production of his works. Thus art is the one and only revelation; there is no other; it is the miracle that must convince all observers of the reality of that system of ultimate categories of a society which in the nature of things tend to remain concealed from the contemporaries of that system. It exhibits the reality of those supreme principles of a society which, since they are conceptual in nature, can never be actual in themselves, but are the cause of the particular structuring of the world by that society.

Thus it is that in art the rationality of man attains objectivity. It would seem that individual thought as such can never acquire universal authority. The single recipient of the deepest collective thought is the artist. The thought of the artist is in its expression as thought transmuted, an expression that translates what seems *like the essence of eternal things into the language of the present. The truth and wisdom of the artist's work are a fragment of that bastion of meaning and value which societal man has built against the dark ocean of the unknown, an ocean which ever threatens to engulf him.*

IX

Keeping in mind the foregoing, the falseness of that theory which would conceive of art as imitation should be evident. This is particularly obvious when we consider the art of music. Superficially, the painter may seem to be imitating the objects of the phenomenal world, but the musician cannot be regarded as copying phenomena. The musician produces that which has no counterpart in nature itself. Thus the function of the artist is not to manufacture a likeness nor to superficially describe one. We now see what the true function of the artist is: to exhibit the universal which society has imposed upon the particular—to show in an unique instance that which is the meaning of the class. The work of the artist is "special" in the ancient meaning of that word, as the revelation of a logical species to a society. Art reveals the meaning with which the society in its collective experience has invested the object. The artist's preoccupation with the individual thing is a preoccupation with its total universal aspects, with its significance as pre-determined by the ultimate conceptual and value system.

The beautiful is the collective representation, the universal, the concept, shining as it were through a sensuous medium (stone, color, sound, or verse). While there are always two factors—the concept and the medium—both are inseparably fused. The material medium expresses nothing but the conceptual thought that animates and illuminates it. Hence, the work of art appears like the fleeting embodiment of eternal beauty for the profounder universals always exhibit themselves as timeless, as if they were, *sub specie aeternitatis,* under the aspect of eternity. When this is not quite achieved the supremely beautiful may be accompanied by remarkable historical feeling flowing from the relatively timeless conceptual system.[13]

It follows that meaning of life as that has been defined in the collective experience of a society is read in its art expressions. The physical dimension is but the instrument that effects the mind's transition from its individual limitations into the almost limitless dimensions of the conceptual structure.

Notes

AGAINST THE DARK OCEAN OF THE UNKNOWN: THE CONCEPTUAL SYSTEM AND THE SOCIOLOGY OF ART

*Written in 1965, this was Stan Taylor's final paper. His own title for the paper was simply "A Contribution to the Sociology of Art."

I selected the new title from p. 12, and the Cassirer quote from endnote 10.

1. "Art may be defined as a symbolic language" (Ernst Cassirer, *An Essay on Man* [Garden City: Doubleday Anchor Books, 1954], p. 214.)

Cassirer's definition while only pointing to the genus to which art belongs is helpful in emancipating one from the conception of art as "mimesis" or "imitation." In the work quoted Cassirer points out that the general theory of imitation still played an important role in the nineteenth century and that Taine defended it in his *Pholosophie de l'art*. However, forms of the symbolic theory of art are very old. The Neo-Platonist, Plotinus, was the first to reinterpret Plato's view of art as the "third remove from reality" by insisting that the artist's so-called imitation of the phenomenal world, which in turn was dependent upon the eternal Ideas, was in fact a symbol—that beauty was the direct expression of reason in the world. Plotinus clearly anticipates the romantic school of aesthetics of Schelling and Hegel with its emphasis upon the metaphysical Infinite and the Absolute as the real object of art, which is expressed in the beautiful in nature and at the conscious level, symbolized in art. See: Bernard Bosanquet, *A History of Aesthetic* (London: George Allen and Unwin Ltd., 1892), pp. 117 ff.

The several forms of the symbolic theory of art imply that art is communication. Note: "... art is not a thing but an act; not an object but a communication. Being a communication, it involves not only an artist, the creator, but an audience and a language familiar to both. This language is a product of society, rather than of the individual, who at best makes a small, if important, addition to it. Since this is so the language changes as society changes. All efforts to call a halt to the change of language have inevitably failed, whether in the realm of words which we usually think of as language, or the realm of sound, rhythm, line, color, and shape, which are the language of music and the graphic arts. Thus, a contemporary communication has a quality not found in one from the past, and the power of a work of art is measured by the effectiveness of its communication rather than by the model it follows" (Sidney Finkelstein, *Art and Society* [New York: International Publishers, 1947], p. 10).

2. See: Emile Durkheim, *The Elementary Forms of the Religious*

Life, trans. J. W. Swain (London: George Allen and Unwin, N.D.).

3. The problem of the relationship between the existential conditions of the origin of a work of art and the standards by which it is aesthetically judged is similar in nature to the problem of the existential determination of the theoretic. Husserl and Mannheim were in opposition upon it, and the latter made the question a central issue of his sociology of knowledge. See: Karl Mannheim, *Ideology and Utopia* (New York: Harcourt Brace and Co., 1949).

4. The distinction that is made here between science and art is the kind of distinction that Aristotle made between science and history. Aristotle did not envisage the aesthetic object as unique, or unusual, but as possessing a certain generality. See: Aristotle, *Poetics,* 9, 3.

Cf. "When we read in the *Poetics* that 'poetry is more philo-sophical (or scientific) than history' we are apt to imagine ourselves in a modern atmosphere...we observe...that the scientific element in poetry lies in its typical generality (Bosanquet, op. cit., p. 59). Cf., also: "Like Plato, he [Aristotle] understands art to be an imitation of reality. However, he does not find the subject of imitation in the several accidental, changeable features, but in the universal and typical aspect of things. The artist is not concerned with what happens at any particular moment, but with what happens always or usually. Hence Aristotle claims that poetry is more philosophical and richer in content than history, that Homer stands above Herodotus" (Rudolph Eucken, *The Problem of Human Life* [New York: Charles Scribner's Sons, 1916], p. 67).

5. "So long as we live in the world of sense impressions alone we merely touch the surface of reality. Awareness of the depth of things always requires an effort on the part of our active and constructive energies. But since these energies do not move in the same direction, and do not tend toward the same end they cannot give us the same aspect of reality. There is a conceptual depth as well as a purely visual depth. The first is discovered by science; the second is revealed in art. The first aids us in understanding the reasons of things; the second in seeing their forms. In science we trace phenomena back to their first causes, and to general laws and principles. In art we are absorbed in their immediate appearance, and we enjoy this appearance to the fullest extent in all its richness and variety. Here we are not concerned with the uniformity of laws

but with the multiformity and diversity of intuitions. Even art may be described as knowledge, but art is knowledge of a peculiar and specific kind" (Cassirer, *op. cit.*, pp. 215 f.).

6. "Croce insists that there is not only a close relation but a complete identity between language and art. To his way of thinking it is quite arbitrary to distinguish between the two activities. Whoever studies general linguistics, according to Croce, studies aesthetic problems—and vice versa. There is, however, an unmistakable difference between the symbols of art and the linguistic terms of ordinary speech or writing. These two activities agree neither in character nor purpose, they do not employ the same means, nor do they tend toward the same ends. Neither language nor art gives us mere imitation of things or actions; both are representations" (Ernst Cassirer, *An Essay on Man* [Garden City: Doubleday Anchor Books, 1954], p. 214).

7. "It is absurd to look at the mind simply from the standpoint of the individual organism; for, although it has it focus there, it is essentially a social phenomenon... "(G. H. Mead, *Mind, Self and Society*, ed. C. W. Morris [Chicago: University of Chicago Press], p. 133).

8. Even the art style in which the values implied in the conceptual structure are expressed has a social base no matter how individualistic it may appear. Note: "Whether we are interested in the art of the present or the past, we must revise our notions of style as a personally inspired creation of the writer out of a dead matter called language. The rudimentary patterns of emotional communication and of complex ideas already exist in language, as it has been built up by society. If the traditions and schools of art have given the writer a finer sensitivity to its individual language elements, and a knowledge of the larger forms that may be built out of it, the language as used by people without any pretense to art gives him the fresh patterns brought by the changing appearances and conditions of life (Finkelstein, *op. cit.*, p. 20).

9. Plato, "Phaedrus," *The Philosophy of Plato*, trans. B. Jowett (3d ed.; New York: Random House, The Modern Library, N.D.), p. 267.

10. "Aesthetic universality means that the predicate of beauty is not restricted to a special individual but extends over the whole field of judging subjects. If the work of art were nothing but the freak and frenzy of an individual artist it would not possess this

universal communicability. The imagination of the artist does not arbitrarily invent the forms of things. The artist chooses a certain aspect of reality, but this process of selection is at the same time a process of objectification. Once we have entered into his perspective we are forced on the world with his eyes. It would seem as if we had never before seen the world in this peculiar light. Yet we are convinced that this light is not merely a momentary flash. By virtue of the work of art it has become durable and permanent. Once reality has been disclosed to us in this particular way, we continue to see it in this shape" (Ernst Cassirer, *An Essay on Man* [Garden City: Doubleday Anchor Books, 1954], p. 187).

11. Cf. "If personality, individuality, originality were as pronounced as it is usually assumed to be, how is it... we find it so difficult to tell where one personality begins and the other ends? It would seem that the only answer to this question is that in art as in all other human activities, the communal, the universal outweighs the individual and particular to such a degree that but for hero-worship, mythology, hagiology, and propaganda, which inflate and distort things out of all relation to facts or to results, the most original genius rarely leaves more than a faint permanent mark on the field of his activity.

Originality (if we may revert to it in passing) is looked for in young emergent artists of our own day, not in those who have already achieved fame, and still less in the artists of the past. This is due to a craving on the part of the public, not for a new way of seeing or hearing but for a new expression of well known things—a visual, verbal, or musical venture, not to outlast a season and not rude enough to stand in the way of a still more recent novelty. Even in Dante's time the public deserted a Cimabue for a Giotti. In our swift moving age, a new painter to escape oblivion must attempt to renew his manner once a year at least. He keeps his reputation on no safer tenure than the Priest of Nemi, the priest who "slew the slayer and shall himself be slain."

Artists take to originality from the moment that they begin to despair of exercising their respective professions within the terms and limits of their art; and I am speaking of the real artist, not of the artificers who are out for success and publicity. They behave like fish out of water, like animals out of their element, and the greatest of them like the aged Michelangelo in sculpture and painting, like Wagner in music, lash about like "Moby Dick" and give vent to their tragic tension in a pathos that transports and inebriates but leaves an aftertaste of rhetoric rather than art" (Bernard Berenson, *Aesthetics and History* [Garden City, N.Y.: Doubleday Anchor Books, 1954], pp. 208 ff.).

12. Cf. "This picture is accessible to analysis just in so far as we are able to appreciate it as a symbol. But if we are unable to discover any symbolic value in it, we have thereby ascertained that, for us at least, it means no more than what it obviously says—in other words, so far as we are concerned it is no more than it seems. I use the word 'seems', because it is conceivable that our own bias forbids a wider appreciation of it. At all events in the latter case we find no motive and no point of attack for analysis. In the former case, however, a phrase of Gerhard Hauptmann will come to our minds almost with the force of an axiom: 'Poetry means the distant echo of the primitive word behind our veil of words.' " (C. G. Jung, "Poetic Art," *Contributions to Analytical Psychology*, trans. H. G. and Cary F. Baynes [London: Kegan Paul, Trench, Trubner and Co., Ltd., 1928], p. 245.)

13. Mueller seems anxious to dissipate the romantic ideology of Schelling, Hegel and Schopenhauer with regard to the arts by insisting on the time-bound character of music and musical taste. Note: By an evolution too complex to rehearse at this point, music was elevated to the most exalted position among the arts; and in its unfettered creativeness, it approximated "pure spirit," universal and absolute Truth. Because of its mystical and supernatural characteristic, it possessed the power to exert a spiritual and ethical influence upon its auditors superior to that of any other medium. Such neo-Platonic doctrines of Hegel and Schopenhauer inevitably place the great musician in a position of ethical leadership; conferred a certain sacrosanct validity on his "inspiration," and elevated him into the realms of near-infallibility. Music, the most exalted art, was not only a reflection of ultimate ideas and sentiments, but was actually a form of thinking in tones—an abstract, subtle, and direct communication superior to crude verbal symbols, independent of the physical actualities of the world and therefore a "universal" language. The inspiration of the artist was thus of higher validity than the uninstructed taste of otherwise intelligent people" (John H. Mueller, *The American Symphony Orchestra*, [Bloomington: Indiana University Press, 1951], p. 291.)

Also: "There are those who may be offended at so prosaic a

treatment of the arts, which suggests that good music is ephemeral and transient, and subject to the material vicissitudes of life. They would prefer to believe that Art secures its sanction from a higher realm, or that it at least possesses some distinctive objective trait to give it permanence and universality in its appeal to the discerning auditor. Such was the fervent faith of Leopold Damrosch, Theodore Thomas, Gericke, and Muck, who laid the foundations of the new traditional standards of taste. It is the long dominance of such a figure as Beethoven, more recently joined by Sebastian Bach, which appears to give plausibility to the faith in a universal Beauty. It is such phenomena which create the illusion of timeless beauty that transcends the ages, passing of which is uncomfortable to contemplate. A well developed historical sense, however, will awaken the realization that a century—or a thousand years—is but a moment in civilization. Bach and Beethoven are not "universal;" they merely have lasted a long time." (Ibid., p. 392.)

Bibliography

Adler, Max, *Das Soziologische in Kant's Erkenntniskritik.* Wien: Wiener Volksbuchhandlung, 1924.

Allport, F. H., *Institutional Behavior.* Chapel Hill: University of North Carolina Press, 1933.

————, "The Nature of Institutions," *Journal of Social Forces,* VI (1927), 167-179.

Alpert, Harry, *Émile Durkheim and His Sociology.* New York: Columbia University Press, 1938.

Bacon, Francis, "Novum Organum," *The English Philosophers from Bacon to Mill.* Edited by E. A. Burtt. New York: The Modern Library, 1939.

————, *The Physical and Metaphysical Works of Lord Bacon.* Edited by Joseph Devey. London: G. Bell & Sons, 1894.

Ballard, L. V., *Social Institutions.* New York: D. Appleton-Century Co., 1936.

Bart, Hans, *Wahrheit und Ideologie.* Zurich: Manesse Verlag, 1945.

Bendix, Reinhard, *Social Science and the Distrust of Reason.* Berkeley and Los Angeles: University of California Press, 1951.

Bentham, J., *Introduction to the Principles of Morals and Legislation.* Edinburgh: Ballantyne & Co., 1843.

Buckle, T., *History of Civilization in England.* New York: D. Appleton-Century Co., 1934.

Burtt, Edwin A., (ed.). *The English Philosophers from Bacon to Mill.* New York: The Modern Library, 1939.

Cailliet, E., *La Tradition littéraire des idéologues.* Philadelphia: The American Philosophical Society, 1943.

Child, Arthur, "The Existential Determination of Thought," *Ethics,* Vol. III, No. 2 (January, 1942).

————, "The Theoretical Possibility of the Sociology of Knowledge." *Ethics,* Vol. II, No. 4 (July, 1941).

Comte, Auguste, *Cours de Philosophie positive.* Edited by E. Littre. 6 vols. 2d ed.; Paris: L. Hachette et Cie., 1864.

————, *Early Essays on Social Philosophy.* Translated by H. D. Hutton. London: Routledge and Sons, 1911.

————, *The Positive Philosophy.* Translated by Harriet Martineau. 2 vols. 2d ed.; London: Kegan Paul, 1890.

Descartes, René, *The Method, Meditations and Selections from the Principles of Descartes.* Translated by John Veitch. 2d ed.; Edinburgh and London: Blackwood and Sons, 1880.

Destutt de Tracy, A. L. C., *Élements d'idéologie.* Paris: Chez Madame Levi, 1825.

————, *Projet d'élements d'idéologie à l'usage des écoles centralies de la Republique Francaise.* Paris: M. Didot, 1801.

Dewey, John, *Essay in Experimental Logic.* Chicago: University of Chicago Press, 1916.

————, *Experience and Nature.* Chicago: Open Court Publishing Co., 1931.

————, *The Quest for Certainty.* New York: Minton, Balch and Co., 1929.

————, "Philosophy," *Research in the Social Sciences.* Edited by Wilson Gee. New York: Macmillan Co., 1929.

Durkheim, Émile, *Les formes élémentaires de la vie religieuse.* Paris: F. Alcan, 1912.

————, (ed.) *L'Année sociologique.* 12 vols. Paris: F. Alcan, 1896-1912.

————, *Les règles de la méthode sociologique.* Paris: F. Alcan, 1895.

————, *Sociologie et philosophie.* Paris: F. Alcan, 1924.

————, *Le Suicide.* Paris: F. Alcan, 1897.

————, *The Division of Labor in Society.* Translated by G. Simpson. Glencoe: The Free Press, 1947.

————, *The Elementary Forms of the Religious Life.* Translated by J. W. Swain. Glencoe: The Free Press, 1947.

Durant, W., *The Story of Philosophy.* New York: Simon and Schuster, 1926.

Eucken, Rudolph, *The Problem of Human Life.* Translated by W. S. Hough and W. Boyce Gibson. New York: Scribners, 1916.

Gehlke, C. E., *Émile Durkheim's Contributions to Sociological Theory*. New York: 1915.

Godwin, W., *An Enquiry Concerning Political Justice*. New York: A. A. Knopf, 1926.

Gurvitch, G., *Initiation aux recherches sur la sociologie de la connaissance*. Paris: Centres d'études sociologiques, 1948.

Hayek, F. A., *The Counter Revolution of Science*. Glencoe: The Free Press, 1952.

Hughes, E. C., "The Study of Institutions," *Social Forces,* Vol. XX (1942).

Hume, David, *A Treatise of Human Nature*. 2 vols. London: J. M. Dent & Sons, Ltd., 1911.

Husserl, E., *Ideas*. Translated by W. R. Boyce Gibson. New York: Macmillan, 1952.

Kant, I., *Critique of Pure Reason*. Translated by Norman Kemp Smith. New York: Humanities Press, 1950.

————, *Prolegomena to Any Future Metaphysic*. New York: Liberal Arts Press, 1951.

Lafitte, P., Materiaux pour servir à la Biographie d'Auguste Comte: "Correspondance d'Auguste Comte avec Gustave d'Eichtal," *La Revue Occidentale,* second series, XII, 19 Année, 1891, Part II, 186 ff.

Lewalter, E., "Wissenssoziologie und Marxismus," *Archiv. für Sozialwissensschaft und Sozialpolitik,* Vol. LIV (Tubingen, 1925).

Locke, John, *"An Essay Concerning Human Understanding," Philosophical Works*. London: G. Bell & Sons, 1901.

Mandelbaum, M., *The Problem of Historical Knowledge*. New York: Liveright Publishing Corp., 1938.

Mannheim, Karl, *Essays on the Sociology of Knowledge*. New York: Oxford University Press, 1953.

————, *Ideology and Utopia*. Translated by L. Wirth and E. Shils. New York: Harcourt Brace and Co., 1949.

Maquet, J. J., *The Sociology of Knowledge*. Translated by J. F. Locke. Boston: The Beacon Press, 1951.

Marx, Karl, *A Contribution to the Critique of Political Economy*. Chicago: Charles Kerr and Co., 1904.

————, *The German Ideology*. Edited by R. Pascal. New York: International Publishing Co., 1939.

Mead, G. H., *Mind, Self and Society*. Chicago: University of Chicago Press, 1934.

Mill, J. S., *Utilitarianism*. London: J. M. Dent & Sons, Ltd., 1910.

————, *On Liberty*. London: J. M. Dent & Sons, Ltd., 1910.

Nietzsche, F., *Thus Spake Zarathustra*. New York: Boni and Liveright, Inc., N. D.

Ortega y Gasset, Jose, *The Modern Theme*. Translated by J. Cleugh. London: C. W. Daniel Co., 1931.

————, *Toward a Philosophy of History*. Translated by H. Weyl. New York: W. W. Norton & Co., 1941.

Panunzio, G., *Major Social Institutions*. New York, 1949.

Parsons, Talcott, *Essays in Sociological Theory*. Glencoe: The Free Press, 1949.

————, *The Structure of Social Action*. Glencoe: The Free Press, 1949.

Picavet, F., *Les Idéologues, Essai sur l'histoire des idées et des théories scientifique, philosophique, religieuses, en France depuis 1789*. Paris: Alcan, 1891.

Pribram, Karl, *Die Enstehung der Individualistichen Socialphilosophie*. Leipzig: C. L. Hirshfeld, 1912.

Rogers, R. A. P., *A Short History of Ethics*. London: Macmillan and Co., 1921.

Rüstow, A., *Das Versagen des Wirtschaftsliberalismus als Religiongeschichtliche Problem*. Instabul: Europa Verlag, 1945.

Schatz, Albert, *L'individualisme économique et social*. Paris: A. Conlin, 1907.

Scheler, M. F., "Probleme einer Sociologie des Wissens," *Die Wissensformen und die Gesellschaft*. Leipzig: Der Neue-Geist Verlag, 1926.

Schwegler, A., *A Handbook of the History of Philosophy*. Translated by J. H. Stirling. 4th ed. Edinburgh: Edmonston & Douglas, 1872.

Sorokin, P. A., "Notes on the Interdependence of Philosophy and Sociology." *Revue Internationale de Philosophie*, No. 13, Juillet, 1950.

Spencer, H., *The Data of Ethics*. New York: American Publishers Corp., N. D.

————, *The Study of Sociology*. New York: D. Appleton & Co., 1893.

Stirner, Max, *The Ego and His Own*. Translated by S. T. Bynington. Boni & Liveright, N. D.

Tylor, E. B., *Primitive Culture*. 7th ed.; New York: Brentano 1924.

Weber, Max, *Gesammelte Aufsatze zur Wissenschaflehre*. Tubingen: J. C. Mohr, 1922.

Whitehead, A. N., *The Organization of Thought*. London: Routledge and Kegan Paul, 1917.

————, *Science and the Modern World*. New York: The New American Library, 1948.

Windelband, W., *A History of Philosophy*. Translated by J. H. Tufts. 2d ed.; New York: Macmillan Co., 1926.

Wirth, L., "Preface" to Karl Mannheim's *Ideology and Utopia*. Glencoe: The Free Press, 1949.

Zimmerman, C. C., *Family and Civilization*. New York: Harper and Co., 1947.

Znaniecki, F., *The Social Role of the Man of Knowledge*. New York: Columbia University Press, 1940.

Index